Anonymous

Hand Book of Honduras

Anonymous

Hand Book of Honduras

ISBN/EAN: 9783337314170

Printed in Europe, USA, Canada, Australia, Japan

Cover: Foto ©Thomas Meinert / pixelio.de

More available books at **www.hansebooks.com**

52D CONGRESS, } SENATE. { Ex. Doc. 149,
1st Session. } { Part 7.

BUREAU OF THE AMERICAN REPUBLICS,

WASHINGTON, U. S. A.

HAND BOOK

OF

HONDURAS.

BULLETIN NO. 57.   1892.

[Revised to March 1, 1894.]

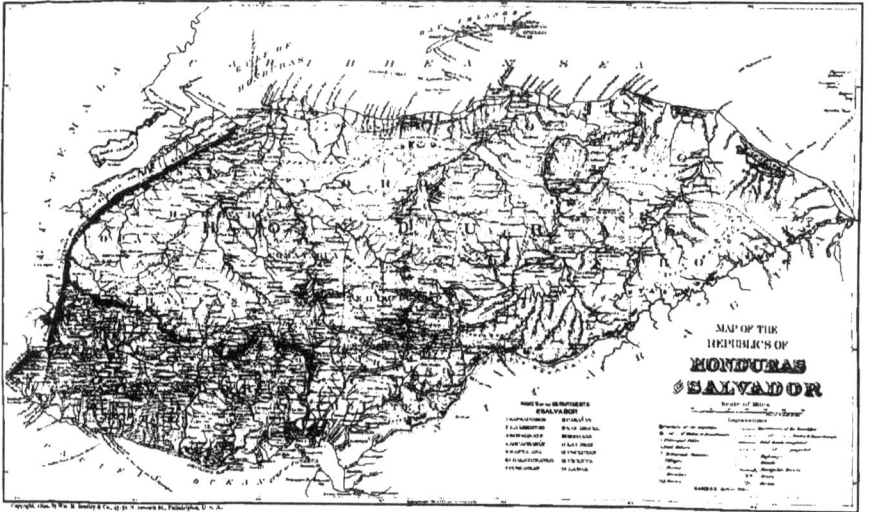

MAP OF THE
REPUBLICS OF
HONDURAS
& SALVADOR

BUREAU OF THE AMERICAN REPUBLICS,
NO. 2 LAFAYETTE SQUARE, WASHINGTON, D. C., U. S. A.

Director.—CLINTON FURBISH.
Secretary.—FREDERIC EMORY.

WASHINGTON, D. C., U. S. A.
GOVERNMENT PRINTING OFFICE.

LIST OF BUREAU PUBLICATIONS.

The above list includes all the publications of the Bureau to April 15, 1894. *Orders for copies based on the above will not be noticed.*

On the following page will be found the price list of Bureau publications.

SALE OF BUREAU PUBLICATIONS.

The following monthly bulletins have been published by the Bureau of American Republics, viz: Coffee in America, October, 1893; Coal and Petroleum in Colombia, etc., November, 1893; Minerals and Resources of Northeastern Nicaragua, etc., December, 1893; Finances of Chile, etc., January, 1894; Costa Rica at the World's Fair, etc., February, 1894; Reciprocity Treaties and Trade, etc., March, 1894; The Republic of Costa Rica, etc., April, 1894, and Mexico; Treasury Receipts, Total Source of Income for Fiscal Year 1894-'95, etc., May, 1894; Import Duties of Guatemala (Revised), June, 1894; American Live Stock, etc., July, 1894.

With the July number will be commenced the second volume of these bulletins, and subscriptions for the year ending June 30, 1895, will be received at the rate of $1 per annum; single copies, 10 cents each. Of the publications of the Bureau, the following will be furnished to applicants upon receipt of the prices named in the list. Money may be sent by post-office money order, payable to the Director of the Bureau of American Republics. All other remittances are at the risk of the sender. *Postage stamps will not be received.*

PRICE LIST.

3. Patent and Trade-mark Laws of America	$0.05
4. Money, Weights and Measures of the American Republics....	.05
6. Foreign Commerce of the American Republics	.20
8. Import Duties of Brazil	.10
10. Import Duties of Cuba and Puerto Rico.	.15
11. Import Duties of Costa Rica	.10
13. Commercial Directory of Brazil	.05
14. Commercial Directory of Venezuela	.05
15. Commercial Directory of Colombia	.05
16. Commercial Directory of Peru	.05
17. Commercial Directory of Chile	.05
18. Commercial Directory of Mexico	.15
19. Commercial Directory of Bolivia, Ecuador, Paraguay, and Uruguay	.05
20. Import Duties of Nicaragua	.10
21. Import Duties of Mexico (revised)	.15
22. Import Duties of Bolivia	.20
23. Import Duties of Salvador	.05
24. Import Duties of Honduras	.10
25. Import Duties of Ecuador	.05
26. Commercial Directory of the Argentine Republic	.05
27. Import Duties of Colombia	.05
28. Commercial Directory of Central America	.10
29. Commercial Directory of Haiti and Santo Domingo	.05
30. First Annual Report of the Bureau, 1891.	.10
32. Hand Book of Guatemala	.35
33. Hand Book of Colombia	.30
34. Hand Book of Venezuela	.35
36. Import Duties of Venezuela	.05
38. Commercial Directory of Cuba and Puerto Rico	.10
39. Commercial Directory of British, Danish, Dutch, and French Colonies	.10

42. Newspaper Directory of Latin America.	$0.05
43. Import Duties of Guatemala	.25
44. Import Duties of the United States	.05
45. Import Duties of Peru	.25
46. Import Duties of Chile	.25
47. Import Duties of Uruguay	.25
48. Import Duties of the Argentine Republic	.25
49. Import Duties of Haiti	.10
50. Hand Book of the American Republics, No. 3	.50
51. Hand Book of Nicaragua	.50
52. Hand Book of Santo Domingo	.50
53. Immigration and Land Laws of Latin America	.40
55. Hand Book of Bolivia	.40
57. Hand Book of Honduras	.50
58. Hand Book of Salvador	.50
61. Hand Book of Uruguay	.50
62. Hand Book of Haiti	.50
63. How the Markets of Latin America may be Reached	.40
64. Hand Book of Ecuador	.50
67. Hand Book of the Argentine Republic..	.50
68. Special Costa Rica Bulletin	.25
69. Import Duties of Guatemala (revised)...	.25

PUBLICATIONS NOT NUMBERED.

Commercial Directory of Latin America,...	.40
Second Annual Report of the Bureau, 1892..	.05
Third Annual Report of the Bureau, 1893...	.15
Manual de las Republicas Americanas, 1892.	.50
Monthly Bulletins, $1 per annum; single copies	.10
Code of Commercial Nomenclature, first volume, 852 pages	3.00

The Code of Commercial Nomenclature, named in the above list, is the first volume of the first edition of the work suggested by the International American Conference. It contains 852 pages, and includes something over 28,000 commercial terms in English, Spanish, and Portuguese. This volume is bound in cloth, and is now ready for distribution.

IV

CONTENTS.

ILLUSTRATIONS.

VI

Chapter I.

That part of Central America now known as the Republic of Honduras was discovered by Columbus during his fourth voyage, about ten years after his first expedition. The locality first seen by him was the island of Guanaja, the most easterly of the group now called the Bay Islands, where he arrived on the 30th of July, 1502. He reached the mainland on the 14th of August at a point which he named Punta de Caxinas, a cape stretching out into the sea and forming what was afterwards known as the bay of Truxillo. Here, the great explorer's foot first pressed the mainland of the continent of America. Some 15 leagues eastward, at the mouth of a river which he named Rio de la Posesión, now known as Rio Tinto, he again landed and took formal possession of the country for Spain.

We next hear of Honduras when Gil Gonzales Dávila, while on a voyage from Santo Domingo to Nicaragua in 1524, steering too far to the westward, reached the coast near the bay now called Puerto Cortez. Having lost some of his horses there, he gave it the name of Puerto Caballos [Port of Horses], but made no settlement.

In the same year, an expedition sent by Cortez from Mexico, under command of Cristobal de Olid, reached the coast about 14 leagues east of Puerto Caballos and founded a settlement, to which was given the name of Triumfo de la Cruz, which was, however, soon aferwards abandoned.

Bull, 57——1

Hernando Cortez, having completed the conquest of Mexico, had, previously to this, sent Pedro de Alvarado with an expedition which reduced to submission the southern Provinces of Mexico, Guatemala, and Honduras. In the meantime, Cortez, doubtful of the loyalty of some of his emissaries, and excited by the glowing accounts brought to him of the wonderful countries to the south, where native tradition located stately cities and treasure-filled palaces, determined to set out himself. He left Mexico in October, 1524, and after a perilous march and great suffering and privation, reached Honduras and planted a colony at Puerto Caballos, which he named Natividad de Nuestra Señora. Since that visit, the bay has been generally known as Puerto Cortez. Cortez next visited Truxillo and sent expeditions into the interior to explore and conquer the country.

From this time, for nearly three centuries, as a province of what was called the Kingdom of Guatemala, the country was under the rule of Spain. War, pestilence, and enforced labor in the mines and plantations swept away the enslaved Indian people, until at last there remained but a mere fragment of its once teeming population.

Futile and desultory attempts at resistance to Spanish rule were made from time to time for several years as echoes of the cry for freedom made by the patriot priest Hidalgo in Mexico in the year 1810, but it was not until 1821, that Central America threw off the yoke of Spain. An act of independence was adopted at Guatemala, and the citizens of the Provinces were invited to choose representatives, on the basis of one for every 15,000 inhabitants, to a national congress, to meet March 1, 1822.

The result of the deliberations of this assembly was the establishment of the Republic of Central America, composed of the territory which is now divided into the five independent States of Guatemala, Salvador, Honduras, Nicaragua, and Costa Rica.

After a wearisome period of internal dissensions and desolating civil wars, the Central American Union was dissolved, and on the 26th of October, 1838, a declaration of independence was promulgated, announcing Honduras to be a free and sovereign State. Since that time, several efforts have been made to reunite the five Republics, but without success, and the federation and unity of Central America still remains an unsolved problem.

For many years after Honduras assumed the responsibilities of independent existence, the country was harassed by revolutions and the efforts of some of its public men to become absolute rulers. In recent years, the prevailing tendency has been toward a more settled state of affairs, and its Presidents have looked more to the general welfare of the country.

Chapter II.

The Republic of Honduras is situated between latitude 13° 10′ and 16° 2′ north; longitude, 83° and 90° west. Its northern frontier, about 350 miles in length, is formed by the Caribbean Sea. On the west it is bounded by Guatemala; on the southwest by Salvador and the Bay of Fonseca, on which it has a frontage of about 70 miles, and on the east and southeast by the Republic of Nicaragua. Its superficial area is about 45,000 square miles, but no exact survey or measurement has ever been made.

The general aspect of Honduras is mountainous; in fact, the greater part of the country is corrugated by disconnected ranges and groups of mountains into which the great continental range is here divided. Many of these mountain ranges are of considerable elevation. Near Omoa, on the north coast, some of the peaks are at least 7,000 feet in height, while Mount Congrejoy, near Ceiba, has an elevation of 7,800 feet and forms a landmark visible for many miles at sea. In the Departments of Intibuca and Gracias, the mountains of Selaque attain in places an elevation of nearly 10,000 feet.

There are extensive alluvions near the coasts, particularly in the northeastern part, comprised in the Departments of Yoro, Colon, and Olancho, which extend inland in the form of broad savannas for many miles, and are covered with luxuriant and nutritious grasses. In near proximity to the coast and at the mouths of the rivers on both sides of the Republic, the land is low and in some places marshy and damp, but with an alluvial soil of almost unsurpassed fertility. Everywhere among the mountains, are high, healthy, wind-swept plateaus and hundreds of beautiful and fertile valleys, some of which are of great extent—such as the valley of Sula, in the Department of Santa Barbara, which extends from the north coast toward the south about 60 miles and averages from 30 to 50 miles in width. In the Departments of Tegucigalpa and Comayagua, are a few valleys of large size, in one of which is situated the city of Comayagua, the ancient capital. The Department of Gracias, on the Guatemala frontier, has also many valleys and plains, which form fine grazing regions.

Although Honduras is so mountainous, it is the only one of the Central American Republics that has no volcanoes, and consequently has never in historic times suffered from their effects, although there are evidences that in prehistoric times volcanoes bore their part in the upheaval and fashioning of the mountainous features of the region. Another striking topographical feature is that the great cordillera, or spinal ridge of the continent, is here so broken and interrupted that between its ranges lies a succession of plains constituting a great transverse valley reaching from sea to sea and offering singular facilities for an interoceanic or trans-isthmian route in an almost direct line and with very easy grades. From this brief description, it will be seen that Honduras has the greatest diversity of surface and elevation. Wide and elevated plateaus, broad plains, fertile valleys, and mountains, many of which are terraced to their summits, present conditions affording almost every possible variety of climate, soil, and productive capacity.

RIVERS.

The divide of the river systems is in close proximity to the Pacific coast. Consequently, that side of the Republic is not so well watered as the Atlantic slope, on which side are situated all the largest rivers, fed by many streams, affording good water power and ample facilities for irrigation during the dry season.

Honduras has some rivers that are of a size that entitles them to special notice, such as the Wanks, Patuca or Patook, Ulua, Chamelicon, Aguan, and Tinto, flowing into the Caribbean Sea; and the Choluteca, Nacaome, and Goascoran, which have their outlets on the Pacific coast. ·

The Wanks, or Segovia, which enters the sea at Cape Gracias á Dios, has its origin in the Department of Nueva Segovia, in the northwestern part of Nicaragua, within 50 miles of the Pacific, and forms for many miles the boundary between Honduras and Nicaragua. This river carries a large body of water, and would form an important avenue for commerce with the interior were it not obstructed by rapids and rocky shallows.

The Patuca or Patook River, which forms the outlet for the watershed of the Department of Olancho, receives the waters of a number of affluents, such as the Guyambre, Guyape, Jalan, and a number of smaller streams. This river, however, above the plains of the coast has a very swift current, and its navigation is interrupted by rocky rapids. At one point, it is narrowed and confined by precipitous walls of rock for a long distance. This place is called by the natives Portal del Infierno, or Hell Gate. Like most of the rivers of Honduras on the Caribbean coast, its usefulness is impaired by a bar at its mouth, which, however, is so limited in extent as to be capable of improvement at a moderate expense.

The Ulua is the most important river in Honduras, and drains a large extent of country. It receives the waters of several considerable tributaries, among which are the Santa Barbara and the Blanco, which latter is the northern outlet for the surplus water of Lake Yojoa. The Ulua is navigable for light-draft steamers for 90 miles from its mouth. It has a bar at its mouth which is dangerous in rough weather, but at other times it can be passed by vessels drawing 6 feet.

The Chamelicon has its origin in the mountains of the Department of Copan on the borders of Guatemala, in the northeastern part of the Republic. It flows through the Sula valley and empties into the Caribbean Sea at only a few miles from the mouth of the Ulua; so near, in fact, that, at times during the rainy season, the low intervening lands are overflowed and the waters of the two rivers intermingle.

The Aguan is a considerable stream which rises in the mountains of Sulaco and falls into the sea a little to the eastward of Truxillo. Its largest tributary is the river Mangualid. It has a bar carrying 5 or 6 feet of water, and can be navigated for light-draft boats for a distance of 80 miles.

The Tinto, which, at a short distance from the sea, takes the name of Poyas, is a stream of considerable volume, having a rapid current. At a point 16 miles from its mouth, the English had a fort and settlement during the last century, which were, however, evacuated in 1786 in conformity with a treaty between England and Spain negotiated in that year. Subsequent attempts were made to found settlements there, particularly by an English company in 1839, under the countenance and support of the British colony of Belize; but all proved failures. It has a bar at its mouth, on which the depth of water varies from 5 to 8 feet, according to the season. It can be navigated by small vessels for a distance of from 40 to 50 miles from its mouth.

The Choluteca has its origin on the northern side of the mountains of Lepaterique, flows eastward until it reaches the meridian of Tegucigalpa, then forms a semicircle, and flowing past that city, describes an extremely circuitous and crooked course and falls into the Gulf of Fonseca on the Pacific. Its upper part is called by the natives Rio Grande. It is navigable for only a few miles from its mouth.

The Nacaome is formed by the watershed of the south side of the Lepaterique mountains. It is not a very long stream, but has a considerable body of water, particularly during the rainy season, when it may be ascended by large canoes as high as the town of Nacaome. Near its mouth, is the settlement of La Brea through which a large portion of the imports on the Pacific side enter the country.

The Goascoran rises among the hills bordering the plain of Comayagua. Its entire length is only about 80 miles, but during the rainy season it carries a large body of water. From the Gulf of Fonseca upward for about 30 miles, it forms the boundary between Honduras and Salvador.

LAKES.

Lake Yojoa is the only lake of any note in Honduras. It lies at an altitude of 2,500 feet above the sea level, at a direct distance of about 50 miles from the Atlantic coast, in the Department of Santa Barbara. It is 22 miles in length from north to south, with an average width of from 6 to 8 miles. Its supply of water must be from internal springs, as no rivers flow into it, while three flow from it. At its extreme northern limit, the river Blanco has its source, but its course, for some distance, is subterranean until it makes its appearance and flows as a narrow, swift, and deep stream to its junction with the Ulua. At the southern extremity, two rivers leave the lake, the Jaitique and the Tacapa. The first named leaves the lake as an ordinary stream, while the Tacapa follows a subterranean passage for upwards of a mile until it reaches the surface in a wildly agitated mass of water, forming a stream 2 to 3 feet deep and 30 feet in width. Both these rivers unite at a distance of about 20 miles from the lake and from the river Santa Barbara, which, after receiving the waters of many other streams, becomes the principal affluent of the Ulua.

RAILROAD STATION, PUERTO CORTES.

PORTS AND HARBORS.

The principal ports on the Atlantic side are Puerto Cortez, Omoa, Ceiba, and Truxillo; on the Pacific, Honduras has but one port, Amapala, in the magnificent Bay of Fonseca.

Honduras is fortunate in possessing, in Puerto Cortez and Amapala, the two best ports in Central America, situated so as to form admirable termini for trans-isthmian traffic whenever the long contemplated interoceanic railroad shall be completed.

The beautiful and spacious harbor of Puerto Cortez was discovered in 1524 by Gil Gonzales Dávila, who named it Puerto Caballos, but made no settlement on its shores. A few years afterwards, it was visited by Hernando Cortez. His quick military eye at once discerned its advantages, and he founded a settlement which he called Natividad, near the site now occupied by the village of Cineguita, opposite the modern town of Puerto Cortez. For more than two centuries, this was the principal establishment on the coast, until it was removed to Omoa, in the year 1752, because the large size of the bay of Cortez and its ease of access made it liable to the attacks of pirates and buccaneers, and the small port of Omoa could be easily defended by a single fort. Cortez, in writing to the King of Spain, gave Puerto Cortez high praise. He said:

It is the best harbor hitherto discovered on all the coast of the mainland from Las Perlas to Florida.

The bay is somewhat in the shape of a horseshoe, with ample depth for large vessels close to the shore and good holding ground for anchorage. Near its apex, there is a small stream giving access to another large landlocked sheet of water, known as Alvarado lagoon. This opening is spanned by a railroad bridge, but with comparatively small expense it could be deepened sufficiently to allow vessels to pass into the lagoon, which has ample depth of water for even the largest ships, and would form a perfect natural dock where they could lie in smooth water in any weather.

Omoa is a small but secure harbor, with good anchorage in from 2 to 6 fathoms of water, and is defended by a fortress, called El Castillo de San Fernando. The town is situated about a quarter of a mile inland. Of late years, the commerce of Omoa has declined, having been largely transferred to Puerto Cortez.

Ceiba owes its origin as a port of entry to the development of the fruit trade on the northern coast. It is now regularly visited by steamers, and does a large export trade in bananas and other tropical fruits.

The ancient port of Truxillo was founded in the year 1524 by Francisco de las Casas of Truxillo in Spain, who gave it the name of his native city. It is situated upon the western shore of a beautiful bay formed by the projecting land of Punta Castilla, sometimes called Cabo de Honduras. It was on this point that Columbus first trod the mainland of the continent of America. He called it Point Caxinas. It has always been an important commercial place, and is the natural outlet for the products of the great Department of Olancho.

There is also good anchorage for ships at the islands of Ruatan, Guanaja or Bonacca, and Utila, members of the group called the Bay Islands, situated about 70 miles to the north of the Atlantic coast. These are also becoming important factors in the foreign trade of Honduras. .   .

The bay of Fonseca is the finest harbor on the entire Pacific coast of America. It is 60 miles in length and 30 in average width, perfectly protected, and capable of sheltering the navies of the world. The three Republics of Salvador, Honduras, and Nicaragua touch upon this splendid bay, although Honduras has the largest frontage.

Capt. M. T. de Lepelier, of the French navy, thus describes it in a report to his Government:

Studded with beautiful islands, this vast and magnificent bay stretches into the land between the mountains of Conchagua and Coseguina. It has no rival on the entire coast of the Pacific, whether as regards its extent, its security, or its naval and commercial position.

E. G. Squier, in his work on Central America, says of this bay:

It seems to have been marked out by the Creator as the ultimate center of the commerce of the Pacific.

On Tigre Island, in this bay, is situated the Honduranean town of Amapala, which occupies a level strip of land on its northern side, while behind, the conical mountain rises to a height of 2,500 feet. The water is so deep that ships of the largest size may anchor within a stone's throw of the shore. The custom-house is located here, and a small steamboat conveys passengers and light baggage to La Brea and San Lorenzo, the two depots on the mainland, which are each about 30 miles distant from Amapala. This vessel also acts as a tug for the bongos or lighters laden with heavy merchandise, although these frequently depend on oars and sails alone.

The Honduraneans have an abiding faith in the great future importance of this port, and rely on the long expected construction of the interoceanic railroad to elevate Amapala into a great commercial depot.

Chapter III.

POLITICAL DIVISIONS—TOWNS—POPULATION.

The Republic of Honduras, since the year 1883, has been divided into thirteen Departments, which, according to the census of 1887, contained 22 cities, 188 towns, 679 villages, and 377 hamlets. Following is a list of the Departments, with their capitals:

Departments.	Capitals.	Departments.	Capitals.
Tegucigalpa	Tegucigalpa.	Comayagua	Comayagua.
Choluteca	Choluteca.	Copan	Santa Rosa.
El Paraiso	Yuscaran.	Gracias	Gracias.
Olancho	Juticalpa.	Intibuca	La Esperanza.
Colon	Truxillo.	La Paz	La Paz.
Yoro	Yoro.	Bay Islands	Ruatán.
Santa Barbara	Santa Barbara.		

By decree, dated March, 1889, the district of Mosquitia was rendered independent of the Department of Colon and placed under the governorship of a superintendent, with full political, military, economic, and judicial authority.

During the year 1893, two new Departments were created, viz, Department of Cortez, to consist of the districts of San Pedro Sula, El Negrito, and Santa Cruz; capital, San Pedro. Department of Valle, consisting of the districts of Nacaome and Goascoran, and the village of Caridad; capital, Nacaome.

DEPARTMENT OF TEGUCIGALPA.

Capital: Tegucigalpa.

Towns: Comayaguela, Santa Lucia, San Antonio de Oriente, Naraita, Tatumbla, Valle de Angeles, San Juan de Flores, San Diego de Talanga, Sabanagrande, Santa Ana, Lepatarique, Ojo-

12

CENTRAL PARK, TEGUCIGALPA.

jona, San Beneventura, Nueva Armenia, La Venta, Reitoca, Alubaren, Curaren, La Libertad, San Miguelito, Cedros, Orica, Santa Rosa de Guaimaca, and Marale.

This Department is situated on the Pacific slope, although it is so near the divide that some of its streams in the northern part find their way to the rivers that flow to the Caribbean Sea. Its main watershed, by the Choluteca River, is toward the Pacific. It is very mountainous, and, although there are many beautiful valleys and small plains adapted to agriculture, its principal industry is mining. In fact, its aboriginal name, Tegucigalpa, means "City of the Silver Hills," and history informs us that silver and gold were plentiful when the Spaniards arrived, and that during the colonial period, for many years, over $3,000,000 were annually exported to Spain in payment of the tribute to the King.

The city of Tegucigalpa is beautifully situated, about 75 miles in a direct line from the Pacific coast, in a pleasant valley, at an elevation of 3,200 feet above the sea, on the eastern bank of the Choluteca River. The latter is here called the Rio Grande, although it hardly deserves so magniloquent a title. It separates the city from its suburb of Villa de Concepción, or, as it is usually called, "Comayaguela." Access to this suburb is had by a handsome stone and brick bridge of ten arches, built in the year 1817. The river at this point is about 200 feet wide. Its bed is full of rocks and bowlders. During the dry season, it carries only a small stream of water, but in the rainy season, it becomes a foaming torrent. A small stream called Rio Chiquito joins it near the bridge, and is itself crossed by a suspension bridge of iron and wood.

Tegucigalpa is the largest and finest city of the Republic. By the census of 1887, it contained 12,587 inhabitants. It is a very old town. The exact date of its founding is not known, but it existed as a native settlement before the Spanish conquest. The first Congress of the Republic, which met at Cedros in August,

1824, decreed that the seat of government should be alternately at Comayagua and Tegucigalpa, but in 1880, during the presidency of Don Marco Aurelio Soto, Congress published a decree declaring Tegucigalpa to be the capital of the Republic. It is laid out with tolerable regularity. The streets are narrow and paved with cobblestones, sloping towards the center, providing surface drainage. There are no sewers. The sidewalks are narrow and paved with bricks or slabs of stone. Lighting is by means of kerosene lamps. The houses are mostly built of adobe, plastered outside and whitewashed or painted, sometimes in gay colors. They are generally of one story in height, although, in the center of the city, some are of two stories. They are built even with the sidewalks, with patios, or inner court yards, which, frequently, are ornamented with pretty flower gardens and orange and pomegranate trees. The windows have no glass nor sashes, but are guarded outwardly by iron gratings and closed on the inside by heavy wooden shutters.

The central point of the city, as in all old Spanish towns, is the plaza, now called Central Park. It is prettily arranged with flowers, shrubbery, trees, and well-kept paths, and is provided with seats for the accommodation of the public. A good military band plays here on Thursday and Sunday evenings. In the center, is a very good bronze equestrian statue of Morazan, the hero of Central American independence. It stands on a lofty marble pedestal, bearing on one side the inscription, "A Francisco Morazan La Patria." Another side has a bronze tablet picturing, in high relief, the battle of La Trinidad, fought in September, 1821. There are four other statues, one at each corner of the park, representing the four seasons. On the east side of the plaza is the principal church or *Parroquia*. It is, with the exception of the cathedral at Comayagua, the largest and handsomest church in Honduras. It was built to replace a more ancient church which was destroyed by fire in 1742, and was completed in 1782. It has two towers and an

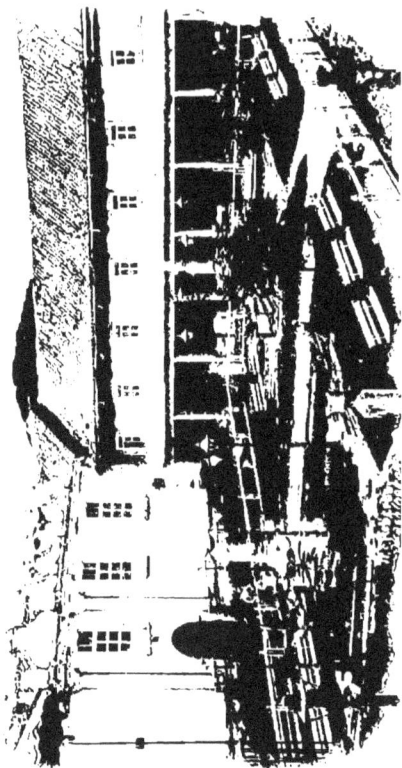

COURT OF THE GOVERNMENT HOUSE, TEGUCIGALPA.

imposing façade, embellished with figures of saints. The roof is cylindrical, terminating in a graceful dome over the altar. The principal altar is an elaborate structure of carved wood richly gilded and adorned with silver ornaments. On the walls, are some ancient paintings. There are four other churches in the city, but none of them specially interesting. On the north side of the plaza, is the Hotei Americano.

In addition to the central plaza, Tegucigalpa has several smaller parks. In that called plaza of La Merced, which adjoins the University and palace or executive mansion, are busts of Gen. Cabañas and José Trinidad Reyes, priest, philosopher, and educator. In another park, called plaza of San Francisco, stands a statue of José Cecilia del Valle, the author of the Honduranean declaration of independence. The principal buildings of the city are the palace, with an adjoining building containing the legislative chamber and offices of the cabinet ministers; the mint, which occupies a building jointly with the Government printing office; the palace of justice, containing the law courts; the general post and telegraph offices; the university; the school of industries and arts; the general hospital, and the penitentiary. There is also, at the plaza Dolores, a well-built public market, divided into three edifices.

For one of the greatest modern improvements, the city is indebted to President Bogran, who, in 1890, made a contract with an American firm, Messrs. Gibson & Cole, for the construction of water-works. Previous to this time, the inhabitants had depended for their water supply on women, who carried it in large "ollas," or earthen jars, upon their heads from the river. The water is now brought into the city a distance of 12 miles from the Rio Jutiapa. The dam at which the pipe line begins is at an elevation of 1,720 feet above the city. The water is carried to a reservoir of 200,000 gallons capacity on the summit of a hill overlooking the city, called the Picacho, at an elevation of 900 feet. From this, the pipe line leads to a second reservoir on a hill called La Leona, 735 feet lower, or 165 feet above the plaza. The work was completed in 1891, and Tegucigalpa now has several fountains, numerous public hydrants, and a house supply of cool clear mountain water. It has been proposed to utilize some of this water to supply the power for lighting the city with electricity, a plan that will probably be carried out when financial conditions permit.

DEPARTMENT OF CHOLUTECA.

Capital, Choluteca.

Towns, Santa Ana de Yusquare, Namacigue, Marcovia, El Corpus, Concepción de Maria, Triunfo, San Marcos, Morolica, Orocuina, Apacilagua, Pespire, San José, San Antonio de Flores, San Isidro Nacaome, San Francisco de Coray, Amapala, Goascoran, Langue, Aramecina, and La Alianza.

This Department is situated in the south of the Republic. It is bounded on the west by Salvador, on the east by Nicaragua, and on the south by the bay of Fonseca. It lies on the western and southern slope of the mountain ranges and is extremely diversified in surface, and, consequently, in climate. In the valleys and lowlands, the heat is tropical. The islands of Tigre and Sacata Grande, in the bay of Fonseca, are within the jurisdiction of this Department. On the former, is located the important seaport town of Amapala, and on the mainland, La Brea and San Lorenzo are the two depots through which passes all the commerce of Honduras on the Pacific. There is considerable mining carried on in the Department, and in colonial times, it bore a great reputation for its production of gold.

Choluteca, the chief town of the Department, is situated in a broad valley on the right bank of the river of the same name. It is a very ancient town, and was a center of population before the Spanish conquest. When, in 1526, Pedro de Alvarado entered Honduras on his victorious march from Mexico and arrived at Choluteca, he met there an expedition that had been dispatched

DEPARTMENT OF JUSTICE, TEGUCIGALPA.

by Cortez from the north coast and another that had entered by way of Nicaragua. The leaders remained here three days in consultation before separating to continue their career of conquest. The city of Choluteca has a national building containing the government offices; a town hall, hospital, college, public school house, and two churches.

DEPARTMENT OF EL PARAISO.

Capital, Yuscaran.

Towns: Guinope, Moroseli, Oropoli, Danli, Jacaleapa, El Paraiso, Teupaceuti, Alanco, Texiquat, Soledad, Liure, Yauyupe, Vado Ancho, San Antonio de Flores, San Lucas.

This Department is situated in the southeastern part of the Republic and is bounded by the Departments of Olancho, Tegucigalpa, and Choluteca, and the Republic of Nicaragua. It was formed from territory separated from the Department of Tegucigalpa by decree of Congress on the 28th of May, 1869. It is extremely mountainous, but has many fertile plains and valleys. The eastern part near the Nicaraguan frontier, particularly in the neighborhood of Danli, is noted for the production of superior grades of coffee and sugar cane. The principal industry of the Department is mining, as it contains many rich veins of gold and silver, as well as extensive deposits of copper and iron. Yuscaran, the chief town, was founded in 1744. It is pleasantly situated at an elevation of 3,400 feet above the sea level, in a valley surrounded by mountains. It has a population of about 4,000 to 5,000, who rely chiefly on the mines for their support. Several mining companies are at work here, among which are the Zurcher Mining Company, the Monserrat, the Guyabillas, and others. The city is abundantly supplied with pure mountain water, which is distributed throughout the streets in wrought-iron pipes. It has a town hall, a hospital, a large and handsome church, and public wash houses.

DEPARTMENT OF OLANCHO.

Capital, Juticalpa.

Towns: Catacamas, Campamento, Manto, San Francisco, Jano-guata, Salamá, Yocon, El Rosario, La Unión, Mangulile, Guyape, Concordia, Silca, San Esteban, Gualaco.

This Department has the largest area of any of the Provinces of Honduras, being larger than the whole Republic of Salvador. It is situated in the northeast of the Republic, and is bounded on the north by the Departments of Yoro and Colon, on the south by El Paraiso, on the west by Yoro and Tegucigalpa, and on the east by Colon and the Republic of Nicaragua.

It is mountainous and undulating, but it possesses wide and extensive plains and fertile valleys, covered with luxuriant grasses and well watered, affording pasturage for great herds of cattle and horses, and constituting the principal wealth of the inhabitants. It is also rich in veins of gold, silver, and copper, and its rivers have long been famous for their gold placers.

Juticalpa, the chief city of the Department, is the second in the Republic in respect of population, which is estimated at 10,000. It is delightfully situated on a small tributary of the river Guyape, not far from the main stream, It derives its support from the cattle trade, agriculture, mining, and gold washing from the streams in its vicinity. It has a military barrack, or *cuartel*, a town hall, and a large and imposing church.

DEPARTMENT OF COLON.

Capital, Truxillo.

Towns: Santa Fé, Sonaguera, Tocoa, La Ceiba, Balfate.

This Department was created by decree of the Government published on the 19th December, 1881. It is situated in the north of the Republic, and is bounded on the north by the Caribbean Sea, on the east by the Republic of Nicaragua, on the south by the Departments of Yoro and Olancho, and on the west its boundary follows the course of the river Cuero, which separates it from Yoro. Its surface in the western part is very broken and is traversed by many lofty ranges of mountains. One of these, the Calentura, runs parallel to the sea and has several very high peaks. There is also, near La Ceiba, a very lofty mountain, called Cangrejos or Congrehoy. These peaks are visible for many miles and form excellent landmarks for navigators. In the eastern part of the Department, are large and fertile plains well adapted for agriculture, the cultivation of fruit, and cattle-raising. On the coast, are several lagoons, some of which are of considerable extent.

Carataska Lagoon is about 36 miles in length, but nowhere exceeds 12 miles in breadth. It is shallow, varying in depth from 12 to 18 feet. It has two entrances, one by a small creek and the other of considerable width, with a bar at the mouth carrying 13 to 14 feet of water. There are three islands of considerable size in this lagoon, and several small streams discharge into it. The land in the vicinity consists of fertile plains affording good pasturage and agricultural facilities.

Brus, or Brewers, Lagoon has a wide mouth, but will not admit vessels drawing more than six or seven feet. Three or four miles from its entrance, is an island about two miles in circumference, which was fortified by the English during their occupancy of this territory. This lagoon abounds in fish, oysters, and water fowl.

Black River Lagoon is about 15 miles long by 7 wide and contains several small islands. On its borders, are extensive plains and pine ridges.

Truxillo, the capital of the Department, is a seaport situated on a beautiful bay and was founded in 1524. Within the next century, it reached a high degree of prosperity, as it was the principal port of entry for ships from Spain. In 1643, it was plundered and burned by buccaneers. It has never recovered its former grandeur, although it is the seat of considerable commerce. It now has about 2,500 inhabitants. Its principal exports are india rubber, sarsaparilla, cattle, and fruit. It has a weekly line of steamers to New Orleans, and steamers from New York call every three weeks. Among its public edifices, are the military barracks, prison, custom-house, Government office building, town hall, a church, and two public schools.

The climate is hot in the summer months, but the refreshing effects of the trade winds render it healthful.

DEPARTMENT OF YORO.

Capital, Yoro.

Towns: Rosa or Siriano, Yorito, Jocón, Sulaco, Tela, El Negrito, Olanchito, Arenal.

This Department is situated in the north of the Republic, and is bounded on the north by the Caribbean Sea and the Department of Colon, on the east by Colon and Olancho, on the south by Olancho, Tegucigalpa, and Comayagua, and on the west by Santa Barbara.

Its surface is very diversified and corrugated by ranges of mountains, between which are rich plains and wide valleys, through which many rivers find their passage to the sea, affording fine pasturage to numerous herds of cattle. These valleys also abound in valuable timber, yielding dyewoods, cabinet woods, and others valuable for building. This Department is preeminently the mahogany district of Central America. All that part of the great Sula Valley which lies east of the river Ulua is in this Department. In the future development of the country, this will prove to be the most attractive region to foreigners from the great variety and richness of its products, its navigable rivers, and its proximity to the ports of the United States.

Yoro, the capital city of the Department, is situated about 75 miles from the seacoast, in a beautiful, extensive, and fertile valley, 45 miles long by 24 in width, bordered by great ranges of mountains. Its climate is very variable. Its inhabitants are principally employed in agriculture and raising cattle.

Among its public buildings, are a handsome modern edifice, containing the Government offices and law courts, a town hall, market, church, and several school buildings. A good road has recently been built from this point to the port of La Ceiba.

DEPARTMENT OF SANTA BARBARA.

Capital, Santa Barbara.

Towns: Ilama, San Pedro Zacapa, Gualala Colinas, Nuevo Celilac, Naranjito, San Nicolás, Trinidad, Chinda, Concepción, Quimistan, Macuelizo, San Marcos, Petoa, Santa Cruz, San Francisco de Yojoa Talpetato, Potrerillos, San Pedro Sula, Omoa, Tuma, Puerto Cortez.

This Department is one of the most important in the Republic from its geographical position, its navigable rivers, and the extraordinary fertility of its lands. It is bounded on the north by the Caribbean Sea, on the east by the Departments of Yoro and Comayagua, on the south by Gracias and Intibuca, and on the west by Copan and the Republic of Guatemala. It is very mountainous, but its great valleys are of wonderful fertility and abound in valuable timber. Fruit-growing, agriculture, timber-cutting, and mining all contribute to the prosperity of its inhabitants. A very large proportion of the commerce of the Atlantic coast passes through its ports and cities.

The city of Santa Barbara, the capital of the Department, is situated on the south bank of the river Cececapa, or Santa Barbara, which is the principal affluent of the Ulua. It is surrounded by hills covered with groves of pine trees, which shut it in so closely that it can only find room for extension in one direction, toward the small plain called El Conejo. Its inhabitants are principally employed in commerce and agriculture, particularly in the cultivation of cacao, fruit, and indigo. It is also famous for its hats, which are similar to the Panama hats, and are made from young palm leaves which, after being bleached in the sun, are divided into threads of which the hats are composed. These hats are made entirely by hand, chiefly by women, who acquire a wonderful dexterity in the work. The principal market for them is in Guatemala.

DEPARTMENT OF COMAYAGUA.

Capital, Comayagua.

Towns: Ajuterique, Lejemani, San Antonio, San Sebastian, Lamani, Opoteca, San Jeronimo del Espino, Siguatepeque, San José, Meambar, Ojos de Agua, La Libertad, Esquias, Minas de Oro, San José del Portrero.

This Department is bounded on the north by those of Santa Barbara and Yoro, east by Tegucigalpa, south by La Paz, west by Santa Barbara. As in the other Departments, the surface is very mountainous and broken, but it has many beautiful plains and valleys and a great variety of climate due to the differences of elevation. Thus, in the great valley of Comayagua, at an average altitude of 1,700 feet, the climate is hot, and all kinds of tropical products grow luxuriantly. It is surrounded by mountains from 5,000 to 6,000 feet in height, covered with pine trees, the slopes producing rich crops of maize, In the plain of Siguatepeque, at an elevation of 3,200 feet, the climate is cool and bracing, and rains are more frequent and prolonged. Wheat, barley, and rye are grown there, and the nutritious grass provides sustenance to large herds of cattle and horses.

Comayagua, the capital of the Department, is situated at the head of an extensive and beautiful valley, which is abundantly watered by the river Humuya and several smaller streams. It was founded in the year 1537 by Capt. Alonzo de Caceres, who was sent by Francisco de Montijo, then governor of Honduras, to subdue some tribes of natives who had revolted against the Spanish authority. He gave it the name of Santa Maria de Comayagua, although it was afterwards known as Valladolid. In 1557, it was raised to the rank of a city and became the capital of the Province, and in 1559, the Episcopal residence was removed from Truxillo to this city, where it has ever since remained.

Its name is derived from the aboriginal word *coma* and the Spanish *y* and *agua* (water), signifying a plain abounding in water. During the colonial times, it attained a high degree of prosperity and was adorned with fountains and monuments and many handsome edifices. Of many of these, only the ruins remain. Previous to the year 1827, it had about 18,000 inhabitants, but in that year, it was captured and many of its buildings burned by the troops of the monarchial faction of Guatemala, and it has never since recovered its former prosperity. In 1873, it again suffered from the effects of siege and capture during the war carried on by Guatemala and Salvador against Honduras.

The removal of the capital to Tegucigalpa in 1880 gave another blow to its fortunes. It has now about 8,000 inhabitants and retains but a vestige of its former importance. It lies, however, in the direct route which an interoceanic railroad must take, and whenever one is built it will do much to resuscitate and restore the fortunes of this ancient city.

Among the public buildings, is the Cathedral, which is the largest and finest church in Honduras. It was commenced in the year 1700 and finished in 1715. The other notable edifices are the bishop's palace, the barracks, town hall, government printing office, post-office, telegraph office, and government offices.

DEPARTMENT OF COPAN.

Capital, Santa Rosa.

Towns: Santa Rita de Copan, Cucuyagua, San Pedro, Corquin, Ocotopeque, Sinuapa, Concepción del Jute, Santa Fé, Trinidad, San Nicolás, Nueva Arcadia, La Florida, San Antonio, San José, Sensenti, Lucerna, San Francisco Chucuyuco, La Encarnación, La Labor, San Marcos.

This Department is bounded on the north by the Department of Santa Barbara, on the east by Gracias and Santa Barbara, on the south by Gracias, and on the west by the Republic of Guatemala. It was created by act of Congress in 1869. Its surface is much diversified and is intersected by several ranges of mountains. Among its most striking topographical features, are the great valleys of Sensenti and Cucuyagua. The former is 30 miles in length and from 5 to 15 wide, and is almost surrounded by lofty mountains. It averages 2,800 feet above the level of the sea.

This department is rich in veins of gold and silver, and veins of bituminous coal 8 to 10 feet in thickness have been found in the district of Sensenti, but the principal wealth of the department is derived from the growth of tobacco, which is of excellent quality and deservedly bears a high reputation. Its cultivation and manufacture are the principal industries. In the Copan Valley, near the Guatemalan frontier, on the right bank of the Copan River, are situated the ruins of Copan, one of the most remarkable remains of an ancient civilization. Among the ruins, are pyramids, innumerable statues, obelisks, and columns covered with singular sculptures, hieroglyphs, and emblematic figures. There are many ancient remains in Honduras, but these ruins are the most extensive and interesting.

Santa Rosa, the capital, was, at the end of the last century, a small village, and owes its subsequent growth and prosperity to the extension of the tobacco industry. In 1795, the colonial authorities built a large tobacco and cigar manufactory, which gave a great impetus to the industry which has ever since been the chief source of prosperity to the city. Santa Rosa is pleasantly situated on a small plain at an elevation of 3,400 feet above the sea level, and enjoys a cool and healthy climate. The public edifices consist of a barracks, which serves as a military headquarters for the Department, government offices, a college, and a church.

San Juancito.

DEPARTMENT OF GRACIAS.

Capital, Gracias.

Towns: La Iguala, Belén, Lepaera, Los Flores, Talagua, Erandique, San Andrés, San Francisco, Candelaria, Virginia, Mapulaca, Piraera, Gualciuse, Guarita, Valladolid, La Virtud, Cololaca, Tomolá.

This Department is bounded on the north by the Departments of Santa Barbara and Copan, on the east by Santa Barbara and Iutibuca, and on the south and west by the Republic of Salvador. It was created in June, 1825, by a decree of Congress, which set forth the political divisions and boundaries of the Republic. Its surface is very diversified, and is remarkable for the various ranges of majestic mountains which traverse it in different directions. One of the highest of these is that of Celaque, which attains an elevation of from 8,000 to 10,000 feet.

The Department is rich in minerals, and in the neighborhood of Erandique, are the celebrated opal mines, which have produced many of these gems of fine quality. Its valleys also present many favorable conditions for raising cattle, which forms one of the principal industries.

Gracias, the capital, is one of the most ancient cities in Honduras. It was founded in 1530 by Juan de Chavez, who gave it the name of Gracias á Dios (Thanks to God). The warlike natives soon compelled the evacuation of the town, but it was reoccupied in 1536 by Gonzalo de Alvarado. It is situated on a handsome plain to the west of the mountains of Celaque, and is watered by the small rivers Arcagual and El Tejar. This city has the distinction of having been the ancient capital of the vast Spanish possessions from the peninsula of Yucatan to the isthmus of Darien. Its climate is moist and warm. It has a large building of two stories used as a barrack and public prison; an extensive edifice containing the Government offices; two churches, a large public school, and in the suburbs, a fortress called the castle of San Cristobal.

DEPARTMENT OF INTIBUCA.

Capital, La Esperanza.

Towns: Intibuca, Yamaranguila, Dolores, San Miguel Guan-capla, San Juan, Camasca, Magdalena, Santa Lucia, Colomon-cagua, San Antonio, Concepción, Jesús de Otoro, Masaguara.

This Department was created by authority of Congress in April, 1883. It is bounded on the north by the Department of Santa Barbara, on the east by La Paz and Comayagua, on the south by the Republic of Salvador, and on the west by Gracias.

The central and northern parts of the Department are extremely rugged and mountainous, but in the south, it is lower and has more level country. Its industries are agriculture and cattle raising. Up to date, no information has been received of any mineral discoveries within its boundaries.

La Esperanza, the capital, is situated in an elevated plain 4,950 feet above the sea level. As a consequence, the climate is cold, the thermometer seldom rising above 62°. Its commerce is confined entirely to agricultural products and the herding and exportation of cattle. Immediately to the north and east, and separated from it only by a street, is the large Indian town of Intibuca, which, from its situation, has sometimes been mistaken for the capital. La Esperanza has a building, two stories in height, in which are the principal offices of the Department; a town hall, a prison, a large schoolhouse for both sexes, and a public park.

DEPARTMENT OF LA PAZ.

Capital, La Paz.

Towns: Cane, Marcala, Santa Maria, Puringla, Yarula, Santa Elena, San José, Chinacla, Opatoro, Guajiquiro, Santa Ana Cacanterique, San Antonio del Norte, Santerique, Caridad, Aguan-queterique, Mercedes de Oriente, San Juan.

SAN JUANCITO.

SAN JUANCITO.

This Department was created by a decree published on the 28th of May, 1869, from territory formerly included in the Department of Comayagua. It is bounded on the north by the Department of Comayagua, on the east by Tegucigalpa and Paraiso, on the south by the Republic of Salvador, and on the west by Intibuca. The greater part of its surface is extremely mountainous and rugged, but the valleys and plains have the advantage of a healthful and pleasant climate and are devoted to agriculture and cattle raising. Very little if any mining is carried on, but in the Lepaterique mountains are many abandoned mines which were profitably worked in colonial times, thus proving the existence of mineral veins which will at some future time attract capital and skill to put them again in profitable operation.

La Paz, the capital, is situated in the western extremity of the extensive and beautiful valley of Comayagua, at the foot of the hills called "Los Manueles." Although founded in 1797, it is only within the past 15 years that it has increased rapidly in size and population. A good stone bridge has recently been built over the river Mura. It has also a very handsome church. Agriculture and cattle dealing are the principal occupations.

DEPARTMENT OF THE BAY ISLANDS.

Capital, Ruatán.

Towns: Guanaja and Utila.

This Department is composed of the islands of Ruatán, Guanaja, Utila, Barbareta, Elena, and Morat, situated at from 25 to 45 miles to the north of the coast of the Department of Colon. The island of Ruatán is the largest of the group, being 30 miles in length by 5 in its widest part. These islands are very fertile and well suited for the cultivation of all tropical products. Cocoanuts, bananas, and other fruits are at present their principal articles of export.

Ruatán, the capital, is situated on the slope of a picturesque hill, the foot of which is bathed by the waters of a well-sheltered bay which forms the harbor. The climate is healthful, and Ruatán is the seat of a considerable and growing commerce, being visited by regular lines of steamships. Among its public buildings, are an edifice containing the Government offices; barracks and military headquarters, custom-house, town hall, law courts, prison, one Catholic and several Protestant churches, and a schoolhouse.

POPULATION.

According to the census taken in 1887, the population of Honduras was as follows ·

Departments.	Population.
Tegucigalpa	60, 170
El Paraiso	18, 057
Choluteca	43, 588
Comayagua	16, 739
La Paz	18, 800
Itibuca	17, 942
Gracias	27, 816
Copan	36, 744
Santa Barbara	32, 634
Yoro	13, 996
Colon	11, 474
Olancho	31, 132
Bay Islands	2, 825
Total	331, 917

Divided by sexes into 163,073 males and 168,844 females. Of this total, 325,750 were Honduraneans and 6,167 were foreigners. Among the most numerous of the latter were—

English	1, 033
Citizens of the United States	185
Spaniards	77
French	72
Germans	43

The greater part of the remainder were natives of the other Central American Republics. It is estimated that the population is now considerably in excess of 400,000. A large proportion of the population are of mixed blood, showing every gradation of color from those of nearly pure Castilian lineage to the Indians. There are also many families that show no admixture of Indian blood. The laboring classes, whether of mixed or pure Indian blood, are, owing to the spread of education, evincing great capacity for improvement. Frugal, patient, industrious, and honest, they have many of the best qualities of a valuable working population, and only lack direction to become an important means for the development and improvement of the country.

The district of Mosquitia, particularly in the neighborhood of the Caratasca Lagoon, contains many of the mixed race of negroes and Indians called *Sambos*. But the most active element of the northern coast are the Caribs, who are the descendants of the Caribs of St. Vincent, who were deported by the English in 1796 and carried en masse to the coast of Honduras. They constitute a good and useful laboring population. They are expert boatmen, and in that vocation, the women are equal to the men. They are also the principal reliance of the mahogany-cutters as axmen.

There are many Indian tribes who still retain their ancient language and many of their primitive habits. As a rule, they are industrious, provident, and peaceable, and as education spreads among them and means of locomotion and intercommunication become more advanced, they will gradually become amalgamated with the Spanish-speaking natives.

Chapter IV.

Honduras is a free, sovereign, and independent republic. The constitution* is extremely liberal, and is largely modeled after that of the United States. It guarantees to all the inhabitants of the Republic, natives or foreigners, inviolability of life, individual security, liberty, equality, and the rights of property. It also guarantees the right of *habeas corpus*. The privilege of self-defense is inviolable. Torture is forbidden. Restrictions that are not absolutely necessary for the security of prisoners are prohibited. Traffic in slaves is a penal offense, and the slave that treads the soil of Honduras becomes free.

The constitution grants no privileges of caste; before the law, all men are equal. All foreigners possess equal privileges and enjoy the same civil rights as natives. Foreigners may, in consequence, buy, sell, locate, and possess all kinds of property, and dispose of it in the form prescribed by law. They may exercise all industries and professions, enter the country freely and leave it with their property, and visit with their ships the ports of the Republic and navigate its seas and rivers.

They are exempt from extraordinary contributions and are guaranteed entire liberty of conscience. They may construct churches and establish cemeteries in any part of the Republic, and their marriage contracts shall not be invalidated by not being in conformity with the regulations of any sect or creed if they

* For translation of constitution in full see Appendix A, page 67

have been legally celebrated. Every inhabitant is free to profess publicly or privately the religion he prefers. The Government acknowledges no official religion.

There is no censorship of the press. No inhabitant may be molested for the expression of his opinions, if such opinions do not infringe the laws, or for any act that does not disturb the public peace. The Republic considers it a sacred duty to promote and protect public instruction in all its branches. Primary instruction is obligatory, secular, and free. No minister of any religious sect is permitted to direct any school or college maintained by the State. No one may be deprived of his property except by course of law or by sentence of law. The domestic hearth is inviolable. Epistolary correspondence, telegrams. private papers, and books used in commerce are inviolable.

Police regulations are exercised solely by the civil authorities. Service in the army is obligatory; every Honduranean between the ages of 18 and 35 years is considered a soldier of the active army, and every one from 35 to 40 a soldier of the reserve. Foreigners are exempt from military service and naturalized citizens are exempt for ten years.

The Government is divided into three branches—the legislative, executive, and judicial.

The legislative power is exercised by a single chamber of deputies, elected directly by the people, which meets in the capital of the Republic every two years between the 1st and the 15th of January. Its sessions last sixty days, unless sooner adjourned by agreement with the executive. Extra sessions may be called at any time, but in that case, no business can be transacted beyond that expressed in the call. The deputies are elected for four years. The constitution provides that one deputy shall be elected to represent every 10,000 inhabitants, but as no congressional districts have yet been established, each department elects three representatives, excepting that of the Bay Islands, which is allowed but one. Three-fourths of the members constitute a quorum. A simple majority determines a question.

The executive power is exercised by a citizen who is styled President of the Republic. He must be a native of Honduras, above thirty years of age, and in possession of all the rights of citizenship. He is chosen by direct vote of the people and his election is declared by Congress. But if, on scrutiny of the vote, no absolute majority is found, Congress shall proceed to elect a President from the three candidates having the largest number of votes. In this case, the election shall be public and must be concluded in one session. The term of office is four years, and the President may be elected for a second term, but can not be chosen for a third term until after the lapse of four years from the termination of his second term of office.

Members of the cabinet are appointed by the President. They may be present at the sessions of Congress and take part in the debates, but have no vote.

The judicial power is exercised by a supreme court and minor tribunals. The supreme court is composed of five judges, which is located in the capital of the Republic, and its jurisdiction extends to all the departments. The presidency of the court is exercised by each judge in turn. Four courts of appeals exercise jurisdiction in the districts allotted to them. A court of letters, presided over by a single judge, is located at the capital of each department. There are also one or two justices of the peace in all the cities and towns of the Republic, according to the number of inhabitants.

Governors of departments are appointed by the President.

The laws are codified. There exists no statute of limitations; therefore, no indebtedness can be outlawed. Gambling and betting debts can not be collected by law, but debts for intoxicating liquors are collectible.

Chapter V.

Within the past few years, the Government of Honduras has made great efforts to extend educational facilities both in the primary and higher grades. Primary education is free and compulsory and as heretofore stated, is entirely secular, no priest or minister of any denomination being allowed to preside over or teach in any school which is supported or subsidized by the Government.

For the higher grades of education, the following establishments exist:

At Tegucigalpa, the Central University, with departments of law, medicine, literature, and science. In connection with the university, there is a free public library which was founded by President Soto in 1880. There are also the National Scientific and Literary Institute, the Female College, with courses in modern languages, music, domestic economy, physiology, and hygiene, a manual training school for mechanic and decorative arts, and an ecclesiastical college and parochial school attached, which is supported by and is under the control of the Roman Catholic Church.

At Yuscaran, college and high school attached. At Danli, high school. At Santa Barbara, college for higher education, including classes in geology, mineralogy, zoology, botany, bookkeeping, and mercantile law and usage. At Santa Rosa, college of sciences and letters, with lower school attached.

The Government has also authorized the establishment of colleges for higher education in the cities of Gracias, Juticalpa, and La Paz.

There is at each capital of a department, a school for secondary education and training of teachers which is subsidized by the Government. There are in the Republic, 640 primary schools, with an attendance of 21,707 pupils, for the maintenance of which the Government paid in the last census year the sum of $100,474.

RELIGION.

The constitution guarantees absolute freedom to all forms of religion. The state does not contribute to the support of any creed, but exercises the right of inspection and control of all, according to the law and the police regulations concerning their external ceremonies. The prevailing religion is the Roman Catholic, but there are Protestant churches at Puerto Cortez, San Pedro, and on the Bay Islands. The whole Republic forms a diocese of the Roman Catholic Church, under the charge of a bishop, who resides at Comayagua, where the cathedral is located.

Chapter VI.

The agricultural resources of Honduras are extremely varied. Almost every vegetable product that flourishes in any part of the hemisphere can be grown within its boundaries, and there is scarcely a limit to the variety of the crops that can be gathered from its fertile soil. In fact, in addition to its wealth of tropical products, most of those grown in the temperate zone can be raised advantageously in some part of the territory of the Republic. This is the effect of the great diversity of climate, due to the peculiar topographical formation of the country. Thus, some landholders may embrace within their territory all the gradations of climate from the northern temperate to the glowing heat of the tropics.

That these magnificent advantages have not been more thoroughly utilized and developed is mainly due to the lack of facilities for transportation. From this cause, there exists, in many localities, little inducement for the agriculturist to raise more than enough to supply his own needs or the demands of some local market which may be within a reasonable distance from his home. To this lack of stimulus which an increased demand would supply, may be largely attributed the primitive system of agriculture practiced by the inhabitants. Ground is cleared and planted in the simplest manner. The *milpas* or maize patches in which the corn is raised which forms the staple food of man and mule, are,

35

if the ground is wooded, merely burned over. A hole is made
in the ground with an iron pointed stick, and a kernel of corn is
dropped into each hole and covered over by a motion of the foot
of the farmer. Such a thing as cultivation of the growing crop is
almost unknown, and even the most fertile plains, if ploughed at
all, are merely scratched a few inches in depth. As a consequence,
the production of cereals is seldom sufficient for home consumption, necessitating the importation every year from the United
States of both corn and flour.

BANANAS.

Within the past few years, the largely increased demand for
tropical fruits in the United States and Europe has led to an
immense development in the cultivation of bananas, on the north
coast of Honduras and in the valley of San Pedro Sula, on lands
within easy reach of ocean transportation. The rapid transit which
has been established by several steamship lines, particularly those
to New Orleans, has given Honduras a great advantage in this
trade, as every day saved in transportation means a saving from
loss by damage, decay, and over-ripening, and consequently the
landing of the fruit in better condition for inland transportation.

In starting a banana plantation, the timber and brush are cut
down and allowed to lie until the warm sun of the dry season has
thoroughly dried them; they are then burned. Then, the sprouts
or suckers, which cost from $1 to $1.50 per hundred, are planted
in shallow holes dug in the soil about 15 feet from each other in
every direction, which allows about two hundred and twenty-five
plants per acre. Nothing else is done except to cut down the
weeds and undergrowth with the machete so as to allow access to
the plants. It would, of course, be better to cultivate the land
and keep it thoroughly clear of weeds, but as good crops can be
obtained without this no one cares to incur the extra expense.
Nine months after planting, the first crop can be cut, and a

monthly harvest can thenceforward be gathered for many years without replanting. The original sprout grows a stalk or tree which bears a bunch of fruit; this is cut down when the fruit is gathered. In the meantime, several young sprouts have been growing. Thus, from a single root, from four to six bunches can be gathered every year. The stalks, as they are cut down, are cut up and thrown around the roots to fertilize the soil.

At a very small expenditure for care or cultivation, a plantation can be safely estimated to yield in the first year 200 bunches per acre, and in the succeeding years, at least three or four times as many. The price varies, of course, according to demand and supply, but even at 37½ cents (3 reals) a bunch, which has been for some years the minimum price, it will be seen that banana-raising is a profitable industry. The banana requires a deep soil, rich in alluvial deposits; it is, therefore, especially adapted to the fertile low lands easy of access to rivers and the sea. In the valley of San Pedro Sula, the exportation of bananas has supplied the bulk of the freight carried on the railroad which extends to the town of San Pedro, 37 miles from the harbor of Puerto Cortez, and the facilities it has offered have led to the establishment of plantations along its line and further from the sea than in other parts of the country.

COFFEE.

Coffee of fine quality is grown on the uplands of the interior of Honduras with great success. The chief obstacle to the progress of this industry has been the lack of means for transportation to the coast. Whenever this question is solved, Honduras will become as great a producer of coffee as any of the other Central American republics, as the country possesses every other element necessary for success in the production of this staple. Coffee grows best at an elevation of from 1,000 to 4,000 feet; consequently, its production must be confined to the highlands of the interior, whence the transportation to the coast is only by mountainous bridle paths on mule-back, at an expense which is prohibitory to raising coffee for exportation.

In starting a coffee plantation, the young plants can be purchased, or, if the planter makes his own nursery, the seeds should be planted not later than the month of May. The young plants should be transplanted when they have attained a height of about 18 inches, which will be in about a year. They are generally set out about 10 feet apart, or about 500 to the acre. The coffee plant, when young, is delicate and requires protection from wind and sun; for this purpose, bananas or other quick-growing trees are planted between the rows. When the coffee tree attains a height of 5 or 6 feet, it is topped to prevent its growing higher, so as to facilitate the gathering of the crop. It blossoms in March; the flowers are pure white in color and very fragrant; the fruit is a fleshy berry, having the appearance of a cherry, which becomes dark red as it ripens. Each fruit contains two seeds, which form the raw coffee of commerce. The trees begin to bear in the third year, and will continue to increase until the sixth or seventh, when a full crop is produced of from 1 to 3 pounds or even more per tree. In November, at the beginning of the dry season, the berries are ripe and ready for the harvest.

The preparation of coffee for the market is a most important part of the work and constitutes the largest item of annual expenditure in its production. The berries are first lightly crushed and washed in running water in tanks, where they are allowed to ferment; by this process, they are freed from the pulpy covering and outer skin. They are then spread out to dry in the open air in specially prepared yards or patios. When thoroughly dried, they are passed through a machine, which frees them from the fine skin which covers each grain. The coffee is then sorted by hand, and all broken and damaged grains are removed. At the prices which have prevailed for some years past, the raising of coffee has been a very profitable industry wherever moderate rates for transportation could be obtained, and even those planters in Honduras who have raised it for home consumption have prospered.

TOBACCO.

The soil and climate of Honduras are well adapted to tobacco culture, as has been thoroughly demonstrated during the past century, particularly in the Department of Copan. The tobacco of Honduras enjoys a high reputation throughout Central America, where it is generally known. Its production, however, has been limited, as it has been a Government monopoly, and could only be cultivated by license and under stringent regulations. From this cause, it has been little known abroad This obstacle to the expansion of the industry has now been removed by a decree published during the past year, allowing tobacco to be cultivated in all the departments of the Republic. By the terms of this decree, planters will have to record the number of their plants. The minimum to be raised on one plantation is 100,000 plants, except in the Department of Copan, where 8,000 is the smallest number allowed. For every 8,000 plants, $20 must be paid to the State.

At the New Orleans Exposition, in 1884, samples of leaf tobacco and cigars, raised and manufactured in Honduras, were exhibited and obtained the highest premium, although exposed to competition with the products of Mexico and Cuba. A Belgian company has recently purchased a large tract of land in the Department of Copan, and is preparing to embark in the enterprise of raising tobacco on a large scale.

On and after July 12, 1894, the export duty to be levied on tobacco will be—

	Dollars.
100 pounds leaf, first class	2. 00
100 pounds leaf, second class	1. 50
1, 000 fine cigars	1. 00
1, 000 ordinary cigars	. 50

INDIA RUBBER.

India rubber is obtained from a tree growing to a height of
50 to 60 feet. It grows more rapidly and is generally taller and
straighter than the rubber-producing trees of Brazil. The native
name for rubber is *ule* and the collectors of it are called *uleros.*
Although the wasteful and destructive methods which have been
used have caused a great loss of trees, the spontaneous production
still goes on, and it will be many years before the natural supply
is exhausted. This industry will doubtless become an important
factor in the future industrial development of the Republic. Where
plantations have been made, about 160 trees have been placed in
each acre. The trees should not be tapped until ten years old;
they will then, with care, continue to produce for many years. It
is estimated that a tree will net to its owner about $6 per year
The success that has thus far attended the few experiments that
have been made proves incontestibly that the rubber tree is susceptible of cultivation. The only drawback, of course, is that the
planter would have to wait ten years for his first return on the
capital invested.

COCOA NUTS.

Cocoanut trees thrive on the seacoasts and around the lagoons.
In making plantations, the trees are usually set 30 feet apart, and
grow to a height of from 40 to 60 feet. In from five to six years,
they commence to bear and continue to do so for many years. Each
tree will produce from one hundred to three hundred nuts annu-
ally. They are a very profitable crop, as they require no care or
cultivation. The nuts ripen throughout the year and are not per-
ishable or liable to damage, as bananas are, by rough handling or
delays in shipping. To anyone who can afford to wait six years
for his first crop, a cocoanut grove is a good investment.

SUGAR CANE.

Honduras is particularly suitable for the production of sugar. The cane attains a size and perfection that would astonish a Louisiana planter. The crop is also perennial. There are many plantations that have not been replanted for twenty-five or thirty years and are still yielding bountiful crops of the finest quality of cane. The sugar cane of Honduras is less fibrous and woody, and is softer than that grown in the United States and yields a larger percentage of saccharine matter. In every valley in the Republic, more or less of it can be seen waving its green ribbons in the breeze. Cattle are very fond of it; everyone who owns stock has a patch of cane for feed, and every traveler looks to it as a provision for his mule when corn is scarce. With proper machinery, as fine sugar could be produced as is made in any part of the world. At present, the only kind made is the coarse brown *dulce*, or common sugar used by the natives. All higher grades are imported, and refined sugar is sold at retail at 25 cents per pound. Aguardiente, or native rum, is also made from it, but this is a government monopoly and the right to manufacture it has to be obtained. There is considerable illicit distilling carried on in remote nooks and corners of the Republic.

COTTON.

The cotton plant grows to perfection in the warm tropical valleys and lowlands of Honduras. It grows into a tall, woody stemmed shrub, and does not require replanting for ten or more years. It is wonderfully productive, and the quality of the fiber is as fine and long in staple as the best produced in the United States. The samples of Honduras cotton shown at the New Orleans Exposition were highly commended and were a revelation to the Southern planters who inspected them.

OTHER CROPS.

Two good crops of corn are raised in Honduras yearly, and in some districts, a third is planted, which, however, is cut before maturity for fodder. Rice, of both the upland and lowland varieties, grows luxuriantly and is of the finest quality. The cultivation of pineapples is becoming more extended than formerly, and this fruit promises to become an important article for export.

Two crops of oranges can be produced per year in Honduras, and the size and quality are such that, with proper attention to cultivation, they could be made equal to the best imported from Sicily. Thus far, little attention has been paid to their culture, but latterly, more interest has been shown in this direction. Lemons, limes, citrons, and shaddocks are also indigenous and would yield good returns by cultivation.

Irish and sweet potatoes, pears, and vegetables of all kinds can be easily grown. Grapes, plums, figs, dates, almonds, olives, and the long list of tropical fruits all grow luxuriantly, and most of them are indigenous.

Sarsaparilla, vanilla, and many medicinal plants and herbs, some of them unknown to our pharmacopœia, abound in the forests, and would amply repay for capital and labor spent in their utilization.

With such a wonderful array of natural resources, all that is needed to give an immense impetus to agriculture is the improvement of the roads and the construction of railroads. With these facilities for marketing its products, the whole face of the country would soon be changed and many a square mile of fertile land now lying idle and unprofitable would be made to blossom as the rose and add its quota to the wealth of the Republic.

The laws of Honduras governing the disposition of the public lands are extremely liberal and afford every facility for obtaining them on very easy terms. A full translation of these laws will be found in Appendix B, page 82.

On the 6th of October, 1893, a decree was published, for the encouragement of agriculture, which grants a bonus of 5 cents on each coffee tree planted, provided that the number is not less than 5,000 trees, and 10 cents on each cacao or India-rubber tree, if not less than 2,000 are planted. Upon satisfactory proof, the amounts are to be paid in cash by the collector of revenue of the district in which the plantation is situated. This decree will not apply to cases where the Government has granted valuable concessions on the condition that coffee, cacao, or India-rubber trees should be planted.

CLIMATE AND SEASONS.

It is almost impossible to describe the climate of Honduras by any general statement. In fact, there exists nowhere in the world outside of Central America such a great variety of climate in so small a space. Owing to the varying elevations of its surface, and consequently, its varying exposures to the winds, Honduras has a variety of climate, temperature, and moisture suited to every constitution and to the cultivation of the products of every zone. The lowlands of the Atlantic coast are the hottest part of the country, or, rather, the heat is felt more oppressively there on account of the humidity of the atmosphere. The heat on the Pacific coast is probably about the same, so far as the actual temperature is concerned, but it is felt less, on account of the greater dryness of the air.

The highlands and plateaus of the interior have a most delightful climate, exceedingly temperate and uniform. Frost and snow are, of course, unknown in any part of the country, and the heat is tempered by the trade winds which sweep across the country from ocean to ocean. On both coasts, heavy dews fall during the night, so that vegetation is always, even in the dry season, profuse and plentiful. On the elevated central plateaus, where the altitude is 3,000 feet and over, the dews are very slight and the nights are as dry as the days. Even in the hottest part of the lowlands, the thermometer rarely rises above 95° or falls below 42°, showing only an extreme range of 53°.

The following table of temperatures, observed in one year at Tegucigalpa, will give a fair idea of the climate of the highlands of the interior:

	Temperature.		Extreme difference.
	Highest.	Lowest.	
	°F	°F	Degrees.
January...	79	54	25
February	84	52	32
March...	88	55	33
April...	89	56	33
May...	90	63	27
June..	86	65	21
July..	84	64	20
August...	84	62	22
September...	84	61	23
October	83	61	22
November	82	61	21
December	81	50	31

There are but two seasons, the wet and the dry. These are much influenced in their commencement and duration by local causes, so that what is true of one part of the country may be only partially true of another. However, the rainy season, called by the natives *invierno*, or winter, generally commences in May and lasts until November, and the dry season, called *verano*, or summer, begins in November and lasts until May.

On the whole, Honduras is a very healthful country. The climate of the coast lands may be trying to a new arrival from the North, but not more so than the lowlands of Louisiana or Mississippi, and with ordinary prudence, no one need suffer from sickness. For the newcomer, it will be well to avoid too much indulgence in tropical fruits, to which he is unaccustomed, not to eat too heartily of animal food, and above all, to be temperate in the use of alcoholic liquors. For all who have weak lungs or are suffering from any affection of the respiratory organs, the interior of Honduras will prove to be a perfect sanitarium.

Chapter VII.

ANIMAL INDUSTRY AND FORESTRY.

Honduras has many and great natural advantages for raising live stock of all kinds. The soil, climate, and natural grasses are all extremely favorable for the business. No epizooty or other serious disease has ever existed among cattle there; no frost injures the grass, no ice closes the streams, no snow nor hard winters injure the herds, and no fierce storms scatter them in this land of perpetual spring and summer, watered by bounteous streams, and rendered fertile by refreshing showers. Large herds of cattle are owned in the Departments of Santa Barbara, Comayagua, and Tegucigalpa, but the greatest development of the business and the largest herds are in the Departments of Olancho, Gracias, Yoro, and Copan, which surpass all others as grazing regions. For centuries, cattle have ranged on the *mesas* and plains of Honduras, where shade is furnished by scattered live oaks and other trees and by the hills. Stock finds nothing to tempt or drive it to stray; consequently, there is no expense for fencing, and there is need for but few men to care for the herds. Notwithstanding all these advantages, and the fact that for centuries the cattle trade has been one of the principal industries of the country, little has been done to improve the stock by the introduction of improved blood or by the selection of the best animals with which to add to size, strength, or quality, as is done by breeders in other countries. The cattle still show evidences of their Spanish origin, and in spite of poor business methods, are profitable to their owners. They are of excellent quality for beef, of good size, and remarkably docile. With improved methods of treatment, they could be made very valuable.

By law, all owners of cattle have the right to graze their stock on the Government lands, but no one has a right to inclose these lands without first obtaining a concession from the Government or becoming their owner by purchase. Ownership of stock is indicated by branding, as in the United States. The various brands are recorded in the districts where the herds are kept, and when sold, the brand is duly described in the bill of sale. A tax of $2 per head is levied by the Government on each sale of cattle, and a municipal tax of 50 cents per head upon slaughtering. A duty of $2 per head is imposed on bulls and steers exported, and $16 for every cow. This latter duty is, of course, prohibitory, as it was intended to be, and it practically prevents the exportation of cows from the Republic. Slaughtering heifers or cows capable of breeding is prohibited by law.

These regulations are causing a rapid increase of the cattle of the country. It is estimated that there are now 600,000 cows in the Republic, and the number of beeves fit for market every year is between 200,000 and 300,000. The markets for the cattle of Honduras are found in the towns and cities of the country and in the adjoining Republics, particularly Guatemala and Salvador. If larger home markets could be created, or if canning factories should be established on the coast, Honduras would be equal to any part of the United States as a cattle-growing region.

The horses of Honduras retain many of the peculiarities of their Arab ancestors introduced by the Spaniards. They are small, of good build, clean of limb, with plenty of courage and intelligence. They are used almost entirely for the saddle, and have great powers of endurance, although they have not been inured to it by hard draft or pack work, for which service mules are almost invariably preferred. The conditions of climate, pasturage, water, etc., are such that, by the introduction of improved stallions, horse breeding might be made a very profitable business.

The burro or ass is not used in Honduras, as in Mexico, as a beast of burden, but is kept solely for the production of mules.

The latter are in universal use for pack animals and very generally for the saddle. Usually, they are rather small in size, but hardy to a wonderful degree. Their surefootedness and sagacity make them invaluable in traversing the difficult and in many places dangerous mountain trails. Mules of large size and well broken for the saddle command high prices, ranging from $100 to $300. Ordinary cargo mules bring from $30 to $75. They are not shod. Eight arrobas (200 pounds) constitute the ordinary load for a pack mule.

The native hog is smaller than the average of the varieties found in the United States. They have long snouts, scanty bristles, short legs, and long body. When crossed with improved varieties, they produce a valuable breed. They are kept universally throughout the country. Raising hogs as a systematic industry would be very profitable in Honduras, as the meat always brings good prices and lard is used for all cooking purposes, as no butter is to be had except that which is imported and which sells at a price that is prohibitory to the majority of the people. Corn, yams, and other food for hogs to supplement what they could find for themselves could be easily and cheaply raised.

FORESTRY.

The forests of Honduras constitute a very large proportion of the natural wealth of the country; they are second only to its minerals in point of value, and are more available, as they require less skill and capital to obtain a profit from them. Cabinet woods of finest quality abound. Notable among these are mahogany, rosewood, ebony, and others almost unknown abroad. The mahogany tree grows in the valleys in nearly all parts of Honduras, but it is found principally on the low lands of the northern coast. It is a magnificent tree, and all others are insignificant in comparison with it. It is of very slow growth. It has been calculated that it requires three hundred years to attain a size fit for cutting. The first men to introduce the industry of mahogany cutting into Honduras came from Belize about one hundred and fifty years ago, bringing with them their slaves and cattle. The remains of some of their camps may still be seen in the depths of the forests.

The timber on Government land is free for anyone to cut, provided that he first obtains a permit and proves that he has means to transport it to market. This provision is to prevent waste, as in former years much was cut and left to decay.

Mahogany can be cut at any season of the year, but it is generally felled during the rainy season, so that the logs may be ready to truck as soon as the dry season commences. A mahogany camp is generally established on the bank of a river, where the underbrush is cleared and cabins built. It is generally composed of from thirty to fifty men, who are divided into companies, each company having a captain. One man, called the hunter, finds the trees fit for cutting. While one company is felling trees, others are cutting truck roads from the trees to the river. No trees are felled of less than 8 feet in circumference. The wages of the men vary, but the average is, for foreman or manager, $60 to $100 per month; captains, $15 to $20; laborers and choppers, $10 to $14 per month and rations. The oxen employed in hauling the logs are fed principally on the leaves of the Masica or bread-nut tree, which forms excellent and nutritious food and grows plentifully in all forests where mahogany is found.

The export duty on mahogany and cedar is $8 per 1.000 superficial feet.

The cedar ranks among the most valuable and useful trees. It is found in all the valleys, but more particularly in those of the principal rivers near the coast. It attains a height of 70 to 80 feet and a diameter of from 4 to 7 feet It is used more extensively than any other wood in Honduras from the fact that it is light and easily worked, as well as ornamental in color and agreeable in smell.

The Ceiba or silk cotton tree is abundant and grows to vast

size. It is frequently used by the natives for making boats, some of which are of large dimensions, by merely hollowing out the trunk. This tree blooms two or three times a year and its vivid red flowers render the forests brilliant. It produces a pod containing a downy fibre or cotton, which may be put to some useful purpose. Its wood is soft and easily worked, which leads to its being largely used for building purposes.

The long-leaved or pitch pine is one of the commonest and most useful trees. It covers all the highlands and mountains of Honduras from sea to sea. The trees do not grow closely together, but stand well apart, permitting the grass to flourish beneath and around them, imparting a park-like appearance to the country and affording good grazing. These trees are rich in resinous material, and the wood is firm, heavy, and durable. The pine forests will in the future be utilized to furnish pitch, tar, and timber for the needs of commerce.

In addition to these woods, the country produces numerous others all more or less useful, such as the guanacasta, live oak, Santa Maria, sapodilla, ironwood, calabash, buttonwood, granadilla, lignum vitæ, and many others. Dyewoods are also abundant, including logwood, Brazil wood, fustic, and others.

Trees and plants producing gums and medicines are not less numerous, including gum arabic, copaiba, liquid amber, ipecacuanha, castor oil, balsam, and last, but not least, the *ule* or rubber tree.

Journeying through Honduras one is never out of sight of a fiber-producing plant; among the most important of these is the *pita*. The great abundance of fibers that can be utilized for the manufacture of various fabrics, from the coarsest cordage and bagging to others as strong as linen and brilliant as silk, or for making all grades of paper, some of which would be strong as parchment, must eventually be utilized and will form a great and wealth-producing industry.

Chapter VIII.

MINERALS AND MINING.

Among the Republics of Central America, Honduras is one of the richest in mineral resources. Of the Departments into which it is divided, there are only two or three that are not rich in the precious metals and other minerals. During the whole period of Spanish rule, mining was the predominant interest, but the political disturbances that followed and were incident to the struggle for independence were ruinous to the industry. Mine after mine was abandoned, and when once the works had suffered from neglect, there was neither the capital nor the energy to restore them. Vast as were the returns from these old mines in the colonial period, the methods used in mining and treating the ores were of the rudest description. The mines were seldom worked to any considerable depth, and there are now hundreds of mines scattered over the country, abandoned and filled with water, which could be profitably worked by the application of proper machinery. But here intervenes the great obstacle which hinders the progress of all industries in Honduras, the lack of railroads or even good wagon roads by which machinery and supplies can be transported at a moderate cost.

Although silver ores are the most abundant, there is no lack of profitable veins of gold, while on the Atlantic slope, almost every stream deposits more or less gold, and placers are numerous. The deposits of copper are of unsurpassed richness and value, but must remain unprofitable until the difficulty of communication is remedied. Iron ores occur in vast beds, much of it highly magnetic and of high grade. If the conditions for marketing the products were favorable, it could be produced in any desirable quantity. Many other minerals have been discovered at different points, but have not been sufficiently explored or developed to ascertain whether they admit of economic production.

Opals of good quality are found, principally in the Department of Gracias. The mines near Erandique, in that Department, have been worked to a large extent and have been very productive.

Within the past ten years, a considerable revival has taken place in mining in Honduras, and in spite of the formidable obstacles to transportation, and consequent great expense, some large reduction mills have been built and a quantity of heavy machinery introduced.

There are now a number of foreign mining companies in more or less active operation in Honduras, among which are the following:

The New York and Honduras Rosario Mining Company, district of San Juancito; The Santa Lucia Mining and Milling Company, district of Santa Lucia; The Suyape Silver Concession (Limited), district of Tegucigalpa; The Victoria Mining and Milling Company, district of Santa Lucia; The Zurcher Hermanos Mining and Milling Company, district of Yuscaran; The Guyabillas Mining Company, district of Yuscaran; The New Guyabillas Company (Limited), district of Yuscaran; The Yuscaran Mining Company of Yuscaran; The Central American Reduction Company of Yuscaran; The Monserratt Mining Company, district of Yuscaran; The Los Angeles Mining and Smelting Company, district of Valle de Angeles; The San Marcos Mining and Milling Company, district of Sabanagrande; The Guasucaran California Mining and Milling Company, district of Guasucaran; The New Orleans and Curaren Mineral Company of Curaren; The Dos Hermanos Mining and Milling Company, district of San Juan del Corpus; The El Salto Mining Company, Santa Barbara; The La Labor Smelting Company, Copan; The Aramecina United Gold and Silver Mining Company (Limited), district of Aramecina; The Central American Syndicate, districts of Tegucigalpa, Paraiso, and Choluteca (Honduranean and French); The San Rafael Mining and Milling Company, district of Gobernado, Nacaome; The Cortland and Honduras Mining Association, district of Nacaome; The Clavo Rico Mining Company, district of El Corpus; The Dakota Mining Company of Minas de Oro; The A. Y. Gold Ledge Company of Quebrada Grande, Olancho; The Guyape Placer Mining Company, district

of Olancho; The Retiro Honduras Gold Mining Company of Olancho; The
Honduras Gold Placer Mining Company, district of Retiro, Olancho; The
Concordia Gold Mining Company, district of Concordia, Olancho; The Olancho Syndicate, district of Olancho; The Rector Mining and Milling Company
of Olancho; The Santa Cruz Mining and Milling Company, district of Santa
Cruz, Santa Barbara; The New York and Camalote Mining Company, district
of Camalote, Santa Barbara.

There is also a syndicate, organized in France, which is engaged
in mining operations at San Martin, near the Pacific coast, and
intends to extend its operations to several other points.

The mines of the first named in the above list, the Rosario
Company, are situated at Juancinto, about 20 miles from Tegucigalpa. The company has a 45-stamp mill and employs about
200 men. It is shipping on an average about $100,000 worth of
bullion every month.

The Government has done everything in its power to facilitate
and encourage mining enterprise and the investment of foreign
capital. The mining laws are very liberal. (A translation of them
will be found in Appendix C, page 97.) Concessions of all kinds
have been granted to miners and speculators with almost too lav-
ish a hand, and the Government has done all that its financial
condition would permit toward improving the roads. It has also
established a department of mining and mineralogy, at the head
of which is Dr. R. Fritzgartner, a scientific mineralogist of reputation both in Europe and the United States, who publishes at
the capital a journal in English called the Honduras Mining
Journal, which has rendered considerable service to the country
by disseminating valuable information as to its resources.

On the 12th of October, 1893, a decree was published imposing an annual tax of 25 cents per manzana (1¾ acres) on all concessions of mineral lands heretofore granted or which may hereafter be granted, payable in the month of January in each year.
The penalty for default in payment is the forfeiture of all rights
and privileges in the said lands.

Chapter IX.

TRANSPORTATION—POSTAL AND TELEGRAPH FACILITIES.

As has been frequently mentioned in preceding pages, in referring to the various resources and industries of Honduras, the whole future development and progress of the country depend upon the improvement of its means of internal communication and transportation. The experience which the country has had in trying to obtain an interoceanic railroad has been particularly unfortunate. Nature has done her part by endowing Honduras with all the conditions indispensable for an interoceanic route, viz:

Good ports at both extremities; an advantageous geographical position with respect to the commercial centers of the world; an interruption or depression in the mountain ranges offering facilities for a direct line and light grades; a healthful and fertile country capable of furnishing supplies and only awaiting the coming of the road to produce material that would afford profitable traffic. But all these natural advantages have been neutralized or held in abeyance for a quarter of a century by the persons who obtained control of the enterprise of building the road.

At first, an attempt was made to organize a company in the United States for that purpose, but this effort having failed, recourse was had to Great Britain, and a company was formed there to undertake the enterprise. The Government of Honduras, realizing the supreme importance of the proposed railroad to the interests of the country, granted a concession of almost unparalled liberality for the construction of a narrow-gauge road from Puerto Cortez to the Gulf of Fonseca, a distance of about 240 miles. This concession granted 10 square miles of land for every mile of road constructed, and such woodcutting and mining privileges that they alone were worth more than the cost of the road. Unfortunately, the Government also granted the privilege of issuing bonds on the completion of a certain number of miles of the road, and, still more unfortunately, no stipulation was made as to the amount to be issued, the Government having confidence in the good faith of the constructors. The result was that, in 1868, the work was begun at Puerto Cortez and about 60 miles of the road was built. Then $30,000,000 worth of the bonds were sold and the work was abandoned, leaving the Government saddled with an enormous debt and unable either to pay it or prosecute the work.

From time to time, the Government has endeavored to come to some agreement with the bondholders, so as to be free to continue the construction of the road, but has always failed in its efforts. In the meantime, the bridge over the Chamelicon River which was constructed on a plan inadequate to meet the contingencies of flood and heavy driftwood in the rainy season, soon collapsed, and still lies an unsightly obstruction in the river. This rendered the 20 miles of road beyond San Pedro useless, thus leaving the 37 miles of poorly constructed road, between Puerto Cortez and San Pedro, all that the Government had in return for the debt which has ever since been an incubus on the country and a bar to its advancement.

The road has since been leased by the Government to several individuals, who never succeeded in rendering it profitable either to themselves or to the country, until a few years since it was leased to Gen. E. Kraft, an American resident of San Pedro, who put it into comparatively good order and developed considerable traffic over it. This gentleman was, unfortunately, drowned in the autumn of 1891; since then, the road has been in the hands of Mr. W. S. Valentine, of New York, who hopes to make it a profitable concern until such time as arrangements can be made to settle, in some way, the claims of the foreign bondholders and to complete the road to the Pacific.

In 1890, a concession was granted to a French company to construct a railroad from Tegucigalpa to San Lorenzo, on the Gulf of Fonseca. The line was surveyed in 1891, but no construction work has yet been done.

Concessions have also been granted for a line from Truxillo to Puerto Cortez, along the north coast, and for another from La Ceiba, in its neighborhood, to Tegucigalpa, but so far nothing has been done towards carrying them out.

Within the past few years, the Government has made an effort to construct and improve wagon roads, and in spite of having been harassed by political troubles and impeded by lack of means, considerable has been done in that direction. A fairly good road has been constructed from the Pacific coast to Tegucigalpa and another from Tegucigalpa to Comayagua, and from thence to Santa Barbara. These have been of great service to the adjacent regions and the country at large; but, unfortunately, the same scarcity of means, which was an obstacle to further extension of these roads, has prevented their being kept in order. Consequently, the heavy rains of the wet seasons have already damaged them considerably and will continue to deteriorate them unless some method is adopted for putting the responsibility of keeping them in repair upon the districts through which they pass.

The routes to the capital are:

From Puerto Cortez by railroad to San Pedro, where mules can be hired for the journey, which occupies about six or seven days, according to the season and condition of the roads. The traveler will need one mule for himself and another for his baggage; he will also require the services of a man to look after the mules, load and unload baggage, and return with the mules. The cost is, for each mule, $20, and for services of man, $15. He will also have to feed both man and mules. From Amapala, the route is by boat to La Brea, thence by mule, by way of Pespire and Sabana Grande. Time, from three to four days.

OCEAN COMMUNICATION.

From New Orleans: By Royal Mail Steamship Company to Puerto Cortez, every Thursday; fare, $30. By Oteri Pioneer Line to Ceiba and Truxillo, four times a month.

From New York: By Honduras and Central America Steamship Company to Puerto Cortez and Truxillo, every three weeks; fare, $70. By Wessels Line to Puerto Cortez, every two weeks; fare, $75. By Pacific Mail Steamship Company to Amapala, via Panama, 1st, 10th, and 20th of every month; fare, $145.

From San Francisco: By Pacific Mail Steamship Company to Amapala, 3d, 13th, and 23d of every month; fare, $75.

POSTAL FACILITIES.

Previous to the year 1877, the postal service of Honduras was in a very disorganized condition and the transmission of internal mails was neither regular nor certain. Since that time, however, great improvements have been made, and the service is now surprisingly prompt and regular, considering the lack of good roads‘ and the fact that the mails are carried by couriers on foot. These men make astonishing trips over mountain trails and swollen rivers, climbing steep hills and fording streams with heavy mail bags on their shoulders, yet generally outstripping mounted travelers and arriving safely at their destination.

In 1879, Honduras entered the Universal Postal Union, and a thorough reorganization was then made and a new tariff of charges was adopted. Postage from the United States is 5 cents for letters not exceeding half an ounce; postal cards, 2 cents; newspapers, 1 cent per 2 ounces. From Honduras to United States: Letters, 10 centavos per half ounce; postal cards, 3 centavos; newspapers and books, 2 centavos per 2 ounces; registration, 10 centavos; charge for return receipt, 5 centavos. Postage to the interior of the Republic, and to Guatemala, Salvador, Nicaragua, and Costa Rica, is as follows: Letters, from 15 to 50 grammes, 5 cents; printed matter, for each 50 grammes, 1 cent; commercial circulars, 5 cents for the first 250 grammes and 1 cent for each additional 50 grammes; samples, 2 cents for the first 100 grammes and 1 cent for each additional 50 grammes; packages, 3, 5, 15, 25 cents for each 450 grammes for the respective distances of 5, 10, 20, 35 leagues; over 35 leagues, 40 cents. Correspondence addressed to the bishop or postmasters is free of postage.

TELEGRAPHS.

The telegraph lines in Honduras were constructed by and are the property of the Government. These, like many other improvements, are of very recent origin, their construction having been commenced only in 1876. From the fact that lack of railways and good roads renders internal communication so slow, the telegraph has proved of inestimable value to the country and is well patronized. There are now between 2,000 and 3,000 miles of lines in operation, and every city and considerable town has its telegraph office. All the operators are natives, who have proved to be apt to learn and soon become efficient operators. The charge is 25 cents for ten words to any part of the Republic. Connection is also made with submarine cable service to any part of the world by land lines to La Libertad in Salvador, and San Juan del Sur in Nicaragua.

Chapter X.

Under the Spanish dominion, the money used in Honduras, in addition to the Spanish coin which found its way to the country, was what was called *moneda cortada ;* that is, coins roughly stamped from sheets of metal, without either border or milling. As the mining industry increased, great difficulty was experienced in obtaining sufficient coin to pay for labor and other expenditures, and recourse was had to small pieces of silver, without stamp or inscription, circulating at their value as bullion, according to weight.

In 1774, the Spanish Government, seeing the difficulty that existed for want of a colonial currency, established a mint in Guatemala, from which source all the coin used in Honduras was supplied until the war of independence put an end to the arrangement.

In 1829, Gen. Morazan sent from Guatemala to Tegucigalpa a press for coining pesetas, reals, and half-reals=25, 12½, and 6¼ cents. These coins had on one side a tree and on the reverse a rising sun. As the revolutionary struggles progressed, and internal strife depleted the treasury and disorganized commerce and mining, the silver currency was alloyed more and more, until at last, money was coined from copper only and circulated at a nominal and fictitious value.

In 1869, the Government ordered a large amount of nickel to be coined in France; but this money soon fell into disrepute until it reached a basis of 50 for 1 of its nominal value.

58

In 1878, a date at which so many reforms were introduced in Honduras, a mint equipped with steam machinery was established at Tegucigalpa, and the peso, ½-peso, peseta, and 10 centavos, were established as a silver coinage, and 1 centavo and ½ centavo in copper.

Gold was never coined in Honduras until the year 1888, when a commencement was made with 20-peso, 5-peso, and 1-peso coins, but only to a limited extent, the total amount of gold coined in 1888 and 1889 being only $1,118. The money of Honduras is now, according to law: Gold, 20 pesos, 5 pesos, and 1 peso; silver, one peso equals 100 cents, medio peso equals 50 cents, peseta equals 25 cents, diez centavos equals 10 cents, cinco centavos equals 5 cents: copper, one centavo equals 1 cent, medio centavo equals ½ cent.

In consequence of the low price of silver, the value of the Honduranean peso is only 51.6 in the United States gold dollar, according to the table issued by the Director of the United States Mint, January 1, 1894. This great depreciation in the value of silver has caused considerable disturbance and loss in commercial and financial affairs. To meet this condition, the Government proposes to devote its attention to so fostering the agricultural and mineral interests of the country as to create larger means of paying with products for goods bought abroad. The first step in this direction has been the removal of restrictions on the free cultivation of tobacco.

In order to throw out of circulation silver coins of other Spanish-American Republics which are not fully equal in value to the Honduranean silver dollar, the following decree was issued on the 5th of July, 1893:

A DECREE

In which are published various measures relating to the depreciation of silver.

Considering: That the fall in the price of silver has caused great disturbance in the circulating monetary medium of all the countries of America, and for this reason it being indispensable to make the best possible arrangement to insure its stability in Honduras, and that in the meantime measures have to be taken to organize properly the National Mint in order to coin a sufficient amount of legal and permanent character for circulation in the country, and meanwhile to make such monetary arrangements with neighboring nations as will facilitate international transactions, it is necessary to make a temporary provision in order to save the Republic from greater losses,

Therefore, in use of the authority with which I am invested,

I decree:

First. To place a duty of 25 per cent on the importation into the Republic of-foreign coins which are not at par with gold in the country of their origin.

Second. Those residents of Honduras who, by virtue of contracts or business pending abroad at this date, are under the necessity of importing silver shall be exempt from paying this tax.

Third. In order to give effect to the foregoing article, it is necessary that the interested parties shall present themselves at the office of the Minister of Finance and exhibit the documents relating to the case, and on sight of the same, the above office shall issue the necessary orders to allow the free introduction. After one month, the aforesaid documents will not be admitted.

Fourth. Amounts less than $200 introduced by travelers at the ports or on the frontiers shall be exempt from payment of the tax.

Fifth. Violations of this decree shall be punished by the forfeiture to the "fiscal" of the amount attempted to be introduced.

Sixth. This decree shall be in force from the time of its publication, and shall become void on the emission of regulations for the circulation of national money.

Dated at Tegucigalpa on the 5th day of July, 1893.

. D. VASQUEZ,
President.

LEOPOLDO CORDOVA,
Minister of Finance.

BANKING.

There is at present only one establishment in Honduras devoted exclusively to banking, that is, the Banco de Honduras at Tegucigalpa, which was formed by a consolidation of the Banco Nacional Hondureño and the Banco Centro Americano. It does a general banking business, discounting and buying and selling exchange. It has the privilege of issuing bills which are a legal tender for all duties, taxes, and debts due to the Government. A concession was granted in 1892 for the establishment of a bank at San Pedro Sula, but nothing has yet been done to utilize it.

REVENUE AND EXPENDITURES.

The revenue of Honduras is derived from indirect taxation, as there are no taxes on real estate or personal property, except such as may be levied for local or municipal purposes. The sources of revenue are customs dues and the monopoly of tobacco, liquors, gunpowder and stamps. One real (12½ cents) on each bottle of native rum (aguardiente) sold by the Government at retail is now dedicated to the maintenance of the public schools. The Government buys the rum from the distillers at 15 cents per bottle. The total amount sold during the year 1892 amounted to 497,858 bottles, which realized 579,836.58 pesos, of which one eighth, or 72,104.57, was devoted to the schools.

The total revenues for the years 1891 and 1892 were:

	1891.	1892.
	Pesos.	*Pesos.*
Customs duties	537, 542. 80	532, 053. 20
Internal revenue	1, 312, 620. 30	1, 232, 079. 40
Total	1, 850, 163. 10	1, 764, 132. 60

The internal revenue for 1892 was derived from the following sources:

	Pesos.
Liquors	622, 062. 20
Tobacco	271, 487. 00
Export of cattle	79, 518. 90
Maritime dues	41, 150. 10
Stamps	60, 509. 70
Sale of public lands	22, 717. 60
Telegraphs	35, 383. 10
Postal	10, 074. 00
Sundries	89, 176. 80
Total	1, 232, 079. 40

The expenditures for 1892 were:

	Pesos.
Public credit	1, 139, 442. 40
War	681, 966. 00
Public works	257, 149. 80
Interior department	150, 109. 90
Finance department	162, 921. 40
Public instruction	92, 717. 30
Justice	88, 388. 40
Foreign affairs	30, 959. 30
Total	2, 603, 654. 50

Showing an excess of expenditures over income of $839,521.90.

The amount of the internal debt of Honduras has been for some years undetermined.' To remedy this, a decree was published on the 5th of December, 1893, calling on all creditors of the Government to appear before January 15, 1894, and file their bonds, coupons, or other evidences of indebtedness for the purpose of registration. The payment of all bonds, etc., not filed within that period will be, *ipse facto*, postponed and all interest shall cease.

COMMERCE.

The commerce of Honduras had, for some years previous to 1891, been gradually increasing and assuming proportions which augured well for the future prosperity of the country. Since that time, a combination of unfortunate circumstances, but principally political disturbances and revolutionary strife, has caused a considerable falling off in the volume of business transacted and a marked depression in all branches of industry.

As the transactions between the United States and Honduras form a large proportion of the whole commerce of the latter country, the following figures in U. S. currency, taken from the United States official returns, will illustrate the situation.

The imports into the United States from Honduras have been:

Fiscal year ending June 30—	Dollars.
1891	1, 159, 591
1892	962, 329
1893	684, 912

The exports from United States to Honduras were:

Fiscal year ending June 30—

1891	649, 921
1892	515, 224
1893	471, 695

When the internal differences of Honduras shall have been settled, there is no doubt that commerce will rapidly recuperate. Honduras is a country too rich in natural resources to remain long in the present depressed condition after the disturbing influences shall have been removed, and it will be well for the merchants of the United States to study the peculiarities of Central American trade so as to secure a still larger share of it. The popularity of American goods is everywhere recognized and acknowledged, and they are so much preferred to those of European manufacture that their trade-marks are imitated. This is particularly the case with sewing machines, revolvers, tools, and hardware. In wines and liquors, it is perhaps within the limit to say that two-thirds of all that are imported from Europe are imitations labeled with famous names and vintages.

The principal reason why American merchants do not secure a much larger share of the business is the lack of proper effort to obtain it. Agencies should be established, or competent men who are acquainted with the language and customs of the people should be sent to Central America to ascertain and comprehend the demands of the market and then faithfully comply with them. One great objection to dealing with the United States is the careless manner in which goods are packed. When goods are ordered for the Central American market, the instructions as to packing should be followed to the letter.

All goods liable to damage by water should be carefully enveloped in some cheap waterproof material and then put into packages not exceeding 125 pounds in weight, but 100 pounds is more desirable. The reason for this is that in the dry season and over tolerable roads, a mule can carry 250 pounds which is divided into two packages of 125 pounds each so as to be slung on the pack saddle, one on each side. When the trails are very bad, mountainous, or muddy from rains, the maximum load is 200 pounds, which will then require two 100 pound packages.

Packing cases and boxes should be made of thin, tough lumber to fit the contents as snugly as possible, and vacant spaces should be stuffed tightly with packing material of the lightest nature. Care should be taken to brace the packages so that they will resist the crushing of the lasso used for lashing the cargo to the saddle. It should be remembered that duties on imports in Honduras are charged by gross weight, packages included; therefore, the two requisites are to combine the maximum of strength with the minimum of weight.

As a rule, European merchants allow much longer credit than is usual in the United States. Six, nine, and twelve months is not unusual. This is rendered necessary by the long time the goods are "en route." The importer has also to extend long credits to country merchants who frequently take their pay in produce and have to wait for the securing of crops, etc. But if collections are slow, failures are very rare, and the laws are so severe on debtors that fraudulent failures are unknown. There is no doubt that, with proper effort, Americans can largely increase their trade with Central America, particularly in cotton goods, for although the English manufacture especially for the market so far as patterns, lengths, packing, etc., are concerned, the natives complain that the cloth is stiffened with starch and when that is washed out a mere rag remains.

The principal articles for which there is a demand are cotton goods, cutlery, axes, machetes, and hoes, kerosene oil, lamps, beer, earthenware, glassware, hats and caps, boots and shoes, jewelry, clocks and watches, paints, perfumery, sewing machines, soaps, musical instruments, wearing apparel, lard, butter, flour, and canned goods. Articles of merchandise shipped from the United States to Honduras do not require consular invoices, but the manifests of vessels must be presented to the consul for certification. Fees are $5 per manifest. Port charges in Honduras are for each manifest $2. Tonnage dues, 25 cents per ton; regular mail steamers are exempt.

On the 11th of December, 1893, a decree was published exempting all steamships visiting the ports on the Atlantic coast of the Republic from the payment of light-house and tonnage dues.

According to the official returns, the total importations into Honduras in the year 1892 amounted in value to pesos 2,005,-025.30. The following list shows the countries from which they came:

	Pesos.		Pesos.
United States	924, 639. 90	British Honduras	31, 813. 40
England	342, 019. 60	Spain	10, 263. 80
France	257, 222. 80	Guatemala	11, 592. 40
Germany	261, 405. 70	Other countries	12, 702. 00
Salvador	114, 478. 60		
Nicaragua	38, 887. 10	Total	2, 005, 025. 30

The exports from Honduras have decreased greatly in value. In 1891, they amounted to pesos 2,781,300; in 1892, they declined to pesos 1,873,800.50, consisting of the following articles:

	Pesos.		Pesos.
Live stock	667, 339. 36	Sarsaparilla	19, 880. 78
Bananas	211, 939. 00	Other agricultural products.	2, 762. 20
Cocoanuts	91, 989. 05	Silver	732, 059. 10
Coffee	41, 393. 85	Gold	19, 657. 00
Tobacco:		Hats (palm leaf)	16, 916. 00
Manufactured	27, 104. 80	Other manufactured articles	6, 930. 85
Unmanufactured	22, 208. 75		
Rubber	6, 861. 12	Total	1, 873, 800. 50
Mahogany and cedar	6, 758. 46		

The division of this amount by countries is as follows:

	Pesos.		Pesos.
United States	1,000,625.60	Nicaragua	13,789.70
Guatemala	506,437.50	France	7,964.30
British Honduras	91,940.10	Spain	7,000.70
Salvador	111,244.70	Other countries	8,628.60
Germany	59,086.20		
England	39,967.20	Total	1,873,800.50
Costa Rica	30,097.90		

During the year 1892, 943 vessels were entered at the ports of Honduras, which are classified thus:

Port.	Steam.		Sailing.	
	Vessels.	Tonnage.	Vessels.	Tonnage.
Amapala	84	102,059	6	2,741
Puerto Cortez	127	83,795	34	2,717
Ruatan	34	19,483	199	6,310
Truxillo	41	24,058	156	3,307
Utilla	30	17,010	232	5,543
Total	316	246,405	627	18,618

These vessels were of the following nationalities:

	Steam.	Sailing.	Total.
United States	175	26	201
England	54	99	153
Honduras	......	493	493
Norway	38	1	39
Italy	28	3	31
Germany	14	1	15
Sweden	7	0	7
Other countries	......	4	4
Total	316	627	943

Appendix A.

CONSTITUTION OF THE REPUBLIC OF HONDURAS.

[Translated for the Bureau of the American Republics, March, 1894.]

Decreed by the Constitutional Convention convoked by the Executive Power 2d of May, 1880.

PART I.—DECLARATIONS, PRINCIPLES, RIGHTS, AND FUNDAMENTAL GUARANTEES.

CHAPTER I.

Declarations and principles.

ARTICLE 1. Honduras considers itself a separate portion of the Republic of Central America. In consequence, it recognizes as its principal duty and its most urgent necessity the return to a union with the other sections of the disunited Republic. In order to attain this capital object, the present constitution shall present no obstacles, as it may be reformed or abolished by Congress in order to ratify the compacts, treaties, and agreements which tend to give or have for a result the national reconstruction of Central America.

ART. 2. The Honduranean Nation is a Republic—sovereign, free, and ndependent.

ART. 3. All public power emanates from the people. The functionaries of the State are its delegates and possess no more powers than those expressly given to them by the law. For it they legislate, administer, and judge, and to it they must give an account of their proceedings.

ART. 4. The Government of the Republic is democratic, representative, alternative, and responsible; and it shall be exercised by three distinct departments: Legislative, Executive, and Judicial.

ART. 5. The boundaries of the Republic and its territorial divisions shall be the subject of a law.

ART. 6. The Constitution guarantees to all the inhabitants of the Republic, whether Honduraneans or foreigners, the inviolability of human life, individual security, liberty, equality, and the rights of property.

Individual security.

ART. 7. (1) The Republic recognizes the guarantee of *habeas corpus*

(2) No order of arrest is legal which does not emanate from competent authority. Detention for inquiry shall not exceed six days, and the justice of the peace shall be obliged, within that time, to liberate or commit the accused.

(3) The delinquent taken in the act may be apprehended by any person for the purpose of delivering him immediately to the authority that has the power of arrest.

(4) Even with a decree of commitment, no person shall be conveyed to prison, or be detained in it if he offers bail, when, for the offense, he is not liable to corporeal punishment.

(5) No one shall be condemned without previous trial founded on law prior to the event which is the motive of the process.

(6) No one shall be tried by special commissions or removed from the judges designated by the law antedating the event which originated the case.

(7) No one shall be compelled, in a criminal case, to testify against himself or against his relations to the fourth grade of consanguinity or the second of affinity.

(8) The right of defense is inviolable.

(9) Torture is forever abolished. Fetters which are not absolutely necessary for the security of prisoners shall not be used.

(10) Solitary confinement of the detained or prisoners shall not be used unless by written order of the judge in the case, and only for a short time and for competent motives. No one shall be imprisoned or detained except in the public places designated for that purpose.

(11) The dwelling place is inviolable. Epistolary or telegraphic correspondence, private papers, or books used in commerce are inviolable.

(12) No inhabitant shall be disturbed or prosecuted for his opinions, of whatever nature they may be, provided that he does not, by direct or positive act, disturb order or infringe the law.

(13) Retroactive laws, orders, provisional judgments, proscriptions, condemnations without trial and defamatory are oppressive, unjust, and of no effect. The authorities who commit such violations shall be responsible with their persons and goods for the consequential damage.

(14) Police powers shall be intrusted only to the civil authorities.

Liberty.

ART. 8. The slave that treads Honduranean territory shall be free. Traffic in slaves is a crime.

ART. 9. All shall have liberty—

(1) To publish their ideas by printing without previous censorship.

(2) To dispose of their property without any restriction by sale, gift, will, or by any other legal method

(3) To profess any religion. The State shall not contribute to the support of any religion. Religions shall be sustained by the voluntary contributions of those who profess them. The State shall exercise the right of supreme inspection over all religions conformably to law and to the police regulations relative to their external ceremonies.

(4) To exercise their profession, business, or industry.

(5) To associate and assemble peacefully without arms. The establishment of all classes of monastic associations is prohibited.

(6) To exercise the right of petition.

(7) To be educated.

(8) To travel in the territory of the Republic, to remain in it, and to leave it without a passport.

(9) To carry on commerce and navigation.

Equality.

ART. 10. (1) Before the law, there are no personal charters or privileges.

(2) All Honduraneans shall be eligible for public office without any other condition than their fitness. Ministers of the different religious societies are not permitted to fill public offices.

(3) Equality is the basis of taxes.

(4) The civil law does not recognize a difference between natives and foreigners.

Property.

ART. 11. (1) Property is inviolable. No one shall be deprived of it except by the power of law or by a sentence founded on law. Expropriation for reasons of public utility shall be qualified by law or by sentence founded on law, and shall not be carried out without previous indemnification.

(2) Congress alone may impose taxes.

(3) No personal servitude can be demanded except by process of law or by sentence founded on law.

(4) Confiscation is abolished forever.

(5) Every author or inventor shall enjoy exclusive proprietorship of his work or discovery.

(6) No armed body shall be allowed to make requisitions.

ART. 12. The laws regulate the use of these guarantees of public rights; but no law shall be made for convenience of regulating or organizing the use of them, which shall diminish, restrict, or corrupt them in their essence.

CHAPTER III.

Public rights granted to foreigners.

ART. 13. (1) No foreigner is more privileged than another. All shall enjoy the civil rights of Honduraneans. Consequently they are permitted to buy, sell, locate, exercise industries or professions; to own all kinds of property and to dispose of them in the form prescribed by law; to enter the country and depart from it with such property; to frequent, with their vessels, the ports of the Republic and navigate its seas and rivers. .They shall be free from extraordinary contributions; they are guaranteed entire liberty of conscience, and are allowed to construct churches and establish cemeteries in any part of the Republic. Their marriage contracts can not be invalidated for not being in conformity with the religious regulations of any belief, if they have been legally celebrated.

(2) They are not compelled to be naturalized.

(3) They are permitted to choose public careers according to the conditions of law, and in no case, shall they be excluded solely on account of their origin.

(4) Naturalization may be obtained by one year's continuous residence in the country [colonists can obtain it without this requisite] by those who settle in places inhabited by natives or on uninhabited lands; by those who commence and carry on important works of general utility; by those who introduce considerable fortunes into the country, and by those recommended by inventions or applications of great utility to the Republic.

ART. 14. Foreigners, on their arrival in the territory of the Republic, must respect the authorities and obey the laws. Also, they must observe the dispositions and regulations of the police, and pay the local taxes and contributions established in consequence of business, industry, profession, property, or possession of goods, as well as those established for the same purpose for the future, whether antecedent ones are increased or diminished.

ART. 15. Laws and treaties may regulate the use of these guarantees without power to diminish or change them.

CHAPTER IV.

Guarantees of order and progress.

Art. 16. Military service is obligatory. Every Honduranean between eighteen and thirty-five years of age is a soldier of the active army, and between thirty-five and forty is a soldier of the reserve. Naturalized Honduraneans are exempt for ten years. The organization of the army shall be regulated by law.

Art. 17. Military jurisdiction is established. Its extension shall be determined by the respective codes.

Art. 18. The public force is essentially obedient; no armed body may deliberate.

Art. 19. Every person or assemblage of persons who assume the title of representatives of the people, arrogates their rights, or makes representations in their name, commits sedition.

Art. 20. All usurped authority is illegal; its acts are void. Every decision agreed to by intimidation, direct or indirect, of an armed body or gathering of the people, is void of right and shall have no legal effect.

Art. 21. Whenever the Republic, or any place in the Republic, is declared in a state of siege, the dominion of the constitution shall be suspended in the locality to which the state of siege refers.

Art. 22. Neither Honduraneans nor foreigners may, in any case, claim from the state any indemnity for damage or injury to their persons or goods caused by revolts.

Art. 23. The President of the Republic, the Judges of the Supreme Court, the Secretaries of State, and the diplomatic agents may be accused before Congress for the crime of treason, or for damaging and violation of the constitution and laws. The political judgment is limited to deposing the accused from his office and delivering him to the regular tribunals.

Art. 24. The State considers it a sacred duty to promote and protect public education in its different branches. Primary education is obligatory, nonclerical, and gratuitous. Secondary and higher education shall also be nonclerical. No minister of any religious society shall be permitted to direct educational establishments sustained by the State.

Art. 25. The State shall provide in every way for the welfare and advancement of the country, promoting the progress of agriculture, industry, and commerce; of immigration, the colonization of vacant lands, and the construction of roads and railroads; the establishment of new industries and the founding of institutions of credit; the importation of foreign capital and the exploration and canalization of the rivers and lakes, by means of laws protective of these objects and temporary concessions of privileges and stimulating recompenses.

ART. 26. The navigation of the rivers is free to all flags.

ART. 27. The present constitution may be amended. The necessity for amendment may be declared by the ordinary Congress, but the amendment can only be effected by a national constitutional convention convened for the purpose. No proposition of amendment shall be efficacious unless approved by a two-third majority of Congress. The case provided for in article 1 is exempt from these requirements.

ART. 28. Every employé or officer of the Republic, on taking possession of his office, shall make the following promise: I promise that I will obey and enforce obedience to the constitution and laws, adhering to their text, whatever may be the orders to the contrary or the authority from which they emanate.

CHAPTER V.

Of nationality, citizenship, and elections.

ART. 29. Those persons are Honduraneans who are born in the territory of the Republic and those who are naturalized in the country according to law.

ART. 30. Honduraneans by birth are:

(1) All persons who have been or shall be born in the territory of the Republic. The nationality of children of foreigners born in Honduranean territory and of children of Honduraneans born in foreign territory shall be determined by the treaties. When no treaties exist, children born in Honduras of foreign parents domiciled in the country are Honduraneans.

(2) Natives of the other Central American Republics shall be considered as native Honduraneans, from the fact of their being found in any part of the Honduranean territory, unless they manifest before the proper authority their intention to preserve their nationality.

ART. 31. Honduraneans by naturalization are:

(1) Spanish Americans domiciled in the Republic who do not preserve their nationality.

(2) Those foreigners referred to in the cases mentioned in section 4 of article 13, provided that they are inscribed in the civic register in the form determined by law.

(3) Those who obtain letters of naturalization from the authority designated by law.

ART. 32. Citizens are:

(1) All native or naturalized Honduraneans above twenty-one years of age who have a profession, office, income, or property which assures them subsistence.

(2) Native or naturalized Honauraneans above eighteen years of age who can read and write or who are married.

Art. 33. The rights of citizenship shall be suspended:

(1) For being under criminal process and sentence of imprisonment.

(2) For notoriously vicious conduct or foi vagrancy legally declared.

(3) For aberration of mind judicially declared.

(4) For sentence of deprivation of political rights.

Art. 34. Honduraneans who enter the employ of other governments without permission of Congress or the Executive lose their rights of citizenship. From this rule are excepted Honduraneans who take offices from the governments of Central America, excepting the case where they render military service or accept military offices without previous permission from the executive power.

Art. 35. The suffrage is irrenounceable and obligatory, and belongs to the citizens in enjoyment of their rights. The suffrage is public and direct. Elections shall be held in the form prescribed by law.

Art. 36. Only citizens in the enjoyment of their rights can be voted for according to law.

Part II.—Departments of the Government.

CHAPTER VI.

Of the Legislative Department.

Section I.—Of its organization.

Art. 37. The legislative power is exercised by a Congress of Deputies, who shall meet by right in the capital of the Republic every two years, from the 1st to the 15th of January, without the necessity of convocation. Its sessions shall last sixty days, with power of adjournment, and of closing earlier by agreement with the Executive. Extraordinary sessions may be held when duly convoked, in which case only the business for which it was called together can be transacted.

Art. 38. A number of Deputies, not less than five, have the power to take the necessary measures to insure the attendance of the remainder. Congress may transact business provided two-thirds of the elected Deputies are present, and a simple majority is sufficient to determine the disposal of a question.

Art. 39. Deputies shall be elected for four years, and may be reelected indefinitely. Congress shall be renewed one-half every two years by drawing lots, which shall be done at the close of the session. Thereafter, renewals shall succeed in order of seniority.

ART. 40. In order to be eligible for election as a Deputy, it is required that the candidate be a citizen in the enjoyment of his rights, and not less than twenty-five years of age.

ART. 41. The following are not eligible for Deputies:

(1) The Secretaries of State.

(2) Soldiers in active service.

(3) Governors and collectors of revenue for the department or electoral district in which they exercise their functions.

ART. 42. Deputies are privileged from arrest. At no time, shall they be held responsible for the ideas, either by word or in writing, which they may utter in the discharge of their duty as legislators.

ART. 43. For the election of Deputies to Congress, the territory of the Republic shall be divided into electoral districts containing ten thousand inhabitants. Each district shall elect one Deputy proper and one alternate. But until this division shall be made, each department shall elect three Deputies and two alternates. The Departments of "the Bay Islands" and "Mosquitia" shall each elect only one Deputy and one alternate.

SECTION II.—*Powers of Congress.*

ART. 44. The Congress has the following powers:

IN THE DEPARTMENT OF THE INTERIOR.

(1) To certify the election of its members and to approve or reject their credentials.

(2) To summon the alternates in case of the death or legitimate disability of members.

(3) To accept the resignation of deputies or alternates presented for legally verified causes.

(4) To make its internal regulations.

(5) To decree, interpret, reform, and abolish the laws.

(6) To create and suppress public employments and to fix their attributes; to grant pensions; to decree honors and concede amnesties and pardons, general or individual, when the public service requires it or the petitioner has in his favor eminent services rendered to the Nation.

(7) To elect the Judges of the Supreme Court of Justice and to accept or reject their resignations.

(8) To make all arrangements concerning the security and defense of the Republic and its advancement and prosperity.

(9) To regulate internal commerce.

(10) To declare the legality of the election of the President of the Republic, to hold such election in the case stated in article 62, and to accept or reject the resignation of the President.

(11) To constitute itself a jury of accusation of the President of the Republic, the Judges of the Supreme Court of Justice, the Secretaries of State, and the diplomatic agents:

IN THE DEPARTMENT OF FOREIGN AFFAIRS.

ART. 45. (1) To provide all that may be necessary for the defense and external security of the country.

(2) To declare war and make peace.

(3) To approve or reject treaties made with foreign nations.

(4) To regulate commerce by land or sea.

IN THE DEPARTMENT OF FINANCE.

ART. 46. (1) To approve or disapprove the accounts for public expenses.

(2) To determine biennially the estimates for said expenses.

(3) To impose or abolish taxes.

(4) To contract national debts, to regulate the payment of those existing, and to make loans.

(5) To establish seaports and create and abolish custom-houses.

(6) To determine the weight, legality, and style of the national money.

IN THE DEPARTMENT OF WAR.

ART. 47. (1) To approve or disapprove of declarations of "state of siege" made during its recess.

(2) To determine biennially the number of sea and land forces to be maintained.

(3) To approve or disapprove a declaration of war which the Executive power may have made.

(4) To permit the departure of national troops beyond the limits of the Republic, and to concede the passage or stationing of foreign troops in the national territory; guarding, in every case, the laws of neutrality.

(5) To declare the Republic, or any part of it, to be in "state of siege" in cases of foreign aggression, internal commotion, or the disturbance of public peace.

ART. 48. Congress may delegate to the Executive legislative powers in the branches of police, finance, war, marine, public instruction, and public works.

Section III.—*Of the formation, approval, and promulgation of laws.*

Art. 49. Laws may be initiated by any member of Congress, by the President of the Republic, and by the Supreme Court of Justice on subjects pertaining to it. Bills shall be presented by Deputies by means of a written proposition, by the President in a message, and by the Supreme Court of Justice by an explanation.

Art. 50. No bill, except in a case of urgency recognized by Congress, shall be passed until it has been read three times. Every proposition which has for its object to declare the urgency of a law must be preceded by an explanation of the reasons on which such proposition is founded.

Art. 51. All bills, after discussion and approval by Congress, shall pass to the Executive, who, if he does not object to them, shall give them his sanction and publish them as laws.

Art. 52. When the Executive declines to give his approval to a bill, it shall be returned to Congress within ten days, with observations as to the reasons on which his disapproval is founded. If, within the said period, it is not returned disapproved, it shall be considered as approved and be published as a law. In case a bill is returned, it shall be discussed again by Congress, and if passed by a two-third majority, it shall be sent to the Executive for promulgation.

Art. 53. When Congress passes a bill at the end of its session and the Executive is in doubt about his approval, he must immediately give notice to Congress so that it may remain in session for ten days, counting from the date of the bill, and if not approved in that time, the bill shall be considered as sanctioned.

Art. 54. When a bill has been rejected or not ratified, it shall not be presented again until the following session.

Art. 55. When the Executive returns a bill to Congress, the voting on it shall be by name and shall be recorded in the proceedings of the day.

Art. 56. The approval of the Executive is not necessary for the following acts or resolutions:

(1) For the elections which Congress holds or ratifies and the resignations which it admits or rejects.

(2) For the declarations which Congress makes as a jury of accusation or impeachment.

(3) For the regulations Congress makes for its internal management.

Art. 57. Every bill passed by Congress shall be written in duplicate and shall be sent to the Executive with this indorsement, "To the Executive power." If he does not approve it, he shall return it to Congress with this endorsement, "Return to the National Congress."

Art. 58. A bill having been received by the Executive, if he finds no objection to it, he shall approve it, returning one copy to Congress and reserving the other to promulgate it as a law within ten days.

Art. 59. The promulgation of the law shall be made in the following terms: "The President of the Republic of Honduras, to its inhabitants, be it known, that the National Congress has ordained the following: (Here the text and signatures). Therefore, let it be executed."

CHAPTER VII.

Of the Executive Department.

Section I.—Of its organization.

Art. 60. The Executive power shall be exercised by a citizen who shall be called the President of the Republic.

Art. 61. The President of the Republic must be a Honduranean by birth, a citizen in the enjoyment of his rights, and above thirty years of age.

Art. 62. The President of the Republic shall be elected by popular vote and his election declared by Congress, as has been prescribed. But when a scrutiny of votes has been made and it is found that no absolute majority exists, the Congress shall proceed to an election from the three candidates who have obtained the largest number of votes. In this case, the voting shall be public and by name, and the election shall be concluded in one session only.

Art. 63. The constitutional period for which the President shall hold his office is four years, and he may be reelected for the succeeding term, but he shall not be elected for a third term until four years shall have elapsed from the conclusion of his second term. The Presidential term shall commence on the 1st of February of the year of renewal.

Art. 64. For the dispatch of business, the President of the Republic shall have one or more Secretaries of State, and he shall designate their respective departments.

Art. 65. To be a Secretary of State it is necessary to be above twenty-five years of age, and a citizen in the enjoyment of his rights.

Art. 66. The Secretary of State shall countersign the decrees of the President of the Republic, without which requisite they shall not be legal; but he shall not exercise this authority alone. He is responsible for the decrees which he legalizes, and jointly for those which he agrees to with his colleagues, except in case he protests against them.

Art. 67. The Secretaries of State shall present to Congress at the commencement of the regular sessions detailed reports and documents upon the acts of the

Executive in every one of the respective branches of the public administration These reports shall serve as a basis whereby Congress may judge of the conduct of the Executive, of all of which it has, by the constitution, tne power to approve or disapprove.

ART. 68. The Secretaries of State shall present biennially to Congress the estimates for the expenditures of their respective departments and the account of the expenditure of the funds voted for the two years preceding.

ART. 69. The Secretaries of State are empowered to attend the sessions of Congress and take part in the debates, but not to vote. They must respond to questions asked them by any Deputy respecting any of the affairs within the authority of Congress, except those relating to war and foreign relations, when the President of the Republic considers secrecy to be necessary.

ART. 70. When the President of the Republic shall take command personally of the armed forces, or when, through sickness, absence from the territory of the Republic or other serious motive, he shall be unable to perform the duties of his office, he shall substitute at his choice either the Cabinet of Secretaries of State or-one of the Secretaries of State to act during the continuance of his disability. In case of the death of the President, the acceptance of his resignation, or other kind of absolute disability which can not cease before the completion of the time wanting to finish the four years of his constitutional term, the Secretary of War shall act as substitute for the President of the Republic, and shall, within the positive time of ten days, call upon the people by means of a decree, to elect a President in conformity with the provisions of the constitution. The President so elected shall remain in office for the term of four years.

SECTION II.—*Of the attributes of the Executive power.*

ART. 71. The President of the Republic is the supreme chief of the nation; he has under his charge the general administrative departments of the country, and his attributes are as follows :

IN THE DEPARTMENT OF THE INTERIOR.

ART. 72. (1) He executes and compels obedience to the laws, issuing the decrees and orders necessary for that purpose, but taking care not to alter their spirit by exceptionary regulations.

(2) He nominates the judges of the courts of appeal on the proposal of the Supreme Court and the judges of district courts in the form prescribed by law.

(3) He receives, during the recess of Congress, resignations of the Judges of the Supreme Court, and in this case, nominates provisionally the judges to act as

substitutes.   Like nominations shall be made in case of death or absolute disability of the members of the Supreme Court.

(4) He nominates the employés of the Executive Department conformably to law.

(5) He watches over the prompt and faultless administration of justice, and over the official conduct of the employés of that branch.

(6) He removes employés and deprives them of office at his discretion.

(7) He grants, during the recess of Congress, amnesties and pardons, general or individual, when public interest demands it, or the petitioner has in his favor important services rendered to the nation.

(8) He commutes the penalties when the superior tribunal which has pronounced the sentence against the criminal recommends such commutation and so expresses in said sentence, and for any of the reasons which the law may point out.

(9) He concedes to employés leaves of absence, superannuations, retirements, or advances of pay, in conformity with law.

(10) He prorogues the regular sessions of Congress and convokes special sessions when a serious national interest requires it.

(11) He gives an account in a message to Congress at the opening of its regular sessions, of the general state of the public administration and the use he has made of the powers delegated to him.

IN THE DEPARTMENT OF FOREIGN AFFAIRS.

ART. 73. (1) He concludes and signs treaties of peace, of commerce, of navigation, of alliance, of neutrality, and other negotiations necessary for the maintenance and cultivation of good international relations.

(2) He nominates the diplomatic and consular agents of the Republic, receives the ministers, and admits the consuls of foreign nations.

IN THE DEPARTMENT OF FINANCE.

ART. 74. (1) He causes the revenues of the Republic to be collected and managed, and orders their expenditure as arranged by law.

(2) He decrees, in case of invasion or rebellion, if the resources of the Treasury are not sufficient, a general extraordinary contribution, of the expenditure of which he shall give account to Congress at its next session.

IN THE DEPARTMENT OF WAR.

ART. 75. (1) The President is the Commandant-General and General-in-Chief of the sea and land forces of the Republic.

(2) He confers all military employments. Of his own power, he appoints to all grades up to that of colonel on the active list. He confers those of brigadier-general and general of division with the concurrence of Congress, and he may confer these grades on the field of battle without that requisite.

(3) He disposes of the military forces, and to him belongs their organization and distribution according to the necessities of the State.

(4) During the recess of Congress, he declares war, and grants privateering commissions and letters of reprisal.

(5) During the recess of Congress, he declares the Republic or any part of the Republic in "state of siege," in case of external aggression, internal disturbance, or if the peace of the country is threatened.

CHAPTER VIII.

Of the Judicial Department.

ART. 76. The judicial power of the Republic is exercised by a supreme court composed of five judges, and by the superior and inferior tribunals established by law.

ART. 77. To be a judge of the supreme court, it is necessary to be a citizen in the enjoyment of his rights, above twenty-five years of age, and an advocate of the Republic.

ART. 78. The faculty of judging and executing judgments belongs exclusively to the tribunals of justice. Neither the President of the Republic nor Congress is able, in any case, to exercise judicial functions, or to advocate pending causes. No public power can revive processes which have been terminated.

ART. 79. The judges of the Supreme Court shall hold their office for four years, continuing by right until the nomination of their successors.

ART. 80. The law regulates the organization and powers of the courts.

ART. 81. The administration of justice in the Republic shall be gratuitous.

PART III.—OF MUNICIPAL GOVERNMENT.

CHAPTER IX.

Of the municipality and the municipal affairs.

ART. 82. Communities which have not less than five hundred inhabitants may be incorporated as municipalities.

ART. 83. The municipality is autonomous, and shall be represented by officers elected directly by the people. The number, conditions, and powers of the municipal officers shall be determined by a special law.

ART. 84. The powers of the municipal officers are limited to local government within their administrative boundaries.

TEMPORARY ARRANGEMENT.

ART. 85. Until the establishment of the penitentiary system is effected, the punishment of death may be imposed in cases designated by law.

Final Article.—This constitution shall commence to be in force on the 1st of December of the current year.

Given in the city of Tegucigalpa, on the 1st of November, in the year 1880, the sixtieth of the independence of Central America.

GOVERNMENT HOUSE, TEGUCIGALPA, 1st of November, 1880.

Let it be published.

MARCO AURELIO SOTO.

Bull. 57——6

Appendix B.

LAND LAWS OF HONDURAS.

The President of the Republic of Honduras—considering that the unappropriated lands of the Republic constitute a source of national wealth, and that the increase and development of agriculture call for the promulgation of an agrarian law which shall guarantee the property and possession of lands, and likewise the correctness and formality of measurements, divisions, setting of boundaries, and other surveying operations connected with the acquisition and peaceful enjoyment of landed property—making use of the powers conferred upon him by the forty-eighth article of the constitution, and the law issued on the 28th of December last, decrees the following ordinances concerning lands:

CHAPTER I.

DIVISION OF LANDS.

ART. 1. The division of land for the purposes of this law shall be into three classes:

(1) Unappropriated lands, which are those that have not been made over to any private individual, towns, or corporate bodies, and which are owned by the State, although it may receive no revenue from the pastures, timber, and other natural products of the land.

(2) Those which are granted to towns as town lands for use of the inhabitants in common, and over which only a right of possession can be acquired.

(3) Lands of private ownership, amongst which must also be comprised those belonging to corporate bodies or definite associations.

ART. 2. The ownership of the possessors of land is guaranteed and protected, whatever may be the time of possession, provided it has been in good faith and with just and lawful title, and in default of document any legal means of proof of the rights of the interested parties is to be so reputed.

ART. 3. The unappropriated lands of the Republic can not be acquired by prescription, except in the case of titles having been given by the Government, without all the conditions of the law having been complied with and their having been in possession of the party acquiring them during a period of ten years.

CHAPTER II.

LAND GRANTS TO TOWNS AND PRIVATE INDIVIDUALS.

ART. 4. The Government, acting in harmony with the present development of agriculture, possesses the power of making grants of land to towns and private

82

individuals, in accordance with the existing laws and ordinances on the subject, or with those that may hereafter be enacted.

ART. 5. To every town which is the capital of a municipal district shall be given gratis, and as town lands, 2 square leagues of land, which must be denounced on the unappropriated lands nearest to the town soliciting them. Town lands of small villages governed by assistant alcaldes, shall not exceed 1 square league; and it is a necessary condition for making such grant that the village concerned in the matter possess a municipal hall, an elementary schoolhouse, and a population of not less than 200 inhabitants.

ART. 6. The towns spoken of in the preceding article shall solicit their town lands in writing from the administrator of revenue of the department to which they belong, through their legal representatives, who in villages are the respective assistant alcaldes. The petition must contain not only a statement of the circumstances which, according to law, are requisite to enable towns and villages to hold town lands, but also of the special condition of the land solicited. The administrator of the revenue shall make a summary investigation, by means of witnesses, in order to demonstrate the correctness of the statements set forth in the petition, the fact of the lands solicited being national property, and whether the petitioners have not already all or part of the town lands to which they have a right. These points being satisfactorily proved, the administrator shall declare, in an official paper, the national ownership of the land and the extent of town lands to which the petitioning village has the right, and shall commission a surveyor or expert to measure off the land in accordance with this law.

ART. 7. On the conclusion of his operations the surveyor shall hand back the documents to the administrator of the revenue, and the latter shall present them to the Government through the Secretary of the Treasury.

ART. 8. After the proceedings have been revised by a special fiscal officer, in the manner hereafter stated, and the whole being approved by the Government, the title shall be made out in favor of those interested without further expense than that of the corresponding stamped paper, and 2 cents, which they shall pay to the public treasury for every "manzana" (100 varas square) called for by the surveyor, and a certificate of the respective payment shall be annexed to the documents.

ART. 9. Town lands of towns and villages are granted for the use of inhabitants in common; their management and distribution belong in towns to municipalities, and in villages to the assistant alcaldes.

ART. 10. Every grantee of land acquires its possession from the moment when, by order of the competent authority, it is measured for him by the surveyor comissioned to that effect. He can make use of the land only after obtaining a title, which the Government shall cause to be made out, with the legal formalities, and without further expense than that of the stamped paper corresponding to the value of the grant.

CHAPTER III.

SALE OF UNAPPROPRIATED LANDS AND PRICES.

ART. 11. All land which is not the exclusive property of any individual, person, or community whatsoever must be reputed unappropriated and the property of the State. Individuals, societies, or towns that wish to acquire the ownership of land of this kind must present themselves to the administrator of the revenue of the department to which the land belongs, denouncing it as unappropriated, and describing it by its best-known names and recognized boundaries, stating its approximate area and the quality of soil; that is, whether it is pasture land fit for cattle-breeding or land suited for agriculture. The officer of the revenue shall admit the denouncement and, without loss of time, shall either himself or by means of the collector of revenue of the same locality examine three fit witnesses as to the following points :

(1) Whether the land denounced as unappropriated is actually or ever has been in possession of any individual or town, and the uses made of it or intended to be made of it.

(2) Whether they know of any one having a right of ownership or possession of said land, or if it is recognized as really unappropriated, and consequently the property of the nation.

(3) The witnesses must also furnish all the information in their power as to the knowledge they have of the locality, in respect to the nature of the soil, its situation as regards navigable rivers, railways, cart roads, and important towns.

ART. 12. After the conclusion of the examination the administrator of the revenue shall formally declare whether the land denounced is or is not property of the State; and in this last case he shall proceed to appoint a surveyor or expert to undertake the operations of measurement, and shall hand to him the respective documents, so that he may act according to the requirement and formalities set forth in a special chapter of this law.

ART. 13. On the termination of his operations the surveyor shall hand back the documents to the administrator of the revenue, who, on receipt of them, shall proceed to value the land in question, taking as a basis for this measure the value set upon lands by law and the report of the surveyor as to its nature, all of which shall be clearly stated in the proceedings.

ART. 14. The administrator shall thereupon decree the sale of the land by public auction, fixing the day and hour for this to take place. The notice of the sale shall be given in a newspaper of the department in three consecutive numbers, or in default thereof in any other newspaper of the Republic having a circulation within the jurisdiction where the land is situated; and it shall express the conditions of the land; its area in manzanas of 10,000 square yards (varas); its value or price, and the date and hour fixed for the sale.

ART. 15. On the arrival of the day and hour fixed for the auction the administrator shall sell the lands to the highest bidder, giving the preference on equal terms to the denouncer. No bid shall be admitted unless accompanied by a sufficient security or cash or guaranty for the amount of the bid. The denouncer is excepted from this condition. The security must be to the satisfaction of the administrator, and the bondsman must make himself jointly responsible as debtor for the amount.

ART. 16. If in the measured land there should be a cultivated piece of arable land, grass piece, etc., formally established, and its possessor should wish to acquire as property the area he occupies and as much more, he has the right to purchase it, whatever may be its extent, at the rate of the valuation set upon it by the administrator, according to the quality of the land occupied, and without overbidding in price being allowed. Of this occurrence separate proceedings shall be drawn up, in which shall be set forth the measures that serve to guarantee the rights of the purchaser, the measurement that comprises the land and so much more, the ground plot, and the report of the surveyor, all at the cost of the interested party; of all of which the respective title shall be given to him with the formalities and requisites of this law.

ART. 17. In every public sale of national lands a deed shall be drawn up in which shall be stated with clearness what took place in the proceedings, the intrinsic value of the land and its increase through counter-biddings, expressing the total amount of the sale, and naming the person or persons in whose favor it is made. The purchasers must bind themselves in a formal and definite manner to the payment of the amount accepted under the legal conditions and with responsibility incurred by back debtors to the public treasury. The proceedings of the sale (auction) shall be signed by the interested parties, the administrator of the revenue, and a notary public, or two assistants who shall be witnesses to the deed.

ART. 18. The sale being concluded in the manner expressed in the preceding article, the functionary who takes cognizance of the proceedings shall remit an account of them to the minister of finance for their revision and approval by the higher authorities.

ART. 19. The Government shall appoint a special official, who must under all circumstances be a surveyor of capacity and probity, to whom the proceedings shall be sent for revision. The decision given by him shall embrace the legal and scientific points raised in the proceedings.

ART. 20. If, from the decision of this official, it should appear that everything has been properly done without material faults or defects, whether in the operations of the survey or in other measures, and the Government accept the opinion of the official, the proceedings shall be forwarded to the Office of the Treasury where the payment has to be made. The certificate of the entry of payment shall be annexed to the proceedings, and after note has been taken in the Comptroller-General's office, and in the office of the director-general of the revenue, the Government shall legalize them. This legalization or testimony of the proceedings constitutes the deed of ownership.

ART. 21. It is to be understood that from the moment when an auction sale of national land takes place it is adjudicated to the purchaser, but the transfer of proprietorship *dominio util* he can acquire only by means of the inscription of the title in the registry office of deeds, in accordance with the provisions of Article 763 of the Civil Code.

. ART. 22. Whenever it be shown by the decision of the official revisor that the survey of a piece of land or of a remeasurement for Government legalization is defective, or that there are similar deficiencies in the administrative proceedings, and the Government adopts said decision, the error shall be ordered to be rectified at the cost of whoever has committed it. The rectified proceedings shall be remitted a second time to the Government for its approbation, and decision.

ART. 23. Every denouncement of national lands shall be dispatched without delay; and if, after three months have passed without sale taking place, the interested party do not press the regular dispatch of the proceedings, he shall be held as desisting from the denouncement, and the Administrator may, under those circumstances, admit a new application for the land. The proceedings shall then be continued in the state in which they are at the time on account of the new petitioner, to whom shall be transferred all the rights of the former one.

ART. 24. If, on making the investigation for the purpose of proving whether an unappropriated land is national property, there should arise the case of the witnesses being in disagreement with some individual who alleges a right to said land, the disagreement shall be settled by the arbitration hereafter spoken of, a hearing being given to the Fiscal of the Treasury, and administrative dispatch of the denouncement must be suspended until the definitive sentence of the arbitrators is given. But if the party alleging the non-nationality of the unappropriated land in question do not make use of his rights within a period not exceeding one month, the Administrator of the Revenue shall, in this case, *ex officio*, make a formal declaration that said land is the property of the State, and shall proceed to the further measures, on the petition of the denouncer.

ART. 25. In the same manner, if, during the operations of the survey, opposition should arise from any of the neighbors of the unappropriated land that is being measured, and according to the data attainable by the commissioner the pretensions of said neighbor may be prejudicial to the Public Treasury, the surveyor shall proceed in accordance with what is set forth in Article 51.

ART. 26. For the purposes of this law, so far as it relates to the grant and sale of national land, the following shall be the unit of measure: The square yard (vara) and the manzana. The latter is equivalent to a square measuring on each side 100 yards (Spanish varas). The league of land, which, to the number of one or two squares, must be measured off as town lands for the towns of the Republic, is a perfect square, whose sides measure 5,000 yards (Spanish varas).

ART. 27. The geometrical map of all land which is surveyed or resurveyed for the purposes of this law shall be estimated in manzanas and square yards, and the calculation must be made by every fiscal revisor who, for any cause, has to examine and decide upon measurements or remeasurements executed prior to the present law. The manzana is the unit that shall regulate all taxes and charges on landed property. The minimum price of lands shall be graduated according to the following classes:

(1) Lands suitable for pasture, whether covered with useful timber or not, shall be valued at the price of 50 cents per manzana.

(2) Fertile lands, suitable for agriculture, not only on account of the facility with which they may be irrigated by streams running through them, but also by reason of the natural conditions of the soil, whether well wooded or not, shall be valued at $1 per manzana.

(3) When the area measured contains the two qualities of land mentioned the surveyor, in his report, shall state the number of manzanas of each kind in his judgment, or their proportion one to the other, so that the Treasury official who has to value the land may have a basis on which to form his estimate.

(4) Lands situated within a league from the banks of navigable rivers, or of lakes connected with them, shall, as a general rule, be valued at $1.50 per manzana. But if such lands excel through other natural or commercial advantages, their value shall then be $2 per manzana. This shall be entirely at the discretion of the administrator, taking into consideration the data acquired in the proceedings.

ART. 28. The total value of the unappropriated lands which it is intended to dispose of shall be fixed by the Administrator of the Revenue, keeping in view what has already been stated.

ART. 29. The Government may prohibit the sale of national land to a distance of 2 leagues in a straight line from the shore of both seas, as also the disposal of islands or quays (cayos). The Government may grant such lands on lease and permit their improvement and cultivation, in accordance with the laws and ordinances promulgated for the encouragement of agriculture and other industries.

CHAPTER IV.

RESURVEY OF LANDS AND RENEWAL OF TITLES.

ART. 30. Whenever a private proprietor, or a town, or any association, on account of loss of title, or any other just cause, may wish to measure their land, they can do so on applying to the Administrator of the Revenue of the respective department, soliciting permission for the resurvey. This shall be granted at once on presentation of the title of the lands or of the documents that prove their right. Proceedings shall be commenced to that effect, and a surveyor or expert shall be commissioned by the administrative authority to carry out the necessary operations on the old boundaries, verified by the unimpeachable testimony of two fit witnesses, who shall give their declaration in presence of the Land Commissioner, and shall accompany him during the whole of his operations, to point out the boundaries and corner posts of the land under measurement.

ART. 31. If it should appear from the legitimate operations of a resurvey that there are differences either in excess or deficiency of the land, in neither case shall the proprietor need to make a fresh transaction with the public treasury.

ART. 32. It is the obligation of every proprietor to mark the boundaries of his land with stone or masonry pillars or other permanent signs, and for this purpose he shall have it measured and marked off by a surveyor or expert, proceeding in the form set forth in another chapter of this law. The same is incumbent on towns, so that they may secure the town and other lands that lawfully belong to them, and be able to defend them perfectly from all trespass attempted either in good or bad faith.

ART. 33. On the termination of the operations of the resurvey of land the surveyor shall return the proceedings to the Administrator of the Revenue from whom he received them, who shall remit them to the Government for the revision and approbation of the fiscal. The title of the resurvey shall be delivered with the same formalities as those provided in the case of the ordinary measurements of unappropriated lands.

ART. 34. In every remeasurement 2 cents shall be charged as fiscal dues for every manzana that results. This fee shall be paid to the Public Treasury, after the proceedings are approved, in order that the certificate of payment may be annexed to the title.

ART. 35. The titles of landed property can be renewed by applying to the Government, which shall order the legalized copy of the respective deed that should be in the general archives of the Republic to be made out. In the new deed there shall be copied the petition requesting it and the final decree granting the renewal of the title, which shall be granted on presentation of the certificate of the payment of 2 cents for every manzana of those expressed in the proceedings to be legalized. The interested party must also pay the expenses of stamped paper, writings, and the copy of the geometrical map, which must be annexed to the deed.

ART. 36. When the person desiring the renewal of a title is owner of the property by bill of sale from one possessor to another, or in virtue of any legal documentary proof, he shall adjoin the documents on which he relies to his petition; and the Government, taking them into consideration, shall admit them, in so far as the law permits, and give orders that on the respective title being extended in favor of the petitioner said documents shall be copied faithfully and in full.

CHAPTER V.

MEASUREMENTS, DEMARKATIONS, SETTING OF BOUNDARIES, AND PARTITIONS.

ART. 37. A surveyor intrusted with the measurement of a piece of land shall, after accepting the commission, receive the papers, and shall mark on them the day for the commencement of operations.

ART. 38. The person commissioned for any survey, resurvey, etc., possesses the authority necessary for acting in the sense of his commission without having to subject his actions to the intervention of the local authorities of the place to which the land belongs. The jurisdiction of the surveyor is in this case of an administrative character, and as agent of the revenue department he should be assisted in the discharge of his duties whenever, with just cause, he calls on the local authorities to this effect.

ART. 39. All operations executed under the law must be authenticated by a notary public or by two attendant witnesses, able to read and write, named and sworn in by the surveyor, who shall state this fact on the proceedings. He shall also appoint a teller and a chain-bearer, who shall keep an exact account of the yards (varas) they measure on each stretch, for the judge of the survey to take note of in due time.

ART. 40. The first operation of the Land Commissioner must be the inspection of the land he is about to survey, and has for its object—

(1) To ascertain what are at the time, or are going to be, the boundaries.

(2) To see whether or not they can be run, and if they are susceptible of material measurement or not.

(3) To inform himself whether the land adjoins private or national property,

and in the former case if the interested parties are in agreement as to their respective boundaries, or there exist doubts or claims regarding them.

(4) To endeavor, with impartiality and earnestness, to have all disagreements that spring up amicably and fairly arranged by the parties themselves.

ART. 41. After the boundaries that the land is to have are decided upon, and the interested parties are in accord regarding them, the measurement shall be proceeded with from boundary post to boundary post, taking the direction and distances in a straight line with a chain or metallic tape-line of 25 yards (Spanish yards), of 835 millimeters to the yard; the Commissioner taking care to avoid all cause of error and to instruct his assistants as to the convenient placing of sights and the carrying the chain accurately along the corresponding line.

ART. 42. At all points where there is a change in the direction of the boundaries and no natural signs exist, temporary marks shall be made by heaps of stones, so that they may not be lost sight of while the formal demarkation of the land is being made.

ART. 43. In the measurement of distances care must be taken to stretch the chain in a straight line, so as to avoid the undulations of the land, or to follow the declivities, in which case the angles of elevation and depression shall be taken and the line reduced to a horizontal.

ART. 44. The variations of the compass shall be ascertained before commencing the survey, the most appropriate spot for making the observation necessary for ascertaining it being selected, and in the proceedings the measures adopted shall be stated.

ART. 45. When lands adjoining others owned by or in possession of private individuals are to be measured, the inspection and measurement of the boundaries must be executed with the knowledge and in presence of the interested parties, and with inspection of their respective documents.

ART. 46. For the effect of the preceding article the judge of the measurement shall officially summon the proprietors or occupiers of the adjacent lands, apponting a period of three days, adding one more for every 5 leagues of distance, so that during that time they may present themselves, either personally or by representative, with their titles, in the place where their presence is required.

ART. 47. A note of these summons shall be entered on the proceedings, expressing the date and place of their issue, the place of residence of the persons to whom they are addressed, and the day fixed for the commencement of the operations at which they should be present.

ART. 48. If, notwithstanding the summons, any of the adjoining proprietors should not appear at his boundary, the surveyor shall proceed with the operations he has to perform thereon, endeavoring for their security to obtain data from other neighbors, or from whosoever can furnish them, for greater exactitude.

ART. 49. When the line to be measured is defined by a river, ravine, fence, or ditch, which from its nature admits of no confusion, the neighboring proprietor or possessor may excuse himself from attending, stating in his answer to the official summons in what his boundary consists. In other cases, where the boundaries are not well defined, it is incumbent on proprietors or possessors to present themselves to point them out, in order that their lawful rights may be respected.

ART. 50. On measuring the recognized boundary of a piece of property it shall be seen whether it is in accordance with the titles or documents from which it proceeds, not so as to alter it in any manner, but with the object that, in the direction and extension it actually has, it may serve as a boundary to the land to be measured.

ART. 51. When the proprietor or possessor of the land adjoining the piece being measured will not agree as to the boundary that the party interested in the survey wishes to establish, the surveyor shall use all effort and impartiality to bring about an equitable arrangement between the parties. If he should succeed, after making an entry to that effect on the proceedings, he shall carry out in conformity therewith the operations necessary for the opening of the line or lines agreed upon. In the contrary case, he shall merely take exact data as to the extension, direction, and other remarkable signs of the lines that each party lays claim to, so that therewith, and with whatever else it may be well to keep in view, the work may be decided by the arbitration hereafter to be spoken of, without on that account suspending the further operations of the measurement.

ART. 52. Should the measurement to be made be of unappropriated land adjoining others of private ownership or legally occupied, the survey shall be carried out, following the recognized boundaries of the owned or occupied lands adjoining.

ART. 53. Should the denounced land be surrounded by others unappropriated, the survey shall be executed in accordance with the terms of the denouncement, endeavoring to follow the natural boundaries of the land.

ART. 54. When lands without defined boundaries have to be measured, so far as topographical circumstances permit, a square or rectangular form shall be given them, the sides of which shall run from east to west and from north to south on a true meridian.

ART. 55. The surveyor shall carry a field-book, in which he shall note down all operations, the direction and length of every straight line measured, the accessory measures adopted to obtain the direction and length of such as are inaccessible, and all the signs met with on the land which demark the boundaries, and corner posts.

ART. 56. With this book before him, and in accordance with the particulars contained therein, and on the corresponding stamped paper the proceedings stating what has taken place every day shall be written out with clearness and precision, both as regards the inspection of the land and the measurement of the boundaries, and also what is expressed concerning them in the documents of the adjoining neighbors, should there be any, and everything else that has been done or may have occurred.

ART. 57. These proceedings shall be signed by the surveyor, by the party interested in the measurement, by the adjoining neighbors whose boundaries are concerned, and by a notary or the attendant witnesses.

ART. 58. As soon as the corresponding calculations for the reduction of the lines that could not be actually measured and for fixing the area are concluded, a statement of the result of said operations shall be entered on the proceedings, declaring the steps taken to obtain it.

ART. 59. Every survey of land must be accompanied by a map, which shall show, in proportional scale with reference to the true meridian, the perimeter of the horizontal plan and the places or objects that help to a fuller understanding of the position of the boundaries and corner posts, nothing the names of these, the area in manzanas and square yards (varas), the adjoining possessions, the variations of the compass, the scale employed, and the date.

ART. 60. There shall also accompany it a record or recapitulation of the whole measurement, in which may be seen at once the direction and length of each line of the perimeter and the magnitude of the angles they form one with another.

ART. 61. Of all that has been done the surveyor shall draw up proceedings, of which he shall give account to the authority from whom his commission emanated, informing him whether the land measured was unappropriated, as to the nature of the land, and other particulars mentioned in Article 27 of this law, and giving the number of the manzanas it contains of the precise kinds, to serve as a basis for the valuation. He shall also make a report as to any disputes that may have occurred, or the way and term for arranging them by means of arbitration, should they have been left open. Under other circumstances the report shall be confined to the matters relating to the object of the commission.

ART. 62. After a sale by auction of unappropriated lands has been effected, or a resurvey of those of private ownership, which the Government has to approve for granting titles, the proceedings shall be revised by the special official, who shall be nominated for that purpose by supreme decree. The fiscal revision of such operations has for its object to observe—

(1) Whether, in carrying out the operations of measurement or remeasurement, all the legal formalities have been complied with.

(2) Whether each and every operation has been performed in accordance with the principles of land survey.

(3) Whether the calculations have been made in accordance with the data obtained on the land, and whether the results are correct.

(4) Whether the maps agree with the data of the survey and of the record referred to in Article 60, and whether they contain the remarks called for in Article 59.

ART. 63. If omissions or errors that can be easily filled up or rectified are met with, the revisor shall do what is necessary, either himself or by agreement with the measuring surveyor; but if this be not possible, the Government, in view of the report made by the revisor of measurement or remeasurement, shall decide what is best to be done, and in that case regard shall be had to the requirements of Article 22.

ART. 64. The maximum error of measurement that can be permitted in the survey of broken land, and of which the perimeter has more than forty sides, is 2 per cent on the whole extent; having only twenty sides, 1½ per cent. Should the error exceed those limits, it will be necessary to resurvey the land.

ART. 65. When a survey of unappropriated lands, or a remeasurement of private ones, has met with a favorable decision from the revisor, and it appears beyond dispute not only that it was executed without any opposition, but also that the interested parties and the adjoining neighbors, if there be any, are satisfied with what has been done, the boundaries indicated shall be considered settled, and shall at once be marked in a formal manner by pillars of masonry, or in some other permanent and secure way, if no natural landmarks exist. This shall be done also on every property and lawful possession of the kind mentioned in Article 32, with permission from the competent authority and in presence of the parties interested, by the same surveyor who measured the land or by another commissioned for the purpose. All that is done with this object shall be stated in proceedings to be drawn up, with the formalities prescribed in articles 56 and 57. When having to do with measurements made prior to this law, a deed shall be made out of all the proceedings of the demarkation, and the originals shall be annexed to the titles of the property marked out, with a certificate from the Administrator of the Revenue, who must intervene for the proper legalization of the different steps.

ART. 66. Surveyors in the exercise of their duties will be under the same criminal and civil responsibility that attaches to other public functionaries; and if—knowingly, through want of skill, and in contravention of what is prescribed in this law, so far as relates to his attributes—a surveyor should incorporate land belonging to a private individual, or lawfully occupied, or should occasion any other injury, he must remedy it at once, making the necessary rectification for the error to be remedied.

ART. 67. If the incorporation or damage treated of in the preceding article arise through the injured proprietor or occupier not having furnished at the proper time the necessary and explanatory data to enable the operations to be fairly performed, the reparation shall be made at the expense of said proprietor or occupier.

ART. 68. In the operations of measurement, remeasurement, running boundary lines, demarkation and division practiced by surveyors in the capacity of experts nominated by judicial or administrative authority, or in those intrusted to them by private individuals, they shall proceed in accordance with the nature and object of the operation, adhering to the spirit of the prescriptions of the present law.

ART 69. Disputes as to doubtful boundaries spoken of in article 51, and likewise those mentioned in articles 24 and 25, that arise between two or more proprietors, whether private individuals, towns, or communities, shall be settled in future by arbitration only; and controversies regarding partitions of land made by a surveyor commissioned for the purpose, and which the contending parties do not wish to accept or to recognize as valid, shall also be settled in the same manner.

ART. 70. The contending parties have the right to name the arbitrators in presence of the administrator who authorized the survey or resurvey of a piece of land, and in other cases in presence of the respective iudge. Those named shall have the authority proper to arbitrators.

ART. 71. In an arbitration suit the contending parties may appear personally or by representative; and the fees of arbitrators and representatives, as well as all other expenses to which these special proceedings may give rise, shall be at the charge of the contending parties.

ART. 72. Each party shall name an arbitrator, and any citizen in the enjoyment of his rights may be such; and the arbitrators thus named shall agree upon a third, who shall decide in case of disagreement without the obligation of this third party being subjected to the approbation of the contending parties.

ART. 73. Whatever questions arise, or any already existing on the publication of this law, must be submitted to arbitration. If either of the parties should fail to name an arbitrator within a month after being called upon to do so by the administrator or judge at the solicitation of his opponent, said functionary may compel him or may name an arbitrator *ex officio* if necessary. The third arbitrator shall be appointed by the administrator or judge, three days after its being declared in writing that the first two can not come to an agreement as to whom to elect.

ART. 74. On the decision being given, in view of the antecedents, the court of arbitrators shall notify the parties; and at request of either of them shall give order of execution and send it, with the proceeding that caused it, to the administrator or judge, for its due enforcement. No appeal can be had from the decision of the arbitrators.

ART. 75. The proceedings in arbitration may last for a period of thirty days, and can not be adjourned. During this period the parties must present the lawful proofs which they are able to obtain, and these must be confined simply to matters relating to the dispute.

ART. 76. Each of the arbitrators shall receive for his fee the amount assigned by the administrator or judge; the arbitrators shall themselves form an account of all other charges arising from the suit, and this, which can not be contested by the litigants, shall be paid one-half by each party.

CHAPTER VI.

GENERAL RULES.

ART. 77. After a surveyor has been appointed to perform a measurement, or any other survey, no other can be appointed for the same purpose, except under the circumstance of the first one having been objected to. When two surveyors are measuring adjoining lands they should come to an understanding before proceeding with the operations, agreeing as to the boundaries and true limits. If they do not agree, they shall institute an arbitration at the expense of the parties interested, so that in view of the antecedents of each one the arbitrators may decide on what is equitable.

ART. 78. Surveyors are those who have obtained their diplomas as such, the professors spoken of in Article 217 of the code of public instruction, and doctors of the faculty of science of the University of the Republic.

ART. 79. For the object of this law, in the part applicable to the circumstances, the following are to be reputed as experts in land surveying: Bachelors of science and letters who are of age, and those citizens who, although not holding a literary diploma, are well known to possess competent knowledge of arithmetic, algebra, geometry, topography, linear drawing, and legal mensuration.

SURVEYORS' FEES.

ART. 80. The fees which surveyors or experts may receive for their operations in surveys, resurveys, demarkations, divisions, and fixing the boundaries of lands, are whatever they may freely stipulate with the respective parties interested.

ART. 81. Failing any stipulation, the fees shall be arranged as follows:

(1) They shall receive $1 per league for every league they have to travel to arrive at the field of operations, reckoning from the place of departure or from the residence of the surveyor.

(2) For inditing the proceedings and drawing the corresponding map, whether

of a survey, fixing boundaries, or division, they shall receive $15, and the cost of the stamped paper used is on account of the interested party.

(3) They shall also receive 10 cents for every manzana of land when the area does not exceed 300 manzanas; but if it should exceed this number the excess shall be computed at 2 cents per manzana.

(4) If for the purpose of dividing a piece of land it should be necessary to re-measure it, the surveyor shall then receive the fees stated in paragraph 1 and in addition 20 per cent. on the total amount that the operation would cost were it a simple measurement; this on account of the proceedings for division, but if no remeasurements should be made, he shall charge only the 20 per cent.

(5) If the boundary marks of the land are fixed at the time the measure-ment is made, and the surveyor directs the operation, he shall receive $2 for every boundary mark that he sets up; but if it should not be done until after-wards, and the surveyor has to go expressly to set up the marks, he shall receive in addition the fees of paragraph 1 and $10 for drawing up the proceed-ings, to be increased to $15 if he has to form the plot of the land.

ART. 82. The witnesses shall receive $1 per day whilst they are employed, and the laborers and chain-bearers 50 cents. The surveyors, shall make out their accounts so that they may be paid by the party interested in the measurement.

ART. 83. The fees for the revision of proceedings of measurements and re-measurements shall be as follows:

(1) Ten cents for each leaf contained in the proceedings to be examined.

(2) Ten cents for each side of polygon that is examined in order to ascertain the exactness of their length, and to prove the correctness of the angles they form, and of their directions in relation to the true meridian.

(3) Twenty-five cents for every triangle comprised in the figure, and if any other method is employed, 20 cents for each side.

(4) Whenever, in order to verify a map, it becomes necessary to form a new one, the revisor shall receive in addition 50 cents for each side.

(5) Three dollars for the decision, if the writing does not exceed one sheet of paper, adding $1 more for every extra sheet, and in addition the value of the stamped paper, if furnished by the revisor.

ART. 84. The present ordinance abrogates all previous laws bearing on lands.

Given in Tegucigalpa on the fifteenth day of the month of May, one thousand eight hundred and eighty-eight.

LUIS BOGRAN.

The Under-Secretary in Charge of the Ministry of Finance,

SIMEON MARTINEZ.

And by order of the President let the above be published and put in force.

MARTINEZ.

Appendix C.

TITLE I.—*Mines and mining property.*

ARTICLE 1. The objects of this code are the mines of gold, silver, copper, platinum, quicksilver, lead, zinc, bismuth, cobalt, nickel, tin, antimony, arsenic, iron, manganese, molybdena, precious stones—whatever be the form of the bed or matrix in which they are found—provided that their development requires works and operations, which may be qualified as mining industry, according to the rules of the art of mining.

The extraction of coal and other fossils, not comprised in the foregoing paragraph, belongs to the owner of the soil, who shall only be obliged to give notice of the same to the administrative authority.

The regulations of Titles X, XII, and XIV shall apply also to these mines as regards to safety, order, and regulation of the works.

ART. 2. The minerals and precious metals. which are found as "float" on the surface of the soil, belong to the first occupant.

ART. 3. The minerals for building purposes or for ornaments, the sands, slates, argil, lime stone, kaoline, peat, marl, and other substances of that kind, which may be found in the uncultivated lands of the State or municipalities, shall be of common use for all individuals who may desire to apply them to.building, agriculture, or to the arts, without prejudice of the right of the State or municipalities to concede them to persons by special contracts, which shall stipulate the extension, the conditions, and the regulations under which they are granted.

ART. 4. The gold bearing and tin bearing sands, and any other mineral production of rivers or placers, shall be for free use, provided they are found in the uncultivated lands of any ownership whatever. However, when they are operated by permanent works, they shall be divided into mining claims.

NOTE.—The above paragraphs are revised as follows:

1. Deposits of coal and other fossils, tin-ores, and precious stones, with the exception of opals, are the exclusive property of the State and can not be denounced.

2. The executive power will promote the exploration of said mines in a manner which is thought most convenient.

(Amendment law of March 9, 1885.)

ART. 5. The dumps, scoria, and tailings of abandoned mines are integral parts of the mines to which they belong; but as long as these mines have not become particular property, they will be considered as common property. Shall also be for common use the scoria and tailings of old reduction works, abandoned by their owners, provided they are situated on grounds that are not enclosed by fence or wall.

ART. 6. The existence of a mine being recognized, the surface grounds are subject to occupation of the extension necessary for the proper working of it, and as the development of the works may require for the establishment of storehouses, dumps, furnaces and machinery, for the extraction of the metals, houses for the use of workmen, and right of way to the public roads, not only for the transportation of the products, but also of the materials necessary for the development of the mine and the reduction of its ores. But the owner of the land is not obliged to allow the establishment of industrial or commercial enterprises for smelting or reducing.

The right of occupation shall be established only after payment, not only of the value of the surface grounds, but also of all damages which may be caused to their owner or to any other person.

ART. 7. The roads open for the development of a mine shall also be free for the use of all others existing in the same locality; in such case the expenses of maintenance shall be divided between them pro rata of the use they make of them.

ART. 8. Not only the superficial lands of the mine, but also those immediately surrounding, are subject to the use of said mine, for pasturing the animals necessary for its working, when said lands are unfenced and uncultivated; also the natural water-supply for the use of workmen and animals.

Those lands are also subject to denouncement to establish reduction machinery, and the works necessary for that purpose. All damages shall be paid or indemnity given, as in the case specified in article 6; and all the dispositions of the same article are applicable to this case.

ART. 9. The water proceeding from the subterranean works of a mine belongs to it.

ART. 10. Mines constitute real estate, distinct and separate from surface land, even when both are the property of the same owner, and the ownership, possession, use, and enjoyment of them are transferable as in the case of other property, subject, however, to the special dispositions of this code.

ART. 11. The materials and objects destined by the owner of a mine to the permanent working of it: as buildings, machinery, pumps, instruments, tools and animals, are integral parts of the real estate of the mine. But the animals and objects used for personal service, or for the transportation or trade of minerals, of products and of articles of necessity, the provisions for the workmen, and other personal property of the owners or lessees, can not be considered as being part of the real estate of the mine.

ART. 12. Mines are not susceptible of natural division. Neither is it permitted to the partners in the ownership to appropriate to themselves exclusively one or more distinct parts. However, it is possible to divide the interests of one or more partners in parts.

ART. 13. The law grants the ownership of mines to individuals, with the condition of working them constantly, subject to the provisions of this code, and to the regulations established for its execution and for their conservation, their security, order, and hygiene; but the loss of this class of property, and its reversion to the State, takes place only in the cases expressly defined by the law.

NOTE.—Compare with Title I, the Decree of the 24 of September, 1888, also Decree No. 27 of February 19, 1889, and Decree No. 34 of March 17, 1887.

TITLE II.—*Exploration or Prospecting.*

ART. 14.—The right to prospect and to excavate in the grounds of whatever ownership, for the purpose of discovering mines, which article 669 of the civil code concedes to individuals, can be exercised freely in lands not fenced in or not dedicated to agriculture.

ART. 15. To execute works of exploration in cultivated lands, the permission of the owner or administrator must be first obtained.

In case of refusal from the owner or administrator, the judge of letters, after hearing the interested parties, and also an engineer of mines, if he thinks it necessary or any of the parties require it, shall have power to grant or refuse the permission; and his decision shall be without appeal.

ART. 16. The permission granted by the judge in accordance with the provisions of the precedent article shall determine the number of persons that may be employed in the exploration, which shall be always conducted according to the following conditions:

1. The prospecting shall be made necessarily when there are no crops growing on the grounds.

2. The prospecting shall not exceed one month, counting from the date of the permission.

3. The petitioner must previously give bonds, if the owner of the land requires it, to secure the payment of all damages which may result to the owner from the prospecting directly or indirectly.

ART. 17. Any person who shall have once obtained a permission from the judge to prospect certain grounds, shall be barred from asking a second permission to prospect the same grounds, under any circumstances.

ART. 18. If, from any just cause, the prospecting could not be performed at the time named, the permission may be transferred to a more opportune time, by virtue of a new decree from the proper authority.

ART. 19. The judge has no power to grant permission to excavate in houses, gardens, orchards, or in any class of irrigated land, or in dry lands planted with trees, or in vineyards.

ART. 20. No excavations, nor any other mining work, shall be opened at a less distance than forty yards of an edifice or a railroad, or on any sloping ground or above or below any public way or canal whatever, without permission of the administrative authority, who shall grant it, if in the opinion of the respective engineer it is not deemed prejudicial, and who shall prescribe the measures of safety that the case may require.

In the same manner, and without prejudice of the provisions of the preceding paragraph, permission shall be asked from the respective military authority to execute said works at a less distance than one thousand and four hundred yards from fortified points.

The same regulation shall apply in case the work should have to be executed at a distance less than one hundred yards from canals, aqueducts, watering places for stock, or any kind of water-course.

The violation of this article shall be punished by a fine of from fifty to five hundred dollars, besides an indemnity due for all damages caused.

TITLE III.—*Persons who are entitled to acquire mines.*

ART. 21. Any person qualified to hold real estate in Honduras has a right to acquire mines in all legal ways, excepting those who fall under the exceptions enumerated in the following article.

ART. 22. The following persons are prohibited from acquiring mines, or holding a part of, or an interest in them :

1. Mining engineers paid by the State, who execute administrative functions in the branch of mining, within the district where they exercise such functions.

2. The governors of departments within the departments they govern.

3. Magistrates of superior tribunals and judges of letters to whom is committed the administration of justice in mining cases, within the territory of their jurisdiction.

4. Undivorced wives, and sons of the above-named officials, while under the father's authority.

This prohibition does not comprise the mines acquired before their appointment to the aforesaid offices, nor those which during the time that they hold them may have been acquired by inheritance by said functionaries, or their wives, or sons. Neither does it apply to those acquired by married women previous to their marriage.

ART. 23. The mine, or portion of a mine, or stock in a mining company, acquired in violation of the provisions of the foregoing article, shall be considered as vacant, and shall be adjudged to whoever may apply for or denounce it.

ART. 24. Outside of those persons and cases expressly excepted by law, no one shall be entitled by right of discovery or denouncement to acquire more than one claim upon the same vein or lode; but any qualified person can acquire by other means any number he may wish, without limitation.

ART. 25. Minors and adult sons of families can, without the consent of their fathers or guardians, acquire the mines they discover, and these shall be incorporated with their own industrial capital.

TITLE IV.—*Discovery of mines, and the method of securing the ownership of them.*

ART. 26. The discoverer of mines in grounds where no other one has been registered within a radius of one league, is entitled to three claims, continuous or discontinuous, upon the principal vein, and to two upon each of the other veins of his discovery.

The discoverer of a vein within the radius of one league of a registered mine is entitled to two claims, continuous or discontinuous upon said vein.

Those claims must be registered separately. But the discoverer is allowed to apply for a treble or double claim, which can at any time be divided into regular claims, subject to the conditions specified in Article 41.

ART. 27. Any person who shall have discovered mineral in a vein, or in any other kind of a deposit, shall make a declaration of his findings before the judge of letters of the department.

In his declaration he shall give his name and the names of his partners, if he has any, the most remarkable landmarks which characterize the site where is to be found the mine-opening, excavation, shaft or work, in which he found the mineral; a sample of it must accompany the declaration, and he shall mention the name which he desires to give to the mine.

The judge to whom is presented the declaration shall note on it the day and the hour on which it was handed to him.

ART. 28. The judge to whom the declaration is presented shall order it to be registered, and the registry to be published.

ART. 29. The registry is a complete copy of the declaration and its contents, and of the certification of the day and hour of its presentation made into the register book of discoveries, which each judge of letters shall keep.

He shall give a copy of this procedure to the party interested, if he asks for it, and the original shall be placed in the archives.

ART. 30. The publication of the registry shall be made by insertion in a newspaper of the department, (if there be any,) three times, at intervals of ten days.

If there is no newspaper in the department, the publication shall be made by means of copies posted for the term of thirty days upon the doors of the office of the judge, and on two of the most frequented localities.

ART. 31. The locator is obliged to uncover the croppings or vein of his discovery within one hundred and eighty days, counting from the day of registry, by opening on the body of the vein a shaft of a depth of no less than five yards, and at its bottom a horizontal gallery of the same length, in order that it may be rendered easy to recognize the class of mineral, the extent, direction, and inclination of the vein, and other circumstances which establish the existence of the mine and serve to characterize it.

ART. 32. In case of a regular deposit, in bed or seam, the shaft should follow towards the greatest dip of the same and the gallery or drift shall extend in the direction of the same, and be of such shape as to show the floor and roof, so that it may be possible to note or recognize with accuracy the same characteristics or circumstances as in the case of veins.

ART. 33. In deposits, scattered or in masses, the locator shall make the same excavation as in the case of a vein, and always open the shaft and drift in the body of the deposit.

ART. 34. Having performed this work, the locator shall complete the registry by a petition directed to the judge of letters, in which he shall describe, from among the circumstances enumerated in the foregoing articles, which ones characterize his mine, and the direction towards which to measure his claim, stating the width he desires on both sides of the shaft, or whether he wants it all on one side of it. The petition shall also be recorded like the denouncement.

ART. 35. The foregoing proceedings shall establish a provisional title of ownership to the mine, until the definitive title be constituted, upon petition of the locator or interested party, by the measurement of the claim, which shall be made by order of the judge in conformity with the provisions of Title VIII. But the contents of this provisional title cannot be used in any case as legal proof.

ART. 36. If the locator does not wish to receive a provisional title, and prefers in its stead a definite one, he shall express his wish in the petition for the ratification of his registry; and it shall be proceeded with in this case according to the forms prescribed in Title VIII.

Art. 37. If the locator, after having made his shaft or performed the legal amount of work desires to open one or two more in different places in the vein, in order to better ascertain and determine the direction, dip, and other charac-teristics of it, and should, before the expiration of the first period of time, solicit a new one to execute this work and ratify his registry, or to make definite the title of ownership of his mine, another equal extension of time shall be granted, which shall continue after the expiration of the first, and he shall be subject, in regard to this new period, to the obligations and penalties established in the fol-lowing article:

Art. 38. If the locator has not excavated the shaft and gallery within legal time, or, having performed that work, and omits to complete his registry, he will be considered as having relinquished his right, and the mine shall be adjudicated to the first person who shall denounce it before the default has been corrected by the locator.

Art. 39. A mistake in any of the circumstances mentioned in the ratification of the registry may be rectified at any time, and the correction shall be entered in the registry. All of which is understood to be without injury to a third party.

Art. 40. In order that discoverers may be enabled to divide in three or two mines their treble or double claims, they shall comply, for each mine, with the conditions of ratification of registry.

Art. 41. Persons claiming a better right to a discovery must present their claims within the time granted to the locator for the ratification of the registry; and they will obtain no hearing if they do so afterwards.

Art. 42. He shall be considered the discoverer who first presents himself for registry, excepting the case wherein it is proved that there was fraud in antici-pating the denouncement or in retarding its presentation by the first discoverer.

Art. 43. He shall not be considered as the discoverer of a mine who has found it while executing mining work by order, or while in the employ of an-other; and the person in whose name he was performing said work shall be the discoverer.

Title V.—*On rights for the exploration of a known vein.*

Art. 44. After a discovery is recorded any qualified person can ask for an extension to prospect the vein, during ninety days, in the direction he may indi-cate on the extension of the vein fixed by the discoverer, but no other individ-ual is allowed to perform work or to acquire the rights of a discoverer on the grounds of that claim.

These petitions shall be recorded in the register in the same manner as the declaration of discovery.

ART. 45. If two or more persons should present petitions of this class on the same line of vein, the first who has presented himself shall have the preference in location, the others following in the order of priority.

ART. 46. Upon his discovering a mineral deposit, the grantee of this class of claims is obliged to register, and shall remain subject to the other rules, respecting discoverers, established by articles 27 and following.

ART. 47. Should the grantee fail in finding mineral or cropping, or in registering within the time specified in article 45, he shall lose his rights; and the claim may be conceded to the first person who applies if in the meanwhile the former has not made any discovery, or failed to register.

ART. 48. If, after having performed well directed and sufficient work in relation to the time specified in article 45, the grantee has not been able to find vein-matter by reason of the ground being much covered up, or from other causes which can not be imputed to him, and he wishes an extension of time, it shall be granted to him, after the report of the engineer upon the case and circumstances, but with the condition that the extension can not exceed the original · time.

TITLE VI.—*Abandonment of mines and their loss by desertion.*

ART. 49. The miner who wishes to abandon his mine shall so declare in writing to the judge of first instance. The judge shall order the insertion of such declaration in the register, and its publication in the same manner and during the same time as the discovery. If there are mortgage debts against the mine, the miner shall notify the holders of his intended abandonment, and transfer his rights to them, should they demand it.

The first-mortgage creditor has the preference to the transfer of the mine to him.

ART. 50. In the meanwhile, if the mine is not abandoned in the manner prescribed in the foregoing article, it shall be considered as the property of the last occupant who shall remain subject to all the charges and obligations inherent to the ownership of it.

ART. 51. An abandoned mine can be registered anew by the first person who demands it, and who proves its abandonment by the registry made of it. He who abandoned it shall also be admitted to registry when the term of the publication of abandonment is over.

ART. 52. The ownership of mines is lost by desertion, as stated in the following articles:

Art. 53. Mines shall be considered deserted—

1. When, during one consecutive year, there shall have been no labor done by four workmen, at least, engaged in interior or exterior works executed for the exploration of the mine.

2. When the labor of four men having been interrupted at intervals without reaching the period of one year, the mine shall not have been worked during four hundred days in two years, counted from the first day of suspension.

Art. 54. It is not necessary that the labor of four workmen required to improve and work the mine should be performed within the limits of the claim, provided that the work performed outside of its limits shall promote its development as shafts, pits, or other works of this class.

Art. 55. No mine can be denounced as deserted during the four months following its desertion, provided that during those four months works have been maintained or resorted to in it which are within the conditions of legal protection.

Art. 56. Desertion does not occur when the suspension of work on the mine results from unavoidable causes, as absolute want of workmen, war, famine, or plague, that affect the territory wherein the mine is situated.

Art. 57. The work in a mine can be suspended for two years without incurring desertion if those who have worked it for two years without interruption pay monthly in advance, from the beginning of the suspension, a local tax not under five and not over thirty dollars, the amount to be determined by the municipality every three years. The payment of this tax shall be equivalent as regards the protection of the mine to the regular working of it from the time when the miner shall have given written notice to the judge of the day on which the suspension commences. Such notice shall be also entered in the register.

Art. 58. Failing to pay the tax for one single period the mine shall be considered as deserted.

Art. 59. Desertion shall be presumed when the indispensable dwellings or offices previously constructed for the service of the mine have been destroyed or rendered unserviceable by the influence of the weather, or when they have not been constructed during the year following the registry, except when the miner is owner of an adjacent claim, the offices of which may be used for the other also.

Art. 60. Several claims located in an old mining property can be worked as one if they belong to the same owner, or if belonging to several owners they have formed a company for the above purpose, and the judge shall authorize them to do so after having received full knowledge of the facts.

To obtain this authorization it is necessary to express the names and dimensions of the claims intended to be operated, the mechanical means which are intended to be employed, and the time at which the work is expected to begin.

It is likewise necessary to make evident the existence of a capital proportionate to the magnitude or extensions of the works which are proposed to be executed.

The judge will cause the engineer, if there is any, or, if there is none, an expert named by him, to inform him, after examination of said mines, as to the convenience of said works, the relation of the capital to the cost of the work intended, and the time needed to begin it, and he will in accordance with this report grant or withhold the authorization petitioned for.

ART. 61. The privilege granted in the foregoing article shall be void—

1. If the work is not commenced within the time fixed by the judge.

2. If the work mentioned in articles 54 and 55 has been suspended eight consecutive months.

3. If the work, having been suspended for alternate periods of time, the claims should have been without work for three hundred days in two years, counting from the first day of suspension.

ART. 62. This privilege shall also be void—

1. By the dissolution of the company organized to perform the work.

2. By the transfer of any of the favored claims to a person who does not work in company with the others.

But in this second case the transfer of title does not cancel the privilege as regards the other claims not thus transferred.

TITLE VII.—*How to constitute new ownership in mines deserted or lost from other causes.*

ART. 63. A deserted mine can be registered by the first person who solicits it and proves legally its abandonment according to the following articles:

ART. 64. Upon a legal declaration of desertion by abandonment the mine reverts to the State and loses its boundaries and individuality, and shall be registered by any one as a new mine subject to registry.

ART. 65. The person denouncing a deserted mine shall present in writing to the judge of letters the name of the place where it is situated, the facts upon which he bases his denouncement, the name of the mine if it is known, that of the mining district where it is found, the class of mineral, and other circumstances which individualize and distinguish it. He shall also give the name of the former owner of the mine if it is known, and those of the actual possessors of the adjacent mines, if there are any.

ART. 66. The judge, having admitted the statement, shall summon the last owner and the owners of the adjacent mines, to appear personally, if they are known, and live in the mineral district or department, or the administrators of those mines, the owners of which live in other parts; and, in case neither the owners nor administrators can be found in the place, he shall notify the former by means of a notice posted for fifteen days on the door of the judge's office, or inserted three times in a newspaper, if there is one in the department.

ART. 67. If no lawful contestant appears within the space of ten days, counted from the date of the summons, the judge shall issue a decree declaring the mine deserted, and order the registry of the petition. If the interested party be outside of the department, the limit time shall be extended with due prudence.

The registry shall be made in a special book, and in the same form as for discoveries.

ART. 68. If a lawful contestant appears, to oppose the demand or denouncement of desertion, the case will be proceeded with until it reaches a sentence, declaring desertion, and allowing the registry, or dissolving the denouncement.

ART. 69. If the person making the denouncement shall allow one complete month to pass without taking any of the measures required to obtain sentence or decree of desertion he loses his preferred rights to register or to acquire the deserted mine, against a posterior denouncer, who may have presented himself, or shall present himself claiming those rights, pending the delayed procedure.

ART. 70. The denouncer shall have ninety days, counted from the date of the decree of desertion and registry, to excavate the shaft and gallery or any vein of the claim denounced, as is prescribed for discoveries in articles 31, 32, 33, and 34, or to perform any equivalent work for the mine.

ART. 71. During that term of ninety days, the former owner of the mine who has failed to appear to oppose the denouncement, may present a petition to . rescind the decree of desertion; but, in this case, he will have to prove, judicially, the illegality of the denouncement. After that time he shall not be heard.

ART. 72. The denouncer or new possessor of a deserted mine is obliged, upon demand of the last owner, to deliver to him, or pay at their just valuation, the machinery, tools, utensils, buildings, and other objects or works which said previous owner may have left in the mine, and which can be removed without injury to it.

ART. 73. The denouncer of an abandoned or deserted mine, which, on account of caving in or other causes, is in such condition that it cannot be operated, except by means of shafts or other preparatory works of great cost, shall be entitled to the same privileges as are conceded to discoverers, without prejudice of those which are due him on account of the kind of works he undertakes, and subject to the regulations established respecting those work.

ART. 74. The denouncement of mines made through the infraction of any law which imposes as penalty their loss, shall be subject to the proceeding established respecting the denouncement of deserted mines, except in what may have been especially determined by the law.

TITLE VIII.—*Mining claims and their boundaries and what constitutes a definitive title of ownership.*

ART. 75. The ground which the law grants to a miner to develop his mine is called mining claim. A claim has an indefinite depth within the limits of its length and breadth.

ART. 76. In regular veins the claim shall consist, when in unoccupied lands, or lands not occupied by other mines previously denounced, of two hundred and fifty yards of horizontal length, and of one hundred to two hundred yards at right angles, or in width, according to the inclination of the vein to the horizon.

ART. 77. The length shall be measured following the course of the vein, and starting from the point of the cropping which the miner designates, so as to leave within the claim the works mentioned in article 31.

ART. 78. The width shall be measured upon a horizontal line perpendicular to the course of the vein.

It can be distributed on one or the other side of the vein, in the proportion that the miner desires. But, if the neighbors oppose it, there shall not be granted more than ten yards against the inclination of the vein.

ART. 79. To fix the width, the following scale shall be observed: From 30° to 45° inclusive, two hundred yards; from 45° to 50° inclusive, one hundred and sixty-five yards; from 50° to 60° inclusive, one hundred and thirty-five yards; from 60° to 65°, one hundred and fifteen yards; from 65° to 90°, one hundred yards.

ART. 80. In irregular deposits or masses, the claim shall form a rectangle, the horizontal section of which shall be equal in surface to a square of two hundred yards a side.

ART. 81. In auriferous sands or tin-bearing sands, and others mentioned in article 4, the claim shall consist of ten thousand square yards, and can be in the form of a rectangle or square, or a series of squares in contact with one another in the form the miner desires, but without intervening openings or spaces. In no case shall the claim have a length of more than three hundred yards.

ART. 82. The administrative authority shall see that two invariable points be fixed in each mining district, of which the line of union shall exactly represent the direction of the astronomical meridian.

ART. 83. In order to proceed with the locating and measuring of a claim, the neighboring owners must be previously summoned to appear, as prescribed in Article 68.

They shall have a term of ten days to claim the preferred measurement of their mine or mines.

ART. 84. The priority of the declaration or denouncement of a mine gives a preferred right to have it laid out and measured over more recent mines; but that right of preference becomes extinct if the mine is found deserted, even before it has been so declared.

ART. 85. The petition for measurement not having been opposed, or the litigation having ended by a final sentence, the judge shall order the engineer of state to execute the measurement, after having notified the parties of the day on which it shall take place.

ART. 86. Each of the interested parties shall have also the right to name before the judge an expert to witness the measurement and laying out, who will watch the operations of the person appointed by the judge, and who will make on the ground the observations and oppositions he may think proper in regard to the proceedings, data, and estimates.

ART. 87. The engineer shall previously examine the mine, and after having ascertained that it contains mineral or a vein, and that the legal amount of labor has been performed, he shall proceed to lay out the claim, distributing the measurement of length to one or the other side of the shaft, in the manner that has been requested by the miner in the ratification of his registry, or as he then desires, if there are no neighboring owners, or if there are any and they make no opposition; but said shaft shall be always enclosed within the limits of the claim.

He should also collect samples of the ore, and mark out the points where he fixes the posts, or boundary marks, that they may be firm, lasting, and easily found.

ART. 88. Mines registered in claims, solicited to explore a vein on the continuation of another known mine, should be laid out, if possible, in such a manner as to leave no vacant space between the one or the other.

ART. 89. A claim must in all cases be continuous. If it should happen that there is not enough ground to fill up the measurement to which it is entitled by reason of the interposition of another claim, the first shall be restricted to the ground which is free, up to the point of interposition, and its measurement shall not be completed by jumping over the interposed mine.

This is understood to be without prejudice of the regulations contained in Article 104.

ART. 90. The engineer or expert shall make use of the magnetic north to fix the courses, and always, if possible, shall determine the position of the legal work, which they will have taken as a basis of their operations, with reference to landmarks easily perceivable on the ground, taking note of their distances. In those places where the astronomical meridian has been determined, the engineer should note carefully the angle of the magnetic declination.

ART. 91. The operation having been completed, the engineer or expert shall draw up a record of the proceedings, containing a description clear and circumstantial of the manner in which they were performed, and of their results, as well as of the observations or objections made by the assistant experts named by the interested parties.

This record, signed by the engineer himself, by the assistant experts, by the interested parties, and by two witnesses, shall be laid before the judge, who, finding it complete and in legal form, shall order its inscription in the register, and shall have the original placed in the archives and a copy given to the interested party; or he shall correct the faults or illegalities which he may discover.

ART. 92. If there should arise any disagreement between the engineer and the experts, upon any point of their examination, the judge shall appoint another engineer or expert who shall act jointly with those disagreeing; and if the new operation results in a majority of similar opinions, the inscription shall be ordered in conformity with the majority and in the manner laid down in the precedent article.

ART. 93. The proceedings mentioned in the preceding articles, shall be immutable and shall constitute a definitive title to the property of the mine, and it cannot be impugned, except in the case of an evident error of experts being found in the record, or of fraud and deceit. However, it can be rectified, on petition of the owner at any time in which are discovered new data which may serve to better determine the direction or dimension of the vein, provided no damage be caused to a third party.

ART. 94. It shall also be rectified, on the petition and at the expense of a miner who should locate in the limits, or vicinity of a laid out claim, and who should allege that it has a greater extension than that assigned in the title.

ART. 95. In rectification, the proceeding shall be the same as in the first location and measurement.

ART. 96. The miner is obliged to maintain and preserve the landmarks of his claim, and can not change or move them under a penalty of a fine of not less than twenty-five dollars, nor more than two hundred and fifty dollars, without prejudice of the criminal responsibility of his action, if he has done it maliciously.

ART. 97. If, by accident, a landmark has fallen down, or has been destroyed, the miner shall inform the judge, that he may have it replaced in its proper position after summoning the neighbors to be present.

TITLE IX.—*A miner's rights upon his claim and intersection of mines.*

ART. 98. The miner is the exclusive owner within the limits of his claim, and in all its depth, not only of the registered vein or deposit, but also of all the other veins, cross-veins, and mineral substances, which exist or may be found in it.

Art. 99. But he is forbidden to follow or work them into some one else's claim.

Art. 100. Every trespass subjects him to restitution of the amount taken out, according to the valuation of experts, without prejudice of an action for theft, should bad faith be proven against him.

Art. 101. Fraud will be presumed when the trespass exceeds twenty-five yards.

Art. 102. In case of the crossing of a registered vein, the miner shall have the right to follow it from the point where it leaves the interposed claim, provided he is able to identify it, and to require, in conformity to the dispositions of article 139, the right of way through the interposed claim, or the right to use it for his purpose.

Art. 103. No one can be accused of trespassing upon a mine which has no claim laid out, nor visible landmarks, as long as it is not legally measured, or its old landmarks are not replaced.

Art. 104. The owners of adjoining or neighboring mines have the right to visit personally, or through an engineer or expert, named by themselves or by the judge, the adjoining mines, when they fear that a trespass has been committed, or is about to be committed, or that any damage whatever is to result, such as an inundation or other damage of that kind, or when by such inspection they believe that they can obtain knowledge which may be useful to them in the prosecution of their respective works.

When the visit has been solicited by reason of suspicion of trespass, or through fear of inundation, the engineer or expert can take measurements of the works adjacent to the mine of the solicitor.

Art. 105. Groundless refusal, the concealing of the work, or any obstacles or difficulties placed in the way of inspection and examination shall be considered as a presumption of bad faith in the trespass.

Art. 106. If the measurements taken by the engineer or expert named by the judge result in proving a trespass, the judge shall order a temporary suspension of the work at the intercrossing and affix seals upon the points of division, while the interested parties carry their cases before the proper tribunals.

Art. 107. If the miner, in his underground works, should have passed the limits of his claim, he shall have the right to enlarge or increase it in the direction in which he thus went out of his limits, and in extent equal to that which might have occurred horizontally with those works, provided that such extension be in vacant lands, or on lands of an abandoned or deserted mine.

The proceedings in regard to this extension shall be the same as for measurement and laying out of claims.

TITLE X.—*Conditions to which is subject the working of mines.*

ART. 108. Mines must be worked and operated according to the rules of the art of mining, and to the regulations of security and order laid down by the President of the Republic.

ART. 109. In order to carry out the dispositions of the precedent article, the mines shall be subject to the inspection of the administrative authority, who shall prescribe the time and manner of inspection, as he may judge convenient.

ART. 110. The miner or occupant must place at the disposal of the engineers or experts, appointed to visit the mine or its works, the articles necessary for that inspection.

He must in the same time show them the books, the plans, the roll of laborers and other data which may serve to make a complete showing, if they desire it.

ART. 111. The owners or administrators of mines must keep their works well ventilated, so that the laborers shall not be choked or suffocated by the accumulated gases or unwholesome air, or by the infiltration or accumulation of water.

ART. 112. The owners or administrators of mines are forbidden under a fine of fifty to five hundred dollars, without prejudice of an action, either civil or criminal, in case of accident, to allow work to be done in places where lamps are burning with difficulty, or are extinguished from the want of sufficient air.

They are also forbidden, under a fine of twenty-five to one hundred and fifty dollars, to allow work to be carried on in the dark.

ART. 113. Miners are obliged to secure the roof and sides or walls of their works in headings and levels, used for carrying ore or material, by means of timber, masonry, or broken stone walls, etc., as the softness or hardness of the work or nature of the ground may require, under a penalty of fifty to two hundred and fifty dollars for the first offense, and for the second of the loss of the mine, if, having been requested by the governor, they fail to execute the work judged to be necessary for its safety, in the time which may have been specially designated in accordance with the engineer's report.

ART. 114. The owner of a mine whose deepest workings have caved in, is obliged to clear them out until the continuation of said works can be carried on, under a penalty of fifty to two hundred and fifty dollars for the first offense, and for the second, the loss of the mine, if he does not begin and conclude this work within a period fixed by the governor according to the examination and report of the engineer.

If, by failing to apply the proper means of drainage, any lower mine shall suffer damages, the miner shall indemnify the injured owners, according to valuation of experts.

ART. 115. The drainage of a mine, by means of works of a lower level, can not be done without permission of the governor. In this permission, which shall be given upon previous advice of the engineer, the proper precautions to avoid accidents shall be determined.

Any infraction of this article shall be fined twenty-five to one hundred and fifty dollars, without prejudice of civil or criminal responsibility in case of accident.

ART. 116. In all headings the inclinations of which exceed 35°, there shall always be a railing, solidly built, to facilitate the entrance and exit of the laborers. If the average inclination of those works reaches to 40°, there must be, besides the railing, a series of footholds in the rock itself, or made artificially.

Any infraction of the present article shall be fined from twenty-five to fifty dollars.

ART. 117. The ladders placed in the transit shafts shall be constructed with a view to the safety of the miners. Any infraction of this article shall be punished by the same fine as that specified in the precedent one.

ART. 118. If the workmen have to go down into the mine, through shafts, in cars or cages, the owners shall use cables of first quality, and apply the apparatus of safety which, to avoid accidents, the governor shall prescribe, upon previous advice of the engineer.

ART. 119. In the working of the mines, safety fuses shall be used for firing powder. In the loading of blasts, only ramrods with points made of soft iron, or copper, or any other material which does not produce sparks by striking, shall be used.

ART. 120. The employment of women, or of children under twelve years of age, in the interior of a mine is prohibited, under a penalty of ten to twenty-five dollars.

ART. 121. The damages caused to a mine by the works of operating another, shall be paid by the owner of the latter, upon a just valuation made by experts, without prejudice of any penalties to which such damages may have given rise.

ART. 122. When, from the visit of inspection of a mine by the commissioned engineer, it shall appear that the life of the workmen, or the security of the works are in jeopardy, from any cause, he shall dictate the measures necessary to remove the cause of danger. Should any reclamation be made, the governor shall hear the report of one or more engineers, employed at the expense of the interested party, and he shall decide in accordance with the opinion of the majority.

If the report of the first engineer shows that there is immediate danger, he shall order the temporary suspension of the work, any reclamation to the contrary notwithstanding.

ART. 123. If, by any accident occurring in a mine, there shall be caused the death or great injury of one or more persons, or the safety of the miners should be compromised, the owners, directors, or administrators must, under a penalty of fifty to two hundred dollars, give immediate notice to the alcalde (mayor) of the municipality, who, together with the engineer or expert who may be in the place, shall proceed, without delay, to make a summary investigation of the occurrence and its causes, and to take the proper measures to avert the danger and its consequences.

To this end he will have the power to use all the tools, the workmen, and the animals belonging to the mine, and anything that he may judge necessary, in order to attain his object. Said alcalde shall also inform immediately the governor and the respective judge of what has occurred.

ART. 124. The penalties which are established in this code shall be imposed by the judge.

TITLE XI.—*Works of excavation and assistance which miners owe to each other.*

ART. 125. The miner who desires to operate his mine by means of drifts, shafts, or inclines, can prosecute his works without previous permission, within the limits of his claim, or outside of them, if the ground is not occupied by other miners.

ART. 126. If, to carry on these works, it should be necessary to commence them in somebody else's claim, or to cross it in all its breadth, or only on a portion, and no arrangements can be made with the owner, the miner must solicit permission from the judge.

The judge will grant it, if, in the opinion of the engineer, the following circumstances are made manifest:

1. That the work is possible and useful.

2. That it cannot be performed on any other point without incurring far greater expenses.

3. That the working of the mine which the excavation has to cross is not rendered impossible or very difficult.

ART. 127. Each of the parties can also name an expert to proceed jointly with the one appointed by the judge, and the judge shall notify them, beforehand, of the day on which the examination of the grounds will take place.

ART. 128. If any disagreement should arise between the engineer and the experts it shall be treated as described in article 94.

ART. 129. The judge, in granting the permit, shall determine the course of the excavation or work, and the maximum of extension which can be given in the other claim, from the opinion of the engineer and experts, and the miner has to conform strictly to that course and extension in the prosecution of his work, otherwise he will have to ask for a new permission, which can not be granted without the advice of the engineer. However, such permission shall not be needed when the variation is accidental and occurs in order to avoid the difficulties which are encountered in the work.

ART. 130. Before commencing the work of excavation the miner shall give bonds to the mine which he intends to cross.

ART. 131. The owner of the crossed mine must not interfere with the shaft or drift which crosses it, nor with its supports; neither can he extract minerals any nearer than two yards, unless he constructs supports, according to regulations. But the miner shall reimburse him the expenses which may be occasioned by this compliance with the rules.

ART. 132. If the party who thus excavates encounters a vein in another claim, he cannot operate and work it, and is allowed only to follow his own excavation across it; and he shall deliver the ores to the owner, after having deducted the cost of extracting them, but he can register and acquire the veins which he may find in vacant ground, by filling the conditions required of discoverers.

In this case the measurement and laying out of the claim will be made on the surface of the ground.

ART. 133. If the party who excavates desires that his works should cross abandoned or deserted mines, he can take possession of them and protect them by the simple fact of his working the excavation, after having denounced and registered them.

ART. 134. In order that the mine or miners should be considered as protected by the works of the excavation, it is necessary:

1. That it should be shown by the report of the engineer that the excavation, or a part of it, is worked in the direction of said mine, and that its development by that means is possible and useful.

2. That, in the prosecution of the work, the excavation does not vary from the course determined, except in the accidental case indicated in article 132.

3. That in the work of excavation, the number of workmen specified for holding mining property shall be maintained, and all other conditions complied with.

ART. 135. The owners of mines which may be drained by the excavation, or the operation of which may be facilitated by it, shall pay to the party who works said excavation, and upon valuation of experts, either the value of the benefits received, or the cost which might accrue, if said benefits were obtained by other means. This disposition applies to drainage by means of shafts.

ART. 136. Mines can be used to facilitate the ventilation of those which may need it, and to allow the underground drainage of other mines in the direction of the general drainage. On the surface they can not stop the necessary transit, and, on the surface as well as underground, they must render to one another those services which, without detriment to any, may be of benefit to others. This is understood to be with payment for damages, to be appraised by experts.

TITLE XII.—*State engineers and mining experts.*

ART. 137. For the administrative service of mines, there shall be, in each mining district, one State engineer who will see to the execution of this law in regard to the safety, order, and regulation of the works, and promote the advancement and progress of mining.

ART. 138. The State engineer shall also attend to the laying out of claims, and to all the acts and relations of miners which might affect the proprietary rights of the State over mines or its direct interest in their operation.

ART. 139. Where there is no State engineer, or in questions or particular indemnities, or other cases in which the State has no interest, the judges or administrative functionaries can appoint experts, selected among the mining engineers, bearers of diplomas, or in default of them, among the most honorable, creditable, and competent miners.

ART. 140. The organization of the corps of engineers, their attributes and their duties, shall be regulated by decree of the President of the Republic.

The President of the Republic shall also determine, after consultation with the respective municipalities, the limits or extent of the mining districts.

TITLE XIII.—*Alienation and prescription of mines and sales of minerals.*

ART. 141. Mines can be alienated between living persons, or conveyed in case of death, in the same manner as any other real estate.

ART. 142. The original property of mines is acquired by legal registry; and after this has been accomplished, the registered mine remains subject to the rules governing recorded property.

ART. 143. For the transfer of laid-out mines, and to constitute vested rights in them, there shall be kept in each department a special recording register, placed in charge of the judge of letters. It shall be kept in the same manner and under the same rules as the recording register of real estate.

ART. 144. The transfer of the mines the registry of which has not been completed, or respecting which a definitive title of property has not been secured, will be done by inscription in the register of discoveries.

ART. 145. The sale of mines shall not be held as complete whilst a public deed has not yet been granted. However, the private writing of contracts of sale shall hold good as a promise to complete and legalize them.

ART. 146. The time of possession necessary to acquire the property of mines by prescription is only two years in the ordinary prescription and ten years in the extraordinary.

ART. 147. There shall not be allowed, in any manner, recovery of minerals bought in the stores of mines, or from a well-known miner, or in presence of the judge, or witnesses not employed by the buyer, or by means of a certificate of the proper authority of the district whence the mineral proceeds, stating that the vendor actually works a mine producing the same mineral as that sold, or that he has acquired such minerals by legal right.

ART. 148. The purchase of stolen mineral accomplished without the conditions of the precedent article, subjects the buyer to the presumption of concealing stolen property.

ART. 149. In this last case it will be sufficient for the claimant to prove that he has been robbed of minerals, and that the ores he claims are similar to those produced by his mine.

TITLE XIV.—*Hiring of workmen by time.*

ART. 150. The contract for hiring the services of workmen for more than one year shall be made in writing, but the workmen shall not be obliged to stay in service more than five years, counted from the date of the contract.

ART. 151. If no time has been stipulated, the services may cease at the option of either party. Nevertheless, in the case of overseers, mechanics, or other operatives of the same class, either party must give notice to the other of his intention of cancelling the contract, although no condition to that effect had been stipulated, at least fifteen days before.

ART. 152. If the workman engaged for a determined time, with a notice stipulation, should leave suddenly without serious cause, he shall pay to his employers an amount equal to one month of his salary, or to the salary equivalent to the time of notice stipulated, or to the days needed to accomplish it, respectively.

ART. 153. The employer who, in the same manner, should dismiss the operative, shall have to pay him a similar sum, besides the travelling expenses of coming and going, if, to engage his services, he made him change his residence.

ART. 154. Shall be considered as serious causes in behalf of the employer, inaptitude, disorderly conduct, or insubordination of the employé, or the fact that the latter has become unfit for work, from any cause, for more than one month.

The employer, however, shall take all the necessary care of the employé who shall have been hurt, or who has become sick in the service of the mine, or who has been disabled from an accident which may have occurred in it.

ART. 155. Shall be considered as serious causes in favor of the employé, bad treatment on the part of the employer, or the failure to pay his salary at the time specified or usual.

ART. 156. The employé who shall run away, after having received an advance on his salary, without giving it back, shall be guilty of fraud for the sum defrauded.

ART. 157. The books of the mine shall be admitted as evidence when kept regularly by an employé, and not by the owner—

1. In regard to the amount of salary.

2. In regard to the payment of the salary and to the time expired.

3. In regard to the amount advanced to the employé for account of current month.

ART. 158. Are not subject to the precedent dispositions, the contracts made for the performance of a special work, nor those which refer to the service of the overseers, of the bookkeepers, or other employés of this category, although these may have been contracted for a specified time.

ART. 159. The salaries and wages due for the current month to the workmen and other employés of the mine, the controller included, shall be paid in preference to all others from the products of the mine. Even the utensils and tools can be sold for that object.

As for the other property of a bankrupt miner the salaries and wages of the laborers and employés shall have the same preference which is granted by common law to those of clerks and servants.

TITLE XV.—*Mines owned in society or community.*

ART. 160. The mine or portion of a mine brought in as property or usufruct shall not be understood as regards to third parties as belonging to the society, unless such fact has been inscribed in the proper register.

ART. 161. Should there be no stipulation, the administration of the society or community belongs to the associates or joint holders who may have the right to vote in the meetings, but the number of administrators can be restricted, and even a third party can be in charge by agreement of those interested.

ART. 162. The administrators shall exercise the same functions which the law confers upon the administrators of civil societies.

ART. 163. The administrators are obliged to keep account books in which shall appear clearly and specifically the investments and products of the mine. The other associates or joint holders shall have the right to examine those books whenever they deem it convenient.

ART. 164. Unless it is otherwise stipulated, the members may alienate their shares, even without consent of their associates, as if there existed no contract of society.

ART. 165. The distribution of the gains or proceeds shall be made monthly, and in values, except in case of agreement or stipulation, or in specie, should one or several of the associates or joint holders, representing more than thirty per cent of the social capital, require it.

ART. 166. But in the case of exception of the preceding article, the administrators shall have the power to alienate a sufficient quantity of ores to cover the working expenses and those which may occur during the following month, unless the associate or joint holder should wish to pay in money the present and anticipated expenses.

ART. 167. The amount and extension of work to be executed in the mine, with the proceeds derived from it, shall be determined by a majority of votes; but an unanimous vote shall be necessary to carry the works beyond what is prescribed in regard to mines which give no proceeds.

ART. 168. In no case can an associate be compelled to contribute to the erection of reduction or smelting works to treat the minerals extracted from the mine, unless it is stipulated otherwise.

ART. 169. If the mine should not give sufficient proceeds the associates or joint holders can not be obliged to contribute more than their corresponding share in the expenses of investigation outside of those necessary to secure the safety of the mine, and the maintenance of the works specified in Title X.

ART. 170. Should any of the members wish to undertake in the mine more expensive works, the usefulness of which may have been shown by experts, he can solicit from the judge an authorization to carry them into effect and may reimburse himself for the amounts expended, with commercial interest, from the first proceeds of the mine.

ART. 171. The associates or joint holders are obligated to pay four months in advance, or in the manner agreed upon or determined, the share assessed against them in the expenses of the mine as agreed upon or stipulated.

Should any of them have failed to pay, and having been requested by any of the contributors, should not present himself to make payment within fifteen days, they can request that the delinquent be considered as having abandoned the community or society and his share in the mine shall accrue proportionally to that of those who have paid their assessments.

Even if there had been no previous agreement or stipulation in regard to the amount of expenses, the same right shall exist in regard to those necessary for the preservation of the mine.

ART. 172. The demand on the delinquent member shall be done judicially and in person if he resides in the department where the mine is situated or has a known representative therein.

If he does not reside in the department and has not therein a known representative it shall be sufficient to publish the demand three times at least, at intervals of ten days, in one of the newspapers designated by the judge, if there is any in the department, or if there is none, by placards which shall be posted within the same intervals on the doors of the judge's office.

ART. 173. The members or joint holders in whose favor the increase shall have been declared, must inscribe in the recording register of mines the portion which has fallen to each.

ART. 174. If there exists a stipulation to work in the mine for a specified time, the members who have contributed have the option between the right of increase, established in the preceding article, or legal prosecution to compel the delinquent to pay his assessment.

ART. 175. The member or joint holder who, without previous consultation with his co-associates or joint holders, shall have executed, at his own cost, the works necessary for the preservation of the mine, shall have only the right to claim from them, proportionally, the reimbursement of his expenses.

ART. 176. In the meetings of the members or joint holders, those shall have a right to vote who own a share or a portion of a share, representing at least one-fourth per cent interest in the ownership of the mine, unless it is otherwise stipulated.

Those who possess minor but uniform shares, can unite to cast as many votes as they can form a sufficient amount of shares.

ART. 177. At the meetings and deliberations of the members or joint holders, legally convocated, the majority of votes of those present shall decide.

The votes shall be counted according to the interest or portion owned by each of the voters in the community or society; but the vote of one alone can never form a majority, but a tie.

ART. 178. In the case of ties the judge shall decide, taking into consideration the equity between the interested parties and the interest of mining.

ART. 179. The notification of meetings shall be made to all the members or joint holders, at the instance of any of them expressing the object of the call, and which must be made in the same form prescribed for notifying delinquent members or joint holders.

ART. 180. Even the members or joint holders who are not entitled to vote shall be called; but a personal summons shall not be necessary for them; a call through newspapers or posters shall be sufficient.

TITLE XVI.—*Advances to mines.*

ART. 181. By contract to furnish advances, a person obligates himself to cover the expenses caused by the working of a mine, and to repay himself only from its proceeds.

ART. 182. Contracts for advances must be in writing, and they will have no effect in regard to third parties, unless they are drawn as a public document and recorded in the register of constitution of vested rights in mines.

ART. 183. Advances may be contracted for quantities or for a determined time, or for the performance of one or more works in the mine.

ART. 184. If the contract does not specify the time or quantity of advances, the contracting parties can cancel it whenever they deem it convenient.

ART. 185. The miner can at any time stop the furnishing of advances by transferring the ownership of the mine to the party advancing money and the latter by renouncing his credit for advances already made.

ART. 186. It can be stipulated that the payment of what is due to the party advancing money may be made in bullion, at the price agreed upon by the interested parties, or appraised by a third person, as in the case of sales or in cash, with the premiums which may be determined.

ART. 187. It may also be stipulated that the party advancing money may become owner of a portion of the mine in payment of his advances. In this case, the contract will be governed by the dispositions which regulate mines in society or community.

But if the advancing party using the right granted by article 188 should stop the furnishing of advances, the portion of the mine of which he became owner, in virtue of the contract, shall revert to the ownership of the miner, without encumbrances or obligations on the part of the latter.

ART. 188. The advances must be furnished by the party advancing, at the time stipulated, or as the works may require; and if, after he has been requested, he refuses to pay the expenses, or delays such payments to the detriment of the works, the miner shall have the option between making a demand in the usual manner in such cases, or receiving money from another party for account of the party advancing, or contract with another whose account shall have preference of payment.

ART. 189. If the miner invests the money or supplies advanced by the party, for a purpose other than was intended without his consent, he will be guilty of abuse of confidence, and the contractor shall have the right to assume the administration of the mine.

The party advancing shall have the same right, if, the mine being insolvent, it could be proved to the miner that the administration of the mine is careless and too expensive, in spite of the advancer's representations and reclamations which he may have made against those abuses.

ART. 190. If, at the expiration of the contract for advances, the mine should be found insolvent, the party advancing shall have the right to retain it, and to continue his advances under his own administration, until he can repay himself, in preference to all other creditors, excepting the holders of anterior mortgages, not only for what was due him, but also for the new advances with the premiums and in the manner stipulated in the contract.

ART. 191. If the mine is in the position indicated in the precedent article, and the party advancing does not wish to continue his advances, the miner shall have the right to contract with other parties, whose accounts shall have preference over the previous ones.

TITLE XVII.—*Sequestration of mines.*

ART. 192. When the sequestration of a mine or of its products occurs sufficient property shall be set aside to pay the expenses of the working. The owner or holder can raise the sequestration by offering security or mortgage to answer for the restitution of the mine, or of said products; but in that case, the sequestrator can claim the appointment of a controller, who shall see that the works are conducted fairly and legally and who shall keep an account of the expenses and proceeds of the mine.

ART. 193. If the proceeds of the sequestrated mine are not sufficient to pay its expenses and the sequestrator refuses to furnish the necessary funds for that, the mine shall be returned to the owner until a definite sentence is reached in the suit which caused the sequestration.

ART. 194. The sequestration of the products of a mine can not be decreed in an ordinary suit, but only after hearing the parties, and in virtue of a title, giving rise to a presumption of ownership or right of the sequestrator, until contrary proof is presented.

TITLE XVIII.—*Seizure of mines.*

ART. 195. In executory judgments, neither the mine of the debtor, nor the tools or provisions introduced for its operation, can be attached or alienated, unless the consent of the miner is expressed in said judgments; but execution can be effected against the minerals on hand which have been extracted from the mine.

ART. 196. If the proceeds of those minerals and of the other effects attached are not sufficient to pay off the debt, the creditor shall have the right to take the mine under his administration as a pledged property, until he can pay himself with the proceeds from it.

ART. 197. The creditor to whom the mine is delivered as a pledge must administer it with the same care and under the same obligations imposed by the law to the associate administrators.

If the mine does not produce enough to pay the expenses of economical and legal operations, he can ask the judge an authorization to make advances, and he shall then enjoy the same rights granted to parties advancing, not only as regards the quantities invested in such advances and the commercial interest, but also as regards his original credit.

ART. 198. Whilst the mine remains in the possession of the creditor, the miner shall have the right to visit it, to inspect the works, to examine the books and vouchers, either personally or through his representative, and to make the observations and corrections which the keeping of accounts and the system of work may suggest to his mind. He may also solicit the appointment of a controller with the powers conferred in article 195.

ART. 199. If the creditor does not work the mine according to the legal requirements, or if it should be shown that his administration is fraudulent, or that it is careless and unduly expensive, although he may have been warned against such an abuse, he will lose the right of administration, and he shall only be allowed to require the appointment of a controller, who shall be in the same time the receiver of the products of the mine.

ART. 200. In the cases of insolvency or bankruptcy of mines, the creditors shall be asked to take on their own account the administration of the mine; and those who will consent to this shall have the same rights and obligations, established in regard to executors.

This is understood to be without prejudice of the rights granted to mortgage holders or parties advancing. The mortgage holders or preferred creditors of the mine shall have a preferred right to have the administration of the mine confined to them.

FINAL TITLE.—*Observance of this code.*

ART. (final). The present code shall enter in force on the first day of January of 1881, and on that date all preëxisting laws or special ordinances on mining, even those which are not contrary to its disposition, shall be abrogated.

On the 24th of September, 1888, the foregoing Code was supplemented and explained by the following decree:

The President of the Republic of Honduras, by virtue of the powers vested in him by article 48 of the constitution and by act of Congress of December 23, 1887, decrees:

ARTICLE 1. By means of denouncement, as established by the mining code, or by concession of the Government, is acquired the possession of mines, working grounds, mineral zones, reduction-work sites, mill sites, and water privileges, necessary for the utilizations of their products as well as other uses.

ART. 2. Therefore, those who have lawfully acquired these rights, previous to the issuance of this decree, or who may acquire them by the same methods in the future, shall be considered as their sole owners and proprietors.

ART. 3. Ownership in sites for reduction works or mills, superficial concessions and water privileges, shall be governed, as to duration, by the same laws and conditions as those relating to mines; it being necessary, in the denouncement of the former, to observe and follow, as far as adaptable, the rules and regulations governing the denouncement of the latter; and the title granted, either by method of denouncement or concession, shall be recorded, as are recorded all deeds for real estate, and shall be considered full and sufficient proof of ownership.·

ART. 4. Mill sites and superficial concessions, intended for the establishment of reduction works, or for the development of mines, shall belong exclusively to those to whom they have been granted, and they shall have full right to ask for their disoccupation, on the part of those who have already or may establish hereafter works thereon, such as farms, fields, dwelling houses, or anything of that class. In case such works or buildings have been placed by authority, or with the knowledge or consent of the rightful owner or proprietor, then their value shall be carefully ascertained by experts, and their owners be indemnified for the same; but in case such works or buildings have not been so placed or located, then no idemnity shall be necessary.

ART. 5. When sites for reduction works, mill sites, superficial concessions, mineral zones, and water privileges belong to owners of mines, they shall have them as accessory holdings, with full ownership, use, and possession of the same.

ART. 6. Reduction sites which do not belong to owners of mines shall be denounceable when abandoned, and the method of denouncement shall be in the same form as that prescribed for abandoned mines.

Mills or other establishments for the reduction of ores shall be considered as abandoned when the buildings are unroofed, and when they do not contain either machinery or tools, and there is not on the ground serviceable lumber for their repair; although the walls of the building or buildings should still remain standing, and even without these reasons or facts they shall still be denounceable and adjudicable, when no formal work shall have been executed there for two consecutive years.

In every case, however, of the denouncement, on account of abandonment of reduction works or other establishments, to which this and article 5 refers, the denouncer must recompense the former owner, the valuation to be made by experts, for everything which, although attached to the soil, may be made serviceable by repair; or the former owner shall be permitted to utilize the same, provided he can so do without notable harm to the succeeding works, or he may remove them provided he should do so within the time which the authority, admitting the denouncement, shall assign.

ART. 7. At the expense of those interested, there shall be published in any newspaper of the capital an extract of each petition made to the Government for the purpose of acquiring any of the vested rights mentioned in article 1, and the judge of letters, in whose jurisdiction said rights may be located, must be officially notified of the fact, and the priority of the petition made to the administrative or judicial authorities shall serve as a base for preference in their adjudication, in case of conflict or opposition between concessionists, or between them and denouncers.

ART. 8. Every concession of mineral zones shall lapse if within two years, dating from their being granted, no formal work shall have been begun, in the form and under the conditions established by the respective code; but the executive power can grant or excuse delays, grounding or basing on the greater or lesser probability of such work being established.

ART. 9. Whenever a mine owner, having several claims in the same district, shall work one of them on a large scale, and on account of the scarcity of labor, or the lack of some other element, shall be impeded in the simultaneous working of the others, the Government, being informed of the cause, shall be able to grant him protection in the ownership of said claims for a determined time.

ART. 10. If the reduction works are to be established on private lands, by private agreement and without making use of the rights mentioned in articles 6, 7, and 8 of the mining code, and also in the decree of 19th March of 1885, then those interested shall have only the rights which may have been granted them by the respective proprietors of the lands, and they shall also arrange with said parties privately in regard to wood and water privileges which they may wish to make use of on the lands of the latter, or of any materials that they may desire to take from the same.

ART. 11. Every owner of mines, without paying any tax or fees, shall have the right to make use of the timber on Government or municipal lands, and shall also have free use of the necessary water, not granted already to others, or any materials which may be necessary for the prosecution of his works.

ART. 12. If various parties should solicit, at the same time, sites for working grounds of mines, and there should not be sufficient space for all, then preference shall be given to those having the largest capital, and who shall give guarantees of working on a large scale; and also, under the same circumstances, attention must be paid to priority of time in the petition.

ART. 13. Any question that may arise between mill-owners, or between them and private parties, or towns, with regard to the use of water, the cutting of wood or timber, or the use of other materials, or with respect to the boundaries of mines, reduction-works, mineral zones, or superficial concessions, or with regard to the occupation of the same, shall be submitted to the decision of a board of arbitrators, which shall be formed in the following manner.

ART. 14. Before the judge, who has to be acquainted with the question, each contending party shall choose a representative, with the power to act as arbitrator. The arbitrators thus named shall choose a third, and, in case of not being able by reason of disagreement to do so, said third arbitrator shall be appointed by the judge. In case one of the contending parties should not wish to respond to the demand for arbitration, or, responding, should refuse to appoint a representative with the quality of arbitrator, then the judge, in such default, shall himself appoint him; but in every case the arbitrators appointed must be capable men.

ART. 15. The tribunal of arbitrators being organized, it shall hear the litigants, who will bring forward the documents and proofs which they may consider necessary, together with the arguments in their behalf; and said tribunal shall proceed with good faith, truth, and care, but without subjecting itself to the rigorous process of ordinary law proceedings.

ART. 16. When said tribunal believes that the contending parties have had full and fair opportunity to present their cases, it shall give the decision which it believes to be just, and from such decision there shall be no appeal.

ART. 17. The proceedings must positively be terminated within one month, except in case that one or both of the contending parties shall prove that some of their testimony or witnesses are outside of the Republic, and in such case the tribunal may extend the proceeding for a period, which shall not exceed three months.

ART. 18. The arbitrament, being arrived at, shall be remitted, with the reasons therefor, to the respective judge, who shall execute it, and he shall fix the fees which the contending parties must pay to the arbitrators; and these latter will make a statement of the expenses incurred in the prosecution of the case, and the litigants are not allowed to question either the accounts of the arbitrators or the fees fixed by the judge.

ART. 19. Suits, however, which shall have been in process of trial in the points indicated in this decree, but prior to the emission of the same, shall be terminated in the tribunal to which they were brought, notwithstanding articles 13 and 19 of this decree.

ART. 20. By this decree shall be tried and adjudged all disputes with regard to mines or other property of which article 1 treats (except those mentioned in article 19), the same having been acquired judicially or administratively before or subsequent to its emission; and said decree shall take effect from the date of its emission; all present laws, however, bearing on the same points, and that do not come in conflict with it, shall remain of full force and effect.

Given in the Government House, at Tegucigalpa, on the twenty-fourth day of September, 1888.

LUIS BOGRAN.

By the President:

FRANCISCO PLANAS, *Secretary of State.*

To further encourage the mining industry in Honduras, two decrees have been issued, one on November 18, 1882, and the other on March 17, 1887, granting several exemptions and privileges of importance to miners and other persons connected with this business.

The text of both decrees reads, respectively, as follows:

DECREE OF NOVEMBER 18, 1882.

Whereas the mining industry is daily acquiring greater importance, and whereas it therefore becomes necessary to favor it, in order that it may attain in as short a time as possible all the development and perfection of which it is capable, therefore the President decrees:

ARTICLE 1. Honduraneans or foreigners who, associated together or as private individuals, engage in the bona fide working of mines which have first been duly enrolled shall enjoy the following concessions:

1. To export free of duty the silver, gold, copper, etc., etc., which they produce.

2. To introduce free of duty and of every kind of imposts machinery for raising weights, stamping and grinding ores, for extracting the metals therefrom, for working iron and steel, and sawing timber, etc., etc., whether the said machinery be moved by steam or water, pumps to extract water, shovels, hammers, plantation knives, axes, drills, wedges, grindstones, machinists' tools, including forges, anvils, etc., etc., powder of all kinds, exploders and fuse to produce the explosion, oils for illuminating and lubricating purposes, materials in bulk, such as steel for augers, iron in plates or bars or cast or in the form of hoops, nails, spikes, screws, tubes of iron, bronze, copper, lead, gutta percha, etc., locks, hinges, ropes made of steel, iron, hemp, or other material, plates of pure or sheet copper, silver and copper in bars for smelting, bronze, tin, lead, quicksilver, or any other metal considered necessary to carry out the work, diamonds in bulk or with teeth, diamond drills if needed to drill rock, all the material used in the art of

assaying ores, such as crucibles, smelting furnaces, chemical ingredients for mixing and analysis, or to be employed in the milling of ores, or to extract therefrom the gold, silver, and copper which they contain; the said ingredients may be acids, sulphur, metallic salts, etc., glass apparatus for chemical operations, stearine or sperm candles, and tents of cloth.

3. The right to use the woods and waters extant in public or vacant lands, without other restriction than such regulations of the Government or which with its approval the respective municipalities may issue concerning the same; and

4. The operatives engaged in mines and mills shall be free from military duty during the time they remain thus employed, but they must engage to serve for at least six months, to which end the managers shall register with the respective departmental commanders the number of operatives which they may need.

Art. 2. The materials specified in article 1, must be ordered from abroad directly by the owners of the mines, or by the superintendents representing them, and they must send a copy of the said order to the secretary of the treasury (secretario de hacienda). These articles shall be brought directly from the ports to the establishment of the mines, to which they belong, and the way-bill for the transit of the same, shall be extended by the administrator of customs and returned by the alcalde of the municipality in whose jurisdiction the establishments are situated.

Art. 3. The managers of the mines are obliged to construct a safe place for storage of powder and other explosives. Such places for storage will not be permitted within the precincts of human settlements.

Art. 4. The managers of mines shall not be permitted to sell the powder or other dutiable articles, which they have introduced free under these concessions, during the time they carry on their operations. The party who violates this rule shall be prosecuted as a smuggler, losing in addition the right of availing himself of the privileges of this decree. But the matriculated miners located in the same mining district, may in cases of urgent necessity make loans and sales among themseves, of such articles as they may require to continue their operations, after previously obtaining permission of the respective judge of the peace.

Art. 5. A mine being abandoned, its owners shall have the right to sell, at a price which shall not exceed the first cost, their machinery, tools, and all comprised in loose fixture (*material volante*), but before executing said sale, the owners must present to the government an inventory of the existing material, in case it would be convenient to buy all, or part of the referred to and existing property, to which the government shall have the first right of preference.

Art. 6. In all the "tercenas" (government stores) will be sold the powder, at six reals per pound, needed by the matriculated miners.

Art. 7. The governors of the departments will keep a register, in which, by solicitation of the interested parties, the governors will inscribe the names of mines which are under exploitation in their respective departments, according to the regulations of the mining code; they will also inscribe the name of the individual or company to which they belong.

The certificate of this register will constitute the matriculation, which, with "anonymous," companies will be extended in favor of the superintendent.

Art. 8. In making the register, the governors will demand the presentation of the definite title of the mining property, also judicial information that the mine is worked. Every four months the governors will remit to the "ministerio de hacienda" a report about the extended matriculations.

Art. 9. The matriculation shall be renewed every four months, otherwise it shall be of no advantage.

Art. 10. The present decree shall not admit of any change during ten years, and all the privileges hereby granted shall be considered in force during that period.

DECREE OF MARCH 17, 1887.

The President of the Republic of Honduras, to the inhabitants thereof, know that the national congress has ordered the following decree, No. 34:

The national congress, with the view of giving to the mining industry a large augmentation, decrees:

Single article.

There is conceded to the miner the exclusive right to use for the working of his mine, all the woods, which are found on the mining claims, that were given to him according to law, and which are in national lands.

Bull. 57——9

Appendix D.

TARIFF OF HONDURAS.

The tariff of Honduras, as here printed, is the latest official publication, but a decree was issued in 1893 augmenting the duties 20 per cent on all merchandise imported into the country. This increase, however, does not apply to imports from the United States, which are regulated by the special reciprocity agreement.

The official tariff of Honduras is arbitrarily divided into eleven classes, according to the rate of duty charged per pound, which is assessed on the gross weight of the merchandise. The following schedules have been arranged alphabetically and include all the articles expressed in the tariff.

The valuations expressed in English are calculated on the basis of the official valuation of foreign coins issued by the Director of the Mint of the United States October 1, 1891, in which the peso is valued at 71.3 cents, United States currency; but the price of silver has since fallen, and on January 1, 1894, the peso was valued at 51.6 cents, United States currency.

ARTICLE OF MERCHANDISE.	Duty per pound in U. S. currency.	ARTÍCULO DE MERCANCÍA.	Derechos por libra en moneda hondureña.
	Dollars.		*Pesos.*
Acetic acid....................	.058	Acido acético.................	.08
Acid, sulphuric............ ...	.0145	Acido sulfúrico...............	.02
Adzes. (See instruments or tools.)	.0145	Azuelas. (Véase herramientas é	
		instrumentos, etc.)..........	.02
Aërated water	.0145	Aguas gaseosas	.02
Albums. (See portfolios, cigar-		Albums. (Véase carteras, taba-	
cases, etc.)	.2175	queras, etc.)................	.30
Almond oil	.0145	Aceite de almendras	.02
Almonds, unshelled or shelled..	.029	Almendras, con cáscaras ó mon-	
		dadas......................	.04
Alpaca. (See cloth, pañete, etc.)	.3625	Alpaca. (Véase paño, pañete,	
		etc.)	.50
Altar-cloths. (See chasubles, etc.)	.58	Manteles. (Véase casullas, etc.)	.80
Altar linen. (See chasubles, etc.)	.58	Paños para cubrir cálices. (Véase	
		casullas, etc.)	.80
Alum, crude	.058	Alumbre crudo...............	.08
Ammunition, small shot, and bul-		Municiones, perdigones y balas.	.04
lets........................	.029		
Anatomical instruments. (See in-		Instrumentos de anatomia.	
struments of surgery, etc.).....	.087	(Véase instrumentos de ciru-	
		gía, etc.)..................	.12
Anchors. (See iron, manufactured,		Anclas. (Véase hierro manu-	
etc.)	.0145	facturado, etc.)	.02
Animals, dissected.............	.058	Animales disecados.	.08

ARTICLE OF MERCHANDISE.	Duty per pound in U. S. currency.	ARTÍCULO DE MERCANCÍA.	Derechos por libra en moneda hondureña.
	Dollars.		*Pesos.*
Aniseed, caraway seed, cinnamon, cumin, cubebs, cloves, marjoram, pepper, and other spices used for seasoning food.	.058	Anís en grano, alcaravea, canela, canelón, comino, cubeba, clavos, orégano, pimienta y demas especias que sirven para sazonar ó condimentar los alimentos.	.03
Anodynes.	.1305	Anodinos	.18
Anvils. (See instruments or tools, etc.)	.0145	Bigornias. (Véase herramientas é instrumentos, etc.)	.02
Appliqué work. (See laces, stripes, etc.).	.58	Embutidos. (Véase encajes, tiras, etc.)	.80
Areometers of all sorts	.1305	Areómetros de todas clases.	.18
Articles not specified	1.088	Alguno ó algunos otros artículos que no esten comprendidos en las clases anteriores	1.50
Articles of German silver or its imitations, such as waiters, trays, bits, muzzles, spurs, stirrups, hinges, buckles, chandeliers, lamps, candlesticks, and others	.3625	Efectos de plata alemana ó metal blanco y sus imitaciones, como bandejas, azafates, frenos, bozales, espuelas, estribos, charnelas, hebillas, arañas, lámparas, candeleros ú otros.	.50
Articles of iron or other metals, gilt or silver-plated	.174	Efectos de hierro ú otro metal, dorados ó plateados.	.24
Articles wholly or in part of gold or silver.	1.088	Los artículos de oro ó plata, ó los que tengan algo de alguno de estos metales	1.50
Augers. (See tools for arts, etc.)	.029	Barrenos. (Véase instrumentos para artes, etc.).	.04
Augers and borers for perforating stones and logs	.0145	Barrenos y taladros para perforar piedras ó troncos	.02
Awls. (See tools for arts, etc.).	.029	Leznas. (Véase instrumentos para artes, etc.).	.04
Axes. (See instruments or tools, etc.)	.0145	Hachas. (Véase herramientas é instrumentos, etc.)	.02
Baby carriages. (See baskets, etc.)	.058	Cochecitos para niños. (Véase canastos, etc.)	.08
Bacon, when not canned	.0145	Tocino, cuando no viene en latas.	.02
Bags or pouches for hunters	.1305	Bolsas ó sacos para cazadores	.18
Bags, traveling, of all sorts	.029	Sacos de viaje, de todas clases.	.04
Baize and ratteen in blankets or by the piece.	.2175	Bayeta, bayetilla y ratina en piezas ó frazadas	.30
Balances of copper, or of which copper is the chief material.	.029	Balanzas de cobre ó que tengan la mayor parte de este metal.	.04
Balances, steelyards, and weights, excepting those made of copper or of which copper forms the chief material.	.0145	Balanzas, romanas y pesos, excepto los de cobre ó que tengan la mayor parte de este metal.	.02
Balconies, iron. (See iron, manufactured, etc.).	.0145	Balcones de hierro. (Véase hierro manufacturado, etc.)	.02
Balusters. (See iron, manufactured, etc.).	.0145	Balaustres. (Véase hierro manufacturado, etc.).	.02
Barley, hulled or ground	.0145	Cebada mondada ó molida	.02

ARTICLE OF MERCHANDISE.	Duty per pound in U. S. currency.	ARTÍCULO DE MERCANCÍA.	Derechos por libra en moneda hondureña.
	Dollars.		*Pesos.*
Barometers	.174	Barómetros	.24
Baskets, baby carriages, and other articles of osier or rushes, there being included in this classification all baby carriages of whatever material	.058	Canastos, canastillos, cochecitos para niños y otras piezas de mimbre ó junco; quedando inclusos en este clasificación los cochecitos para niños, de cualquier materia que sean ...	.08
Batiste. (See muslin, batiste, etc.)...........	.58	Batista. (Véase muselina, batista, etc.)..................	.80
Batiste or cambric, of linen or of linen mixed with cotton, or any other fine fabric of linen or linen mixed with cotton, not included in other classes..............	1.088	Holán batista ó claron de lino ó mezclado con algodon, ó cualquiera otra tela fina de lino ó mezclada con algodon, no incluida en las clases anteriores	1.50
Battens, picture frames, or moldings of wood, painted, varnished, gilded, or silver plated..	.029	Listones, cañuelas, cenefas ó molduras de madera, pintadas, barnizadas, doradas ó plateadas.....................	.04
Beads and bugles of glass, porcelain, steel, wood, or any other material, excepting gold and silver.....................	.1305	Abalorios, cañutillos y cuentas de vidrio, porcelana, acero, madera y cualquiera otra materia, excepto las de oro y plata	.18
Bedspreads. (See huckaback etc.).....................	.087	Colchas. (Véase alemanisco, etc.)	.12
Beer of all sorts, however put up.	.0145	Cerveza de todas clases y en cualquier envase	.02
Bell metal. (See steel, copper, etc.)...................	.029	Metal campanil. (Véase acero, cobre, hierro, etc.)	.04
Bellows of all sorts. (See instruments or tools, etc.)..........	.0145	Fuelles de todas clases. (Véase herramientas. é instrumentos, etc.)..................	.02
Belts, cotton. (See ribbons braids, etc.).................	.174	Fajas de algodon. (Véase heladillas ó cintas, etc.).........	.24
Belts, linen, etc. (See laces stripes, etc.).................	.58	Fajas de lino. (Véase encajes, tiras, etc.)...............	.80
Belts, woolen, etc. (See understockings, stockings, etc.).....	.2175	Fajas de lana. (Véase calcetas, medias, etc.)	.30
Bench-screws. (See tools for arts, etc.)...................	.029	Tornos y tornillos de banco. (Véase instrumentos para artes, etc.).................	.04
Bene seed....................	.0145	Ajonjoli	.02
Billiard balls of ivory, when imported without the table.......	1.088	Bolas de marfil para billares, cuando vengan sin estos......	1.50
Billiard-cue tips..............	.058	Puntas de suela para los tacos de billar..................	.08
Billiard cushions	.058	Bandas de billar..............	.03
Billiard tables, with all their appurtenances, including the balls and the cloth for each billiard-table, when imported with the table.......................	.058	Billares con todos sus enseres, inclusas las bolas y el paño correspondientes á cada mesa de billar cuando vengan juntamente con los billares........	.08

ARTICLE OF MERCHANDISE.	Duty per pound in U. S. currency.	ARTÍCULO DE MERCANCÍA.	Derechos por libra en moneda hondureña.
	Dollars.		*Pesos.*
Binocles. (See eyeglasses, etc.)..	.3625	Gemelos ó binóculos. (Véase anteojos, etc.)	.50
Bits. (See articles of German silver, etc.)	.3625	Frenos. (Véase efectos de plata alemana, etc.)	.50
Bits. (See iron, manufactured, etc.)	.0145	Brocas. (Véase hierro manufacturado, etc.)	.02
Bituminous applications of all sorts	.0145	Betunes de todas clases, excepto él de calzado	.02
Blank books	.0145	Libros y libretines en blanco....	.02
Blankets, cotton. (See huckaback, etc.)	.087	Frazadas de algodon. (Véase alemanisco, damasco, etc.)....	.12
Blankets or coverlets of wool or mixed with cotton, white or colored	.174	Frazadas, mantas ó cobertores de lana ó mezclada con algodon, blancas ó de color	.24
Blondes. (See laces, stripes, blondes, etc.)	.58	Blondas. (Véase encajes, tiras, etc.)	.80
Blunderbusses. (See swords, sabres, etc.)	.3625	Trabucos. (Véase espadas, sables, etc.)	.50
Boar's bristles, for shoemakers...	.058	Cerda de jabalí para zapateros..	.08
Bombazine. (See cloth, pañete, etc.)	.3625	Alépin. (Véase paño, pañete, etc.)	.50
Boneblack	.0145	Carbon animal	.02
Bone, ivory, mother-of-pearl, jet and its imitations, tortoise shell and its imitations, rubber, gum elastic, horn, and talc, manufactured into articles not included in other classes	.174	Hueso, marfil, nácar, azabache y sus imitaciones, carey y sus imitaciones, caucho, goma elastica, asta ó cuerno, y talco manufacturado en cualquier forma, no comprendidos en otras clases	.24
Bonnets. (See jerkins or doublets, etc.)	.1305	Gorras. (Véase almillas, etc.)..	.18
Books. (See blank books.)	.0145	Libros y libretines. (Véase libros y libretines en blanco.)..	.02
Boot hooks	.058	Tirabotas	.08
Bosoms, paper. (See paper lanterns, etc.)	.058	Pecheras de papel. (Véase farolillos de papel, etc.)	.08
Bottle-stands	.087	Porta-botellas	.12
Bougies	.1305	Candelillas ó sondas	.18
Bows. (See understockings, stockings, etc.)	.2175	Lazos. (Véase calcetas, medias, etc.)	.30
Boxes, candy. (See figures, ornaments, etc.)	.058	Envases para dulces. (Véase figuros, adornos, etc.)	.08
Boxes for watches or jewelry, even when empty and separately imported	1.085	Las cajitas vacias preparadas para relojes y prendas finas, aunque vengan por separado..	1.50
Boxes, money. (See iron, in wire, etc.)	.0145	Cajas para guardar dinero. (Véase hierro manufacturado, etc.)	.02
Brabant. (See canvas, brabant, etc.)	.058	Bramante. (Véase cañamazo crudo, etc.)	.08
Braids. (See laces, stripes, etc.)..	.58	Trenzas. (Véase encajes, tiras, etc.)	.80

ARTICLE OF MERCHANDISE.	Duty per pound in U. S. currency.	ARTÍCULO DE MERCANCÍA.	Derechos por libra en moneda hondureña.
	Dollars.		*Pesos.*
Braids, cotton. (See ribbons, braid, etc.)...............	.174	Trencillas de algodon. (Véase hiladillos ó cintas, etc.)......	.24
Brass, manufactured. (See steel, copper, etc.),...............	.029	Laton ó azófar manufacturado. (Véase acero, cobre, etc.)....	.04
Brass, unwrought. (See steel, bronze, etc.)...............	.0145	Latón en pasta, etc. (Véase acero, bronce, etc.)..........	.02
Breast-pumps.................	.1305	Mamaderas	.18
Bricks, bristol or scouring.......	.0145	Ladrillos para limpiar cubiertos..	.02
Bristles. (See boar's bristles.)...	.058	Cerda. (Véase cerda de jabalí, etc.).....................	.08
Bristol brick	.0145	Ladrillos para limpiar cubiertos..	.02
Bronze in powder and in little books, for bronzing..........	.3625	Bronce en polvo y libritos, para broncear..................	.50
Bronze, manufactured. (See steel, copper, etc.).......	.029	Bronce manufacturado. (Véase acero, cobre, etc.)............	.04
Bronze, unwrought. (See steel, copper, etc.).................	.0145	Bronce, en pasta, etc. (Véase acero, bronce, etc.)..........	.02
Brooches. (See pins, etc.)	.087	Broches. (Véase alfileres, etc.).	.12
Brooms and brushes of bristles...	.058 *	Escobas, escobillas y escobillones de cerda.............	.08
Brooms of palm, rushes, or vegetable material	.0145	Escobas de palma, junco ú otra materia vegetal.........	.02
Brushes. (See tools for arts, etc.).	.029	Cepillos. (Véase instrumentos para artes, etc.)............	.04
Brushes, common, for animals..	.029	Cepillos ordinarios ó bruzas para las bestias.............	.04
Brushes for the teeth, the head, the clothes, the shoes, and for any other use, excepting those included in the third class.....	.087	Cepillos para los dientes, la cabeza, la ropa, el calzado, y para cualquier otro uso, excepto los comprendidos en la tercera clase	.12
Brushes of palm, rushes, or other vegetable material	.0145	Escobas, escobillas y escobillones de palma, junco ú otra materia vegetal	.02
Brushes, painters', of all sorts ...	.1305	Brochas y pinceles de todas clases.....................	.18
Buckles. (See articles of German silver, etc.).................	.3625	Hebillas. (Véase efectos de plata alemana, etc.)..........	.50
Bullets. (See ammunition, etc.)..	.029	Balas. (Véase municiones, etc.).	.04
Burins. (See tools for arts, etc.)..	.029	Buriles. (Véase instrumentos para artes, etc.)	.04
Busts, iron. (See iron, manufactured, etc.)	.0145	Bustos. (Véase hierro manufacturado, etc.)	.02
Butter	.029	Mantequilla..................	.04
Buttons of all kinds, excepting those of silk, shell, silver, or gold	.1305	Botones de todas clases, excepto los de seda, concha, plata y oro	.18
Buttons, shell	.2175	Botones de concha	.30
Cables......................	.0145	Cables......................	.02
Cages for birds. (See wire, manufactured, etc.)	.087	Jaulas para pájaros. (Véase alambre manufacturado, etc.).	.12
Calendars, perpetual	.087	Calendarios perpetuos	.12

ARTICLE OF MERCHANDISE.	Duty per pound in U. S. currency.	ARTÍCULO DE MERCANCÍA.	Derechos por libra en moneda hondureña.
	Dollars.		*Pesos.*
Cambric, lace, zephyr, l i n e n tarlatan, muslin, a n d a n y other fine linen fabrics made up into neck-cloths, ruchings, caps, skirts, sleeves, c a p e s, chemisettes, gowns, or o t h e r articles not included in other classes......................	1.088	Holán batista,clarín, punto, céñro, lino, tarlatán, muselina y cualesquiera otras telas finas de lino, preparadas en gorgueras,ruches, gorras, faldellines, manquillos, pelerinas, camisitas, camisones ú otras piezas ú adornos no incluidos en las clases anteriores............	1.50
Cambric, linen...........:........	.174	Cambray del obispo............	.24
Camera lucida or camera obscura, for drawing or photography, and other such apparatus......	.1305	Cámaras claras ú oscuras, para dibujo ó fotografia, y demas aparatos semejantes	.18
Canary seed....................	.0145	Alpiste	.02
Candlesticks, not specified. (See chandeliers, globes, etc., articles of German silver, etc.).....	.1305	Candeleros n o especificados. (Véase aranas, bombas, etc., efectos de p l a t a alemana, etc.).................	.04
Candles, sperm, paraffin, or stearin	.029	Velas de esperma, de parafina, de composición ó estearicas ..	.04
Cane, unmanufactured	.029	Juncos ó junquillos, sin manufacturar...................	.04
Canes.........................	.1305	Bastones.....................	.18
Canned foods. (See sausages, etc.)	.058	Conservas alementicias en latas. (Véase salchichones, etc.)....	.08
Canvas and raven's duck of cotton	.058	Lona y loneta de algodon.......	.08
Canvas, brabant, and other similar ordinary cloths	.058	Cañamazo crudo, b r a m a n t e y otras telas .ordinarias semejantes....................	.08
Canvas, cotton, for embroidering.	.087	Cañamazo de algodon para bordar........................	.12
Canvases prepared for portraits and pictures in oil, and also stumps for drawing..........	.058	Telas preparadas para retratos y pinturas al óleo, y tambien el esfumino para dibujos.....	.08
Cap-boxes, for hunters.........	.1305	Pistoneras	.18
Capers.......................	.029	Alcaparras	
Capes. (See cambric, etc.).....	1.088	Pelerinas. (Véase holán batista, clarín, etc.)...........	1.50
Capes. (Seejerkins or doublets, etc.) .... \.............	.1305	Birretes. (Véase almillas, etc.).	.04 .18
Caps, fulminating. (See swords, sabers, etc.)	.3625	Fulminantes ó pistones. (Véase espadas, sables, etc.).....	.50
Caps, linen. (See cambric, batiste, etc.)	1.088	Gorras de lino. (Véase holán batista, clarín, etc.)	1.50
Caps, woolen. (See understockings, stockings, etc.)..........	.2175	Gorras de lana. (Véase calcetas, medias, etc.)............	.30
Capstans. (See instruments or tools, etc.)	.0145	Cabrestantes. (V é a s e herramientas é instrumentos, etc.)..	.02
Capsules. (See swords, sabers, etc.)	.3625	Cápsules. (Véase espadas, sables, etc.)	.50

ARTICLE OF MERCHANDISE.	Duty per pound in U. S. currency.	ARTÍCULO DE MERCANCÍA.	Derechos por libra en moneda hondureña.
	Dollars.		*Pesos.*
Caraway seed. (See aniseed, etc.)	.058	Alcaraboa. (Véase anís en grano, etc.)	.08
Carbonate of lead	.0145	Albayalde ó carbonato de plomo	.02
Cardboard, fine, or thick paper, for offices, for cards, or for any other use, including impermeable paper for presses	.029	Cartón fino ó papel grueso para escritorio, para tarjetas y para cualquier otro uso, incluyendo en esta clasificación el papel impermeable para prensa	.04
Cardboard, manufactured or prepared for boxes, large or small, and in any other form except in toys for children, in masks, in boxes for watches or fine jewelry, and in some other articles which, like the foregoing, are included in other classes	.058	Cartón manufacturado ó preparado para cajas y cajitas, y en cualquier otra forma, excepto en juguetes para niños, en máscaras, en cajitas preparadas para relojes de faltriquera y prendas finas y en algunos otros artículos que como los anteriores están comprendidos en otras clases	.08
Card cases. (See portfolios, cigar cases, etc.)	.2175	Tarjeteros. (Véase carteras, tabaqueras, etc.)	.30
Cards, playing	.087	Naipes ó barajas	.12
Cards, visiting	.2175	Tarjetas para visita	.30
Carpenters' braces. (See tools for arts, etc.)	.029	Berbiquíes. (Véase instrumentos para artes, etc.)	.04
Carpets, of wool, separate or by the piece, and footcloths of all kinds	.2175	Alfombras sueltas ó en piezas, de lana, y gualdrapas de todas clases	.30
Cartridges. (See swords, sabers, etc.)	.3625	Cartuchos. (Véase espadas, sables, etc.)	.50
Cases containing small articles for embroidery, toilet, drawing, painting, and other purposes	.174	Estuches con piececitas de acero, cobre ú otro metal, para bordar, para limpiar la dentadura, para las uñas, para dibujos ó pinturas, etc	.24
Cassimere. (See cloth, pañete, etc.)	.3625	Casimir. (Véase paño, pañete, etc.)	.50
Chains. (See iron, manufactured, etc.)	.0145	Cadenas. (Véase hierro manufacturado, etc.)	.02
Chalk for polishing and also for billiard cues	.029	Pasta ó tizate para lustrar, y tambien él que sirve para las puntas de los tacos de billar.	.04
Chalk, tailors'	.0145	Jabon de piedra, llamado de sastres	.02
Chalk, white or red, crude or powdered	.0145	Creta blanca ó roja en piedra ó polvo	.02
Chalks for slates	.0145	Tizas de pizarra	.02
Chandeliers. (See articles of German silver, etc.)	.3625	Arañas. (Véase efectos de plata alemana, etc.)	.50

ARTICLE OF MERCHANDISE.	Duty per pound in U. S. currency.	ARTÍCULO DE MERCANCÍA.	Derechos por libra en moneda hondureña.
	Dollars.		*Pesos.*
Chandeliers, globes, glass shades, candlesticks, lanterns, lamps, excepting those made of gold or silver, which belong to the 11th class, and those of German silver, gilt or silver plated, which belong to the 9th; all adjuncts or accessories to said articles to be appraised with the latter when imported with them.................	.029	Arañas, bombas, briseras, candeleros, candelabros, fanales, girándulas, lámparas, linternas, palmatorias, guardabrisas y quinqués, con excepción de los que tengan oro ó plata, que corresponden á la 11ª clase y los de plata alemana, dorados ó plateados, que corresponden á la novena; debiendo aforarse en las clases á que correspondan los artículos expresados, todo lo que les corresponda ó sea anexo á dichos artículos cuando vengan junto con ellos...........	.04
Charcoal powder..............	.0145	Carbon vegetal en polvo........	.02
Chasubles, capes, corporals, altar-cloths (frontales), dalmáticas, stoles, maniples, altar linen, bands, and other ornaments for priests and churches..	.58	Casullas, capas pluviales, bolsas de los corporales, manteles ó frontales, dalmáticas, estolas, manípulos, paños para cubrir cálices, bandas y demas ornamentos para uso de los sacerdotes y las iglesias..........	.80
Cheeses of all sorts.............	.029	Quesos de todas clases.........	.04
Chemicals not specified under óther classes. (See drugs, medicines, etc.)..................	.174	Productos químicos no incluidos en las clases anteriores. (Véase drogas, medicinas, etc.) ...	.24
Chemicals for preserving skins..	.0145	Venenos para preservar pieles...	.02
Chemises. (See muslins, fine, etc.).	.2175	Camisetas. (Véase muselinas finas, etc.)................	.30
Chemisettes, linen. (See cambric, etc.)...................	1.088	Camisitas de lino. (Véase holán batista, etc., preparada.).....	1.50
Chess, checkers, dominoes, roulette, and other such games....	.1305	Juegos de ajedrez, de damas, de dominó, de ruleta ú otros semejantes.................	.18
China ink.....................	.0145	Tinta de China...............	.02
China or porcelain ware, or imitation of it in any form........	.029	Loza de china ó de porcelana, ó sus imitaciones en cualquier forma...................	.04
Chintz, calico, cretonne, collars or ruching (carlancanes), "brillantina," French plaids, "malvinas," "lustrillos," and any other fabric of cotton colored similar to those indicated and mentioned in other classes.....	.1305	Zarazas, calicones, cretonas, carlancanes, brillantina, listado frances, malvinas, lustrillos; y cualquiera otra tela de algodon de color, semejante á las indicadas y mencionadas en otras clases.............	.18
Chisels. (See tools for arts, etc.).	.029	Escoplos. (Véase instrumentos para artes, etc.).............	.04
Chloride of lime..............	.0145	Cloruro de cal...............	.02
Chromate of lead.............	.058	Amarillo inglés ó cromato de plomo	.08
Chronometers	.174	Cronómetros................	.24

ARTICLE OF MERCHANDISE.	Duty per pound in U. S. currency.	ARTÍCULO DE MERCANCÍA.	Derechos por libra en moneda hondureña.
	Dollars.		*Pesos.*
Cigar-cases. (See portfolios, cigar-cases, etc.)..............	.2175	Tabaqueras. (Véase carteras, tabaqueras, etc.).............	.30
Cigarette-cases. (See portfolios, cigar-cases, etc.)..............	.2175	Cigarreras. (Véase carteras, tabaqueras, etc.)	.30
Cigarettes, of paper or corn-leaves......................	.58	Cigarrillos de papel ú hoja de maíz......................	.80
Cinnamon. (See aniseed, etc.)..	.058	Canela. (Véase anís en grano, etc.)......................	.08
Clay, glazed or unglazed, in any shape......................	.0145	Barro vidriado ó sin vidriar, en cualquier forma.............	.02
Cloaks (ponchos). (See sleeves, sheepskin garments, etc.)......	.174	Ponchos. (Véase mangas, chamarras, etc.)	.24
Cloaks. (See understockings, etc.)......................	.2175	Abrigos. (Véase calcetas, medias, etc.)...................	.30
Clocks, table or wall, alarm, and any other, not including watches or steeple clocks..............	.174	Relojes de mesa ó pared, despertadores y cualquiera otra clase de reloj, excepto los de faltriquera y los de torres.....	.24
Cloth. (See handkerchiefs, shawls, etc.)......................	.58	Paños. (Véase pañuelos, pañolones, etc.)..................	:80
Cloth or knit-goods for slippers, excepting those of silk........	.2175	Géneros y tejidos para chinelas, excepto los de seda.........	.30
Cloth, "pañete," cassimere, "casinete," muslin, satin, lace, flannel, bombazine, alpaca, "cambrón," merino, serge, "cúbica" and damask, of wool or wool mixed with cotton, and any other fabric of wool, or of wool mixed with cotton, not mentioned in other classes........	.3625	Paño, pañete, casimir, casinete, muselina, raso, franela, alepín, alpaca, cambrón, m e r i n o, sarga, cúbica y damasco, de lana ó mezclado con algodon, y cualquiera otra tela de lana ó mezclada con algodon, no mencionada en otras clases...	.50
Clothing. (See skirts, fustians, etc.)......................	.174	Ropa. (Véase enaguas, fustanes, etc.)......................	.24
Clothing, ready-made. (See shirts, linen, etc.)..................	.2175	Ropa hecha. (Véase camisas hechas, etc.).................	.30
Cloths or textiles of cotton, hemp, "esparto," or linen, for covering the floor, though they may contain some wool.............	.058	Telas ó tejidos de algodon, cañamo, esparto ó lino, para cubrir el suelo, aunque tengan alguna mezcla de lana..............	.08
Cloves. (See aniseed, etc.)......	.058	Clavos. (Véase anís en grano, etc.)	
Clyster pumps.................	.1305	Clisobombas..................	.08
Coats. (See shirts, linen, etc.) ..	.2175	Casacas. (Véase camisas hechas, etc.)..·................	.18
Cocoa in the grain.............	.0145	Cacao en grano...............	.30
Cocoanut oil..................	.0145	Aceite de coco................	.02
Cod-liver oil. (See train oil, etc.).	.0145	Aceite de higado de bacaláo. (Véase aceite de pescado, etc.).	.02
Coffee	.0145	Café en grano.................	.02
Collars, paper. (See paper lanterns, etc.)	.058	Cuellos de papel. (Véase farolillos de papel, etc.)..........	.02
Collars, shirt-bosoms, and cuffs of linen or cotton for men.....	.2175	Cuellos, pecheras y puños de lino ó de algodon para hombres	.08
			.30

ARTICLE OF MERCHANDISE.	Duty per pound in U. S. currency.	ARTÍCULO DE MERCANCÍA.	Derechos por libra en moneda hondureña.
	Dollars.		*Pesos.*
Columns. (See iron, manufactured, etc.)	.0145	Columnas. (Véase hierro manufacturado, etc.)	.02
Compasses. (See tools for arts, etc.)	.029	Compases. (Véase instrumentos para artes, etc.)	.04
Compasses, magnetic, of all sorts.	.174	Brújulas de todas clases	.24
Cook-stoves, portable, of iron or other material	.0145	Cocinas portatiles de hierro ú otra materia	.02
Copal	.087	Resina de copal	.12
Copper, manufactured. (See steel, copper, etc.)	.029	Cobre manufacturado. (Véase acero, cobre, etc.)	.04
Copper, old, in odd pieces	.0145	Cobre viejo en piezas inutilizadas	.02
Copper, unwrought. (See steel, bronze, etc.)	.0145	Cobre en pasta. (Véase acero, bronce, etc.)	.02
Copes. (See chasubles, etc.)	.58	Capas pluviales. (Véase casullas, etc.)	.80
Coral in any form, except when set in gold or silver	.3625	Coral en cualquier forma, excepto cuando venga montado en oro ó plata	.50
Cordage	.0145	Cordería ó mecate	.02
Cords, linen. (See laces, stripes, etc.)	.58	Cordones de lino. (Véase encajes, tiras, etc.)	.80
Cords, woolen. (See understockings, stockings, etc.)	.2175	Cordones, de lana. (Véase calcetas, medias, etc.)	.30
Corduroy, cotton plush, velveteen, by the piece or in strips	.174	Pana, panilla, y felpa de algodon, imitación de terciopelo, en piezas ó en cintas	.24
Cork, in tablets or stoppers, or any other form	.058	Corcho en tablas, en tapones ó cualquier otra forma	.08
Corkscrews	.058	Tirabuzones	.08
Corporals. (See chasubles, etc.)	.58	Bolsas de los corporales. (Véase casullas, etc.)	.80
Corsets of all kinds	.3625	Corsés de todas clases	.50
Cosmoramas. (See stereoscopes, etc.)	.1305	Cosmoramas. (Véase estereoscopios, etc.)	.18
Cotton. (See curtains, hangings, etc., laces, strips, etc.)	.58	Algodon. (Véase cortinas, colgaduras, etc., encajes, tiras, etc.)	.80
Cotton. (See muslin, batiste, etc., handkerchiefs of linen, etc., handkerchiefs, shawls, etc.)	.58	Algodon. (Véase muselina, batista, etc., pañuelos de lino, etc., pañuelos, pañolones, etc.)	.80
Cotton. (See neckties of cotton, etc.)	.58	Algodon. (Véase corbatas de algodon, etc.)	.80
Cotton. (See shirts, linen, etc.)	.2175	Algodon. (Véase camisas hechas, etc	.30
Cotton. (See textiles or fabrics, ordinary, etc.)	.087	Algodon. (Véase telas or tejidos ordinarios, etc.)	.12
Cotton clothing. (See skirts, fustian, etc.)	.174	Ropa hecha de algodon. (Véase enaguas, fustanes, etc.)	.24
Cotton fabrics, not specified	.087	Telas de algodon, no especificadas	.12

ARTICLE OF MERCHANDISE.	Duty per pound in U. S. currency.	ARTÍCULO DE MERCANCÍA.	Derechos por libra en moneda hondureña.
	Dollars.		*Pesos.*
Cotton fabrics, white, such as madapolams, "estrivillos," family goods, "bogotanas," jeans, croydon, imperial, glazed, lining ("holandilla"), Rouen, Irish, and other similar fabrics........................	.087	Tejidos blancos de algodon, como madopollanes, estrivillos, género de familia, bogotanas, coquillo, croydon, imperial, holandilla, ruan, irlanda, y otros semejantes.............	.12
Cotton linings. (See lutestring, etc.)........................	.1305	Forros de algodon. (Véase sándalos, lustrinas, etc.)........	.18
Cotton, raw....................	.0145	Algodon en rama..............	.02
Cotton stuffs. (See drills, jeans, etc.)........................	.087	Tejidos de algodon. (Véase driles, coquí, etc.)...........	.12
Counterpanes. (See huckaback, etc.)........................	.087	Sobrecamas. (Véase alemanisco, etc.).................	.12
Coverlets. (See huckaback, etc.).	.087	Cobertores. (Véase alemanisco, etc.)...................	.12
Covers or stoppers with crowns of metal, glass, crystal, or porcelain	.087	Tapas con coronillas de metal, vidrio, cristal ó porcelana....	.12
Crackers of all sorts............	.0145	Galletas de todas clases........	.02
Crayons and charcoal pencils for drawing....................	.0145	Creyones y carboncites para dibujar...................	.02
Creas. (See drills, linens, creas, etc.)........................	.1305	Creas. (Véase driles, creas, etc.).	.18
Crockery, ordinary	.0145	Loza ordinaria	.02
Cruet stands, excepting those which are wholly or partly of gold or silver, which belong to the eleventh class, and those of German silver, gilded or silver-plated, which belong to the ninth class	.087	Aceiteras, angarillas ó aguaderas y porta-vinagreras, excepto las que sean ó tengan algo de oro ó plata, que corresponden á la 11ᵃ clase, y las de plata alemana, doradas ó plateadas, que corresponden á la 9ᵃ clase................	.12
Cruppers........'...............	.3625	Gruperas.....................	.50
Cubebs. (See aniseed, etc.).....	.058	Cubeba. (Véase anis en grano, etc.)......................	.08
Cuffs, linen or cotton. (See collars, shirt-bosoms, etc.)........	.2175	Puños de lino ó de algodon. (Véase cuellos, pecheras, etc.).	.30
Cuffs, paper. (See paper lanterns, etc.)......................	.058	Puños de papel. (Véase farolillos de papel, etc.).	.08
Cumin. (See aniseed, etc.)......	.058	Comino. (Véase anis en grano, etc.)	.08
Cupping glasses................	.1305	Ventosas.....................	.18
Curtains, etc., wool............	.3625	Cortinas, etc., de lana, etc	.50
Curtains, hangings, and musquito net, of linen or cotton.	.58	Cortinas, colgaduras y mosquiteras de lino ó de algodon	.80
Curtains, etc., silk	r.088	Cortinas, colgaduras, etc., de seda, etc....................	1.50
Cushions, not including those made of silk. (See billiard cushions.)...................	.058	Cojines, excepto los de seda. (Véase bandas de billar.)......	.50
Daggers. (See swords, sabres, etc.).........................	.3625	Puñales. (Véase espadas, sables, etc.)....................	.50

ARTICLE OF MERCHANDISE.	Duty per pound in U. S. currency.	ARTÍCULO DE MERCANCÍA.	Derechos por libra en moneda hondureña.
	Dollars.		*Pesos.*
Dalmaticas. (See chasubles, etc.).	.58	Dalmáticas. (Véase casullas, etc.)	.80
Damask. (See cloth, pañete, etc.).	.3625	Damasco. (Véase paño, pañete, etc.)	.50
Damask, cotton. (See huckaback, etc.)	.087	Damasco de algodon. (Véase alemanisco, etc.)	.12
Dates, dried. (See prunes, dates, etc.)	.058	Dátiles pasados. (Véase ciruelas pasas, etc.)	.08
Dioramas. (See stereoscopes, etc.)	.1305	Dioramas. (Véase estereoscopios, etc.)	.18
Dish-covers, wire	.087	Tapaderas de alambre para las viandas	.12
Door-mats	.0145	Felpudos ó limpiapiés	.02
Doors, iron. (See iron, manufactured, etc.)	.0145	Puertas de hierro. (Véase hierro manufacturado, etc.)	.02
Doors, iron	.0145	Puertas de hierro	.02
Drawers, cotton stockinet. (See jerkins or doublets, etc.)	.1305	Calzoncillos de punto de media de algodon. (Vease almillas, etc.)	.18
Drawers, others. (See shirts, linen, etc.)	.2175	Calzoncillos, otros. (Véase camisas hechas, etc.)	.30
Dress patterns of cotton prints. (See sleeves, sheepskin, etc.)	.174	Cortes de cotón. (Véase mangas, chamarras, etc.)	.24
Dressing and traveling cases	.174	Indispensables y neceseres de viaje	.24
Drills, jeans, napped stuffs (borlón), sheeting, satin, satinet, "mantadril," ticking, "mantalona," and other similar cotton textures	.087	Driles, coquí, borlón ó grano de oro, cotí, brin crudo, raso, rasete, mantadril, cotínes, mantalona y cualquier otro tejido de algodon semejante..	.12
Drills, linens (creas), pure or mixed, tablecloths, napkins, and hand-towels, of linen or mixed with cotton	.1305	Driles, creas puras ó mezcladas, manteles, servilletas y toallas de mano, de lino ó mezclado con algodon	.18
Drugs, medicines, and chemical products not specified under other classes	.174	Drogas, medicinas y productos quimicos, no incluidos en las clases anteriores	.24
Dusters	.087	Plumeros para limpiar	.12
Dye. (See hair-dye.)	.0145	Tinta. (Véase tinta de teñir el pelo.)	.02
Dynamite for blasting	.0145	Dinamita para esplotación de minas y canteras	.02
Earthenware. (See clay, glazed, etc.)	.0145	Loza de barro. (Véase barro vidriado, etc.)	.02
Earthenware, glazed or unglazed.	.0145	Loza de barro vidriado ó sin vidriar	.02
Elastics for shoes	.087	Cinta de goma ó elástica para el calzado	.12
Emery stone or powder	.0145	Esmeril en piedra ó polvo	.02
Engravings on paper	.174	Láminas ó estampas en papel	.24
Envelopes for letters	.0145	Sobres para cartas	.02

ARTICLE OF MERCHANDISE.	Duty per pound in U. S. currency.	ARTÍCULO DE MERCANCÍA.	Derechos por libra en moneda hondureña.
	Dollars.		*Pesos.*
Epaulets. (See understockings, stockings, etc.)	.2175	Charreteras. (Véase calcetas, medias, etc.)	.30
Epsom salts	.0145	Sal d'Epson	.02
Essences and extracts of all sorts.	.174	Esencias y extractos de todas clases	.24
Extracts. (See essences and extracts, etc.)	.174	Extractos. (Véase esencias y extractos.)	.24
Eyeglass cases.. (See portfolios, etc.)	.2175	Cajitas para anteojos. (Véase carteras, etc.)	.30
Eyeglasses, spectacles, binocles, spyglasses, lenses, telescopes, and microscopes, excepting those framed in gold or silver, including the crystals or lenses when separately imported	.3625	Anteojos, espejuelos, gemelos ó binóculos, catalejos, lentes, telescopios y microscopios, excepto los que tengan guarnición de oro ó plata, quedando incluidos en esta clase los cristales ó lentes cuando vengan por separado	.50
Eyelets. (See pins, etc.)	.087	Ojetes. (Véase alfileres, etc.)..	.12
Eyes, artificial	1.088	Ojos artificiales	1.50
Fabrics of materials other than silk, if containing some admixture of silk. (See silk, pure or mixed, etc.)	1.088	Telas ó tejidos de materias que esten mezcladas con seda. (Véase seda pura ó mezclada, etc.)	1.50
Fans, ivory	1.088	Abanicos de marfil	1.50
Fans of all kinds, excepting those of ivory, which belong to the 11th class	.3625	Abanicos de todas clases, excepto los de marfil que corresponden á la 11ª clase	.50
Feathers for ornamenting hats, caps, etc	1.088	Plumas para adorno de sombreros, gorras, etc	1.50
Fencing foils, masks, breast-protectors, and gloves	.1305	Floretas, máscaras, petos y guantes para esgrima	.18
Figs, dried. (See prunes, etc.)..	.058	Higos (pasados). (Véase ciruelas, etc.)	.08
Figures, ornaments, and boxes for candies, of any sort	.058	Figuras, adornos y envases para dulces, de cualquier clase que sean	.08
Filberts, shelled or unshelled...	.029	Avellanas, con cáscara ó mondadas	.04
Files. (See tools for arts, etc.)...	.029	Limas. (Véase instrumentos para artes, etc.)	.04
Filters	.1305	Mangas ó filtros	.18
Filters, water	.0145	Aparatos ó filtradores de agua..	.02
Firearms. (See swords, sabres, etc.)	.3625	Armas de fuego. (Véase espadas, sables, etc.)	.50
Fire-crackers	.087	Triquitraquis	.12
Fire-works	.1305	Fuegos artificiales	.18
Fish-glue	.1305	Cola de pescado	.18
Fish, pickled, salted, or smoked.	.0145	Pescado salpreso, salado ó ahumado	.02
Flannel. (See cloth, pañete, etc.).	.3625	Franela. (Véase paño, pañete, etc.)	.50
Flat-irons. (See iron, manufactured, etc.)	.0145	Planchas para aplanchar. (Véase hierro manufacturado, etc.)...	.02

ARTICLE OF MERCHANDISE.	Duty per pound in U. S. currency.	ARTÍCULO DE MERCANCÍA.	Derechos por libra en moneda hondureña.
	Dollars.		*Pesos.*
Flax, raw	.0145	Lino en rama	.02
Flints	.0145	Piedras de chispes	.02
Flower-pots, iron. (See iron, manufactured, etc.)	.0145	Floreros (de hierro). (Véase hierro manufacturado, etc.)...	.02
Flowers, artificial. (See lutestring, sandalos, etc.)	.1305	Flores artificiales. (Véase sándalos, lustrinas, etc.)	.18
Flowers, artificial, and the materials for making them	.58	Flores artificiales y los materiales para las mismas	.80
Foot-cloths. (See carpets, of wool, etc.)	.2175	Gualdrapas. (Véase alfombras sueltas, etc.)	.30
Forges. (See instruments or tools, etc.)	.0145	Fraguas. (Véase herramientas e instrumentos, etc.)	.02
Forks, not specified	.1305	Tenedores, no especificados	.13
Forks, plated, etc. (See knives and forks, etc.)	.3625	Tenedores de plata alemana, etc. (Véase cuchillos y tenedores, etc.)	.50
Frames, for pictures, etc. (See battens, picture frames, etc.)...	.029	Cenefas. (Véase listones, cañuelas, etc.)	.04
French linen. (See linen fabrics, medium fine, etc.)	.174	Royales. (Véase tejidos entrefinos de lino, etc.)	.24
Frieze blouses. (See sleeves, sheep-skin garments, etc.)	.174	Gerga. (Véase mangas, chamarras, etc.)	.24
Fringes. (See ribbons, braid, etc.)	.174	Fluecos. (Véase hiladillos ó cintas, etc.)	.24
Fringes. (See understockings, stockings, etc., laces, stripes, etc.)	.2175	Fluecos. (Véase calcetas, medias, etc., encajes, t i r a s, etc.)	.30
Frock-coats. (See shirts, linen, etc.)	.2175	Levitas. (Véase camisas hechas, etc.)	.30
Fruits, artificial	.58	Frutas artificiales	.80
Fruits, including nuts, dried, with the shell or shelled	.029	Frutas secas con cáscara ó mondadas	.04
Fruits, such as prunes, dates, figs, and raisins. (See prunes, etc.)..	.058	Frutas. (Véase ciruelas, etc.)..	.08
Frying-pans. (See iron, manufactured, etc.)	.0145	Sartenes. (Véase hierro manufacturado, etc.)	.02
Funeral crowns and other such ornaments	.3625	Coronas fúnebres ú atros adornos funerarios semejantes....	.50
Furniture, iron. (See iron, manufactured, etc.)	.0145	Muebles de hierro. (Véase hierro manufacturado, etc.).....	.02
Furniture of wood, of osier, of straw, or of cane	.0145	Muebles de madera, de mimbre, de paja ó de junco	.02
Fuses for blasting	.0145	Espoletas para esplotación de minas y canteras	.02
Fustians, cotton. (See skirts, fustians, wrappers, and gowns, etc.	.174	Fustanes. (Véase enaguas, etc., de algodón)	.24
Fustians, linen. (See skirts, etc., linen, etc.)	.3625	Fustanes. (Véase enaguas, etc., de lino)	.50
Galloons. (See wire, spangles, etc.)	.3625	Galones. (Véase alambrillos, lantejuelas, etc.)	.50
Garters of all kinds	.3625	Ligas de todas clases	.50
Gasoline	.0145	Gasolina	.02
Gelatin of all kinds	.029	Jelatina de todas clases	.04

ARTICLE OF MERCHANDISE.	Duty per pound in U. S. currency.	ARTÍCULO DE MERCANCÍA.	Derechos por libra en moneda hondureña.
	Dollars.		*Pesos.*
German silver. (See articles of German silver, etc.)..........	.3625	Plata alemana. (Véase efectos de plata alemana, etc.).......	.50
German silver in any form not specifically mentioned........	.3625	Plata alemana en cualquiera forma no especificada..........	.50
Girths........................	.3625	Cinchas......................	.50
Glass or crystal manufactured in in any shape, not specified in other classes	.0145	Vidrios ó cristalos manufacturados en cualquier forma, no comprendidos en otras clases.	.02
Glass or goblet stands..........	.087	Portavasos	.12
Glass shades. (See chandeliers, globes, etc.)	.029	Briseras. (Véase arañas, bombas, etc.)....................	.04
Glass sheets without mercury....	.0145	Vidrios ó cristales planos sin azogar...................	.02
Glauber salts..................	.0145	Sal de Glauber	.02
Globes. (See c h a n d e l i e r s, globes, etc.)	.029	Bombas. (Véase arañas, bombas, etc.)	.04
Gloves. (See jerkins and doublets, etc.).....................	.1305	Guantes. (Véase almillas, etc.).	.18
Gloves. (See laces, stripes, etc.).	.58	Guantes. (Véase encajes, tiras, etc.)......................	.80
Gloves. (See understoc k i n g s, stockings, etc.)	.2175	Guantes. (Véase calcetas, medias, etc.)	.30
Gloves, kid	1.088	Guantes de cabritilla	1.50
Gloves of skins, for driving......	.58	Manoplas de piel para camino ..	.80
Glue, common.................	.087	Cola ordinaria	.12
Gold, articles of	1.088	Los artículos de oro, etc......	1.50
Gold, imitation. (See wire, spangles, etc.)	.3625	Oro falso. (Véase alambrillo, etc.)......................	.50
Gold lace imitation. (See wire, spangles, etc.)	.3625	Galones ó pasamanería de oro falso. (Véase alam b r i l l o, etc.)......................	.50
Gold leaf. (See wire, spangles, etc., gold or silver leaf, etc.) ...	.3625	Hojilla de oro. (Véase alambrillo, etc., libritos con hojillas, etc.)...................	.50
Gold or silver leaf, real or imitation, in little books, for gilding or plating	.3625	Libritos con hojillas de oro ó plata, finos ó falsos, para dorar ó platear..................	.50
Gold thread, imitation..........	.3625	Hilo de oro falso	.50
Gouger. (See tools for arts, etc.).	.029	Formones. (Véase instrumentos para artes, etc.)..........	.04
Gowns. (See cambric, etc.)......	1.088	Camisones. (Véase holán batista, clarín, etc.).............	1.50
Gowns. (See skirts, f u s t i a n s, wrappers, pillowcases, etc.)....	.3625	Túnicos. (Véase enaguas, fustanes, fustansones, etc.).......	.50
Gowns, cotton. (See skirts, fustians, wrappers, and gowns, etc.).	.174	Túnicos de algodon. (Véase enaguas, fustanes, batas, etc.) .	.24
Gratings. (See iron, manufactured, etc.),..................	.0145	Rejas. (Véase hierro manufacturado, etc.)	.02
Gridirons. (See iron, manufactured, etc.)	.0145	Parrillas. (Véase hierro manufacturado, etc.)	.02

ARTICLE OF MERCHANDISE.	Duty per pound in U. S. currency.	ARTÍCULO DE MERCANCÍA.	Derechos por libra en moneda hondureña.
	Dollars.		*Pesos.*
Gum arabic	.087	Goma arábiga	.12
Gum elastic. (See bone, ivory, etc.)	.174	Goma elástica. (Véase hueso, marfil, etc.)	.24
Gums or resins not included in other classes	.087	Toda clase de goma ó resina, no comprendida en otras clases...	.12
Gutta percha, worked or un-worked	.087	Guta-percha, labrada ó sin labrar.	.12
Gypsum, in pieces or powdered..	.0145	Yeso en piedra y en polvo	02
Hair. (See horse-hair.)		Pelo. (Véase cerda ú crin.)....	
Hair-dye	.0145	Tinta de teñir el pelo	02
Hair, human, or its imitations, manufactured or not	1.088	Cabello ó pelo humano y sus imitaciones, manufacturado ó no.	1.50
Hairpins. (See pins, etc.)	.087	Horquillas. (Véase alfileres, etc.)	.12
Hairsprings. (See hands, etc.)..	.2175	Muellecitos de relojes. (Véase minuteros, etc.)	.30
Hammers. (See instruments or tools, etc.)	.0145	Mandarrias. (Véase herramientas é instrumentos, etc.)	.02
Hammers. (See tools for arts, etc.)	.029	Martillos. (Véase instrumentos, para artes, etc.)	.04
Hammocks. (See huckaback, etc.)	.087	Hamacas. (Véase alemanisco, damasco, etc.)	.12
Hams	.029	Jamones	.04
Handkerchiefs, cotton. (See skirts, fustians, etc.)	.174	Pañuelos de algodon. (Véase enaguas, fustanes, batas, etc.) .	.24
Handkerchiefs of linen or of linen mixed with cotton	.58	Pañuelos de lino ó mezclado con algodon	.80
Handkerchiefs, shawls, scarfs, cloth, carpets, shirts, and jerkins or underwaistcoats, of wool or wool mixed with cotton, plain or embroidered with any material	.58	Pañuelos, pañolones, chales, paños, carpetas, camisas, y almillas ó guardá-camisas de lana ó mezclado con algodón, lisos ó bordados en cualquier materia	.80
Hands, keys, regulators, springs, and other parts of the works of clocks or watches, not of gold or silver	.2175	Minuteros ó manecillos, llaves, muelecitos, resortes y otras piezas para el interior de los relojes, que no sean de oro ó plata	.30
Hatboxes of sole leather	.087	Cajas de suela para sombreros..	.12
Hatchets. (See instruments or tools, etc.)	.0145	Hachuelas. (Véase herramientas é instrumentos, etc.)	.02
Hats and caps of all sorts of plush, of straw or felt, for men, women, or children, and of any material not specified, excepting those with high crowns, which belong to the 10th class, and those of rushes, which belong to the 11th class	.174	Sombreros y gorras de todas clases de felpa, sombreros de paja y de fieltro, para hombres, mujeres y niños, y de cualquiera otra materia no especificada, con excepción de los con copa alta, que pertenecen á la 10ª clase, y los de junco, que corresponden á la 11ª.....	.24

ARTICLE OF MERCHANDISE.	Duty per pound in U.S. currency.	ARTÍCULO DE MERCANCÍA.	Derechos por libra en moneda hondureña.
	Dollars.		*Pesos.*
Hats of black silk stuff, with high crowns, known as black silk hats, and all other hats of the same shape, whatever their material or color................	.58	Sombreros de felpa de seda negra, copa alta, llamados sombreros de pelo negro, y los demas sombreros de esta misma forma, de cualquier materia y color que sean..............	.80
Hats of rush or Panama hats....	1.088	Sombreros de junco ó jipijapa..	1.50
Head stalls...	.3625	Cabezadas...................	.50
Hemp. (See textiles or fabrics, ordinary, etc.)..............	.087	Cáñamo. (Véase telas ó tejidos ordinarios, etc.).............	.12
Hemp or oakum, in the fiber or twisted, for calking..........	.0145	Cáñamo ó estopa en rama ó torcida para calafatear ó estopar..	.02
Hinges. (See articles of German silver, etc.)...................	.3625	Charnelas. (Véase efectos de plata alemana, etc.)..........	.50
Holsters.....................	.3625	Cañoneras ó pistoleras........	.50
Hones for sharpening razors.....	.087	Piedras finas para amolar navajas	.12
Honey.......................	.0145	Miel de abejas...............	.02
Hooks. (See pins, etc.)........	.087	Anzuelos. (Véase alfileres, etc.)	.12
Hops.......................	.0145	Lúpulo ó flor de cerveza.......	.02
Horn. (See bone, ivory, etc.)....	.174	Asta ó cuerno. (Véase hueso, marfil, etc.)................	.24
Horse-hair....................	.058	Cerda ó crin.................	.08
Horse-hair fabrics for covering furniture....................	.087	Telas de cerda para forrar muebles	.12
Huckaback, damask, piqué, coverlets, blankets, carpets by the piece or rugs, towels, bedspreads, counterpanes, hammocks, napkins, tablecloths, and any other damasked or quilted cotton cloth..........	.087	Alemanisco, damasco, piqué, cobertores, frazadas, alfombras sueltas ó en piezas, paños de mano, colchas, sobrecamas, hamacas, servilletas, toallas de mano, manteles y cualquier otro tejido adamascado ó acolchado de algodon...........	.12
Hydrochloric or muriatic acid....	.058	Acido hidroclórico ó muriatico..	.08
Hydrometers..................	.174	Hidrómetros	.24
Illuminating oils	.0145	Aceites para alumbrar.........	.02
Images or effigies not made of gold or silver.....................	.087	Imágines ó efigies, que no sean de oro ó de plata	.12
Implements, domestic. (See iron, manufactured, etc.)	.0145	Utensilios para el servicio doméstico. (Véase hierro manufacturado, etc.)..............	.02
Incense......................	.058	Incienso	.08
India-ink	.0145	Tinta de China	.02
Ink of all sorts, except printing ink........................	.0145	Cualquiera clase de tinta, excepto la de imprenta.........	.02
Ink powders for writing........	.0145	Polvos de tinta para escribir....	.02
Inkstands	.0145	Tinteros	.02
Ink, writing.................	.0145	Tinta para escribir............	.02
Insertings. (See ribbons, braid, etc.).......................	.174	Tiras bordadas y caladas. (Véase hiladillos ó cintas, etc.)	.24

ARTICLE OF MERCHANDISE.	Duty per pound in U. S. currency.	ARTÍCULO DE MERCANCÍA.	Derechos por libra en moneda hondureña.
	Dollars.		*Pesos*
Instruments of surgery, and also anatomical and mathematical ones, and scientific instruments generally, not included in other classes	.087	Instrumentos de cirugia, y tambien los de anatomía, matemáticas y otras ciencias, no incluidos en otras clases......	.12
Instruments or tools for agriculture or other uses, with or without handles, such as spades, adzes, pruning hooks (chicuras, chicurones), levers, weed hooks, axes, hatchets, machetes, mallets, hammers, shovels, picks (tasies), capstans, forges, bellows of all sorts, jacks for lifting weights, grindstones, large screws for blacksmiths' anvils, and all similar tools or instruments..........	.0145	Herramientas é instrumentos para agricultura ú otros usos, con cabos ó sin ellos, como azadas, azuelas, calabozos, chicuras, chicurones, barras, escardillas, hachas, hachuelas, machetes, mazos, mandarrias, palas, picos, tasíes, cabrestantes, fraguas, fuelles de todas clases, gatos para levantar pesos, mollejones tornillos grandes para herreros, bigornias, yunques, y toda otra herramienta ó instrumento semejante á los indicados	.02
Instruments, such as barometers, hydrometers, chronometers, etc	.174	Instrumentos semejantes á los barómetros, hidrómetros, etc..	.24
Iron, manufactured: in wire, except for fences; in chains and anchors for ships; in boxes for keeping money; in mortars; in furniture; in presses for copying letters and stamping paper; in nails, tacks, bits, rivets, tarpaulin nails; balconies, doors, balusters, gratings, and columns; statues, urns, flower-vases, busts, and any other such ornament for house or garden; weights for weighing; flatirons for ironing; posts for railings; stoves, "budares," kettles, gridirons, pots, frying pans, and all other domestic implements, whether tinned or not and with or without a lining of porcelain	.0145	Hierro manufacturado: en alambres excepto los de cercos; en cadenas y anclas para buques; en cajas para guardar dinero; en morteros ó almireces; en muebles; en prensas para copiar cartas y timbrar papel; en clavos, tachuelas, brocas, remaches y estoperoles; en balcones de hierro, puertas, balaustres, rejas y columnas; en estatuas, jarrones, floreros, bustos y cualquier otro adorno semejante para casas y jardines; en pesas para pesar; en planchas para aplanchar; en postes para empalizadas, y en anaíes, budares, calderos, parrillas, ollas, sartenes y toda otra pieza para el servicio doméstico, esten ó no estañadas, y tengan ó no baño de loza	.02
Iron manufactures. (See steel, copper, etc.)..................	.029	Manufacturas de hierro. (Véase acero, cobre, etc.)............	.04
Iron, round or square, in sheets, plates, or other form of the raw material, and old iron in odd pieces	.0145	Hierro redondo ó cuadrado, en platinas, en planchas ó láminas y en cualquiera otra forma bruta y el hierro viejo en piezas inutilizadas.............	.02

ARTICLE OF MERCHANDISE.	Duty per pound in U. S. currency.	ARTÍCULO DE MERCANCÍA.	Derechos por libra en moneda hondureña.
	Dollars.		*Pesos.*
Iron wire, excepting for fences ..	.0145	Hierro manufacturado en alambres, excepto los de cercos...	.02
Ivory. (See bone, ivory, etc.) ...	.174	Marfil. (Véase hueso, marfil, etc.)	.24
Ivory. (See fans, ivory.)	1.088	Marfil. (Véase abanicos de marfil.)	1.50
Jackets. (See shirts, linen, etc.).	.2175	Chaquetas. (Véase camisas hechas, etc.)	.30
Jacks for lifting weights. (See instruments or tools, etc.)	.0145	Gatos para levantar pesos. (Véase herramientas é instrumentos, etc.)	.02
Jeans. (See drills, jeans, etc.)...	.087	Coquí. (Véase driles, coquí, etc.)	.12
Jerkins or doublets, scarfs, caps, understockings, drawers, trousers, stockings, bonnets, gloves, and all fabrics of cotton stockinet	.1305	Almillas ó guarda-camisas, bandas, birretes, calcetas, calzoncillos, pantalones, medias, gorras, guantes y todo tejido de punto de media de algodon.	.18
Jet, crude	.087	Azabache en bruto	.12
Jet, manufactured. (See bone, ivory, etc.)	.174	Azabache, manufacturado. (Véase hueso, marfil, etc.)...	.24
Jewels	1.088	Joyas, alhajas	1.50
Kerosene oil	.0145	Aceite de kerosene	.02
Kettles, iron. (See iron, manufactured, etc.)	.0145	Calderos de hierro. (Véase hierro, manufacturado, etc.)..	.02
Keys, watch. (See hands, etc.).	.2175	Llaves de reloj. (Véase minuteros, etc.)	.30
Knives and forks, excepting those with handles covered with gold or silver leaf, which belong to the 11th class, and those of german silver, or silver plated, or gilt, which belong to the 10th class	.1305	Cuchillos y tenedores, excepto los que tengan manga de hojilla de oro ó plata, que corresponden á la 11ª clase, y los de plata alemana, plateados ó dorados, que corresponden á la 10ª clase	.18
Knives and forks with handles of german silver or white metal, gilded or silver plated	.3625	Cuchillos y tenedores con mango de plata alemana ó metal blanco, plateados ó dorados ..	.50
Knives, hunting. (See swords, etc.)	.3625	Cuchillos de monte. (Véase espadas, etc.)	.50
Knives, sharp pointed, with or without sheath	.1305	Cuchillos de punto, con vaina ó sin ella	.18
Knives with handles of wood or other common material, for fishermen, shoemakers, beltmakers, and, generally, all such as are used in the arts or trades.	.058	Cuchillos con mango de madera ú otra materia ordinaria, para pescadores, zapateros, talabarteros, jardineros, tabaqueros y en general los que se emplean en las artes ú oficios ...	.08
Labels, printed or lithographed ..	.2175	Etiquetas y rótulos impresos ó litografiados	.30
Lace. (See cambric, etc.)	1.088	Punto. (Véase holán batista, clarin, etc.)	1.50
Lace. (See cloth, pañete, etc.)...	.3625	Punto. (Véase paño, pañete, etc.)	.50

ARTICLE OF MERCHANDISE.	Duty per pound in U. S. currency.	ARTÍCULO DE MERCANCÍA.	Derechos por libra en moneda hondureña.
	Dollars.		*Pesos.*
Lace or tulle, of cotton or pita, plain or embroidered	.2175	Punto ó tul de algodón ó pita, liso ó bordado	.30
Laces. (See ribbons, braids, etc.).	.174	Encajes. (Véase hiladillos ó cintas, etc.)	.24
Laces. (See understockings, stockings, etc.)	.2175	Encajes. (Véase calcetas, medias, etc.)	.30
Laces, strings, and twisted cords of all kinds	.3625	Cuerdas y entorchados de todas clases	.50
Laces, stripes, blondes, appliqué work, ribbons, sashes, purses, shoulder straps, tassels, cords, fringes, socks, belts, braids, gloves, and trimmings, of linen or of linen mixed with cotton..	.58	Encajes, tiras, blondas, embutidos, cintas, bandas, bolsas para dinero, charreteras, borlas, cordones, fluecos, escarpines, fajas, trenzas, guantes y pasamanería de lino ó mezclado con algodón	.80
Lampblack	.0145	Negro humo	.02
Lamp-chimney cleaners	.087	Limpiadores para tubos	.12
Lamps. (See articles of German silver, etc.)	.3625	Lámparas. (Véase efectos de plata alemana, etc.)	.50
Lamps. (See chandeliers, globes, etc.)	.029	Lámparas. (Véase arañas, bombas, etc.)	.04
Lancets	.1305	Lancetas	.18
Lanterns. (See chandeliers, globes, etc., paper lanterns, etc., stereoscopes, etc.)	.029 / .058 / .1305	Fanales, lanternas ó farolillos. (Véase aranas, bombas, etc., farolillos de papel, etc., estereoscopios, etc.)	.04 / .08 / .18
Lard	.029	Manteca	.04
Lavender	.029	Alhucema ó espliego	.04
Lawn, long. (See linen fabrics, medium fine, etc.)	.174	Estopillas. (Véase tejidos entrefinos de lino, etc.)	.24
Lead. (See steel, copper, etc., steel bronze, etc.)	.029 / .0145	Plomo. (Véase acero, cobre, etc., acero, bronce, etc.)	.04 / .02
Lead, carbonate	.0145	Albayalde ó carbonato de plomo.	.02
Leather tips for billiard cues	.058	Puntas de suela para los tacos de billar	.08
Lemonades	.0145	Limonadas	.02
Lenses. (See eyeglasses, etc.)...	.3625	Lentes. (Véase anteojos, etc.)..	.50
Levels. (See tools for arts, etc.).	.029	Niveles. (Véase instrumentos para artes, etc.)	.04
Levers. (See instruments or tools, etc.)	.0145	Barras. (Véase herramientas é instrumentos, etc.)	.02
Linen. (See drills, linens, etc.)..	.1305	Lino. (Véase driles, creas puras, etc.)	.18
Linen. (See shirts, linen, etc.)..	.2175	Lino. (Véase camisas hechas, etc.)	.30
Linen. (See textiles of fabrics, ordinary, etc.)	.087	Lino. (Véase telas ó tejidos ordinarios, etc.)	.12
Linen. (See curtains, hangings, etc., laces, stripes, etc.)	.58	Lino. (Véase cortinas, colgaduras, etc., encajes, tiras, etc.)...	.80
Linen. (See cambric, etc.)	1.088	Lino. (Véase holán batista, clarín, etc.)	1.50

ARTICLE OF MERCHANDISE.	Duty per pound in U. S. currency.	ARTÍCULO DE MERCANCÍA.	Derechos por libra en moneda hondureña.
	Dollars.		*Pesos.*
Linen fabrics, medium fine, such as nankeen, French linen, Irish linen, long lawn, "bretañas," and other similar goods........	.174	Tejidos entrefinos de lino, como coletillas, royales, irlandas, estopillas, bretañas y otros semejantes..................	.24
Linen fabrics not specified in other classes .... :....	.3625	Tegjidos de lino no especificados en otras clases..............	.50
Linseed, in the grain or ground..	.0145	Linaza en grano ó molida	.02
Linseed oil....................	.0145	Aceite de linaza..............	.02
Lint for wounds	.1305	Hilos para heridas............	.18
Liquor-flask stands, of any material other than German silver, the latter belonging to the 11th class......................	.087	Licoreras de cualquiera materia, con excepción de las de plata alemana, que pertenecen á la 10ª clase..............	.12
Liquor-flask stands of German silver......................	.58	Licoreras de plata alemana	.80
Liquors, various kinds, such as cognac,absinthe,rum,gin, "rossolis," "mistea," champagne, chartreuse, and others not specified, and bitters of all sorts....	.058	Aguardiente fuerte ó dulce,como coñac, agenjo, ron, ginebra, rosolio, mistela, champagne, chartreuse y otros no especificados y amargos de todas clases.....................	.08
Litharge	.058	Litargirio	.08
Lithographic stone.............	.0145	Piedras de litografiar.........	.02
Locks, gun. (See swords, etc.)..	.3625	Llaves de las armas de fuego. (Véase espadas, etc.)........	.50
Looking glasses. (See mirrors, etc.)........	.058	Espejos. (Véase espejos de todas clases).................	.08
Lutestring, "sándalos," and other such cotton fabrics used for linings and flowers...........	.1305	Sándalos, lustrinas y demas telas semejantes de algodon que se usan para forros y flores	.18
Macaroni	.029	Macarrones	.04
Machetes. (See instruments or tools, etc.)	.0145	Machetes. (Véase herramientas é instrumentos.)	.02
Machines and apparatus not specified in the first class........	.0145	Máquinas y aparatos no especificados en la primera clase.....	.02
Machines for aërated waters.....	.087	Máquinas para aguas gaseosas..	.12
Magic lanterns. (S e e stereoscopes, etc.)..................	.1305	Linternas mágicas. (Véase estereoscopios, etc.)............	.18
Magnets	.1305	Imán	.18
Maizena(fine corn meal,prepared).	.0145	Maicena, ó sea harina fina de maíz preparada.............	.02
Mallets. (S e e instruments or tools, etc.)	.0145	Mazos. (Véase herramientas é instrumentos.)............	.02
Manganese, mineral	.058	Manganesio mineral .... ᵔ....	.08
Maniples. (See chasubles, etc.).	.58	Manípulos. (Véase casullas,etc.).	.80
Marjoram. (See aniseed, etc.)...	.058	Orégano. (Véase anis en grano, etc.)	.08
Marking ink	.0145	Tinta de marcar..............	.02
Masks or false faces, of all sorts.	.058	Máscaras ó caretas de todas clases	.08
Match boxes. (See portfolios, etc.)	.2175	Fosforeras. (Véase carteras, etc.).	.30

ARTICLE OF MERCHANDISE.	Duty per pound in U. S. currency.	ARTÍCULO DE MERCANCÍA.	Derechos por libra en moneda hondureña.
	Dollars.		*Pesos.*
Match rope for blasting........	.0145	Mechas para esplotación de minas y canteras............	.02
Match sticks..................	.0145	Palitos para hacer fósforos......	.02
Matches of wood, wax, or tinder.	.058	Fósforos de palillo, de cerilla ó de yesca...................	.08
Mathematical instruments. (See instruments of surgery, etc.)...	.087	Instrumentos de matemáticas. (Véase instrumentos de cirùgía, etc.)...................	.12
Mats for the table..............	.0145	Esterilla para mesas............	.02
Matting, floor	.0145	Estera, esterilla y petate para pisos	.02
Mattresses	.029	Colchones y gergones..........	.04
Measures, of leather, tape, or paper, with or without cases	.029	Medidas de cuero, cinta ó papel, sueltás ó en estuches........	.04
Meat, salt, pickled, or smoked, when not canned	.0145	Carne salada, salpresa ó ahumada,cuando no viene en latas.	.02
Medicines. (See drugs, medicines, etc.)..................	.174	Medicinas. (Véase drogas,medicinas, etc.).................	.24
Mercury......................	.0145	Azogue ó mercurio vivo	.02
Merino. (See cloth, pañete, etc.).	.3625	Merino. (Véase paño, pañete, etc.)	.50
Metallic articles, gilded or silverplated	.174	Efectos de metal, dorados ó plateados	.24
Microscopes. (See eyeglasses, etc.).........................	.3625	Microscopios. (Véase anteojos, etc.)	.50
Millet	.0145	Mijo.........................	.02
Mills for coffee, corn, etc........	.0145	Molinos para café, maiz, etc....	.02
Millstones. (See instruments or tools, etc.)	.0145	Piedras de molino. (Véase herramientas é instrumentos, etc.).	.02
Mineral waters	.0145	Aguas minerales	.02
Minium. (See red lead)........	.058	Minio. (Véase azarcón ó mínio)..	.08
Mirrors of all sorts, framed or not........................	.058	Espejos de todas clases y las lunas azogadas................	.08
Molasses	.0145	Miel de azúcar	.02
Moldings. (See battens, picture frames, etc.)..................	.029	Molduras. (Véase listones, cañuelas, etc.)................	.04
Mortars. (See iron, manufactured, etc.)	.0145	Morteros. (Véase hierro manufacturado, etc.)..............	.02
Mosquito net. (S e e curtains, hangings, etc.)................	.58	Mosquiteros. (Véase cortinas, colgaduras, etc.)............	.80
Mother-of-pearl. (S e e bone, ivory, etc.)..................	.174	Nácar. (Véase hueso, marfil, etc.).......	.24
Mufflers, cotton................	.087	Rebozos de algodon...........	.12
Music books..................	.058	Colecciones de música....:.....	.08
Musical instruments and their parts, of all kinds, excepting pianos and organs............	.087	Instrumentos de música ó cualquiera de sus partes ó accesorias, exceptuandose los pianos y órganos..................	.12
Muskets. (See swords, etc.)....	.3625	Escopetas. (Véase espadas, etc.).	.50
Muslin. (See cloth, pañete, etc.).	.3625	Muselina. (Véase paño, pañete, etc.)	.50

ARTICLE OF MERCHANDISE.	Duty per pound in U. S. currency.	ARTÍCULO DE MERCANCÍA.	Derechos por libra en moneda hondureña.
	Dollars.		*Pesos.*
Muslin. (See cambric, etc.)	1.088	Muselina. (Véase holan batista, clarín, etc.)	1.50
Muslin, and any other fine fabric of linen mixed with cotton, unbleached or in colors, by the piece or cut for dresses	.58	Muselina, batista y cualquiera otra tela fina de lino mezclado con algodon, cruda ó de color, en piezas ó en cortes de vestido	.80
Muslin, book	.174	Linoes	.24
Muslins, fine, dotted or embroidered with wool or cotton, by the piece or cut, chemises, yokes, and other such articles, embroidered, large cotton shawls of all sorts	.2175	Muselinas finas de mota ó bordadas con lana ó algodon, en piezas ó en cortes, camisetas, golas y demas piezas bordadas semejantes; pañolones de algodon de todas clases	30
Muslins, smooth, embroidered, white, or printed	.174	Gasas lisas, labradas, blancas ó estampadas	.24
Mustard	.029	Mostaza en grano ó molida	.04
Muzzles. (See articles of German silver, etc.)	.3625	Bozales. (Véase efectos de plata alemana, etc.)	.50
Nails, iron. (See iron, manufactured, etc.)	.0145	Clavos de hierro. (Véase hierro manufacturado, etc.)	.02
Nankeen. (See linen fabrics, medium fine.)	.174	Coletillas. (Véase tejidos entrefinos, etc.)	.24
Napkins. (See drills, linens, etc.)	.1305	Servilletas. (Véase driles, creas, etc.)	.18
Napkins. (See huckaback, etc.).	.087	Servilletas. (Véase alemanisco, damasco, etc.)	.12
Napped cotton stuff. (See drills, jeans, etc.)	.087	Borlón. (Véase driles, coquí, etc.)	.12
Neck-cloths. (See cambric, batiste, etc.)	1.088	Gorgueras. (Véase holán batista, clarín, etc.)	1.50
Neckties of cotton, horse-hair, or wool	.58	Corbatas de algodon, cerda ó lana	.80
Needles. (See pins, etc.)	.087	Agujas. (Véase alfileres, etc.)	.12
Nets. (See ornaments for the head, etc.)	1.088	Redecillas. (Véase adornos de cabeza, etc.)	1.50
Netting of iron wire, not included in other classes	.058	Telas ó tejidos de alambre de hierro, no comprendidos en otras clases	.08
Nipple glasses	.1305	Pezoneras	.18
Nipples, gun. (See swords, etc.).	.3625	Chimeneas. (Véase espadas, etc.).	.50
Nipples for nursing bottles	.1305	Picos de teteros	.18
Nursing bottles	.1305	Teteros	.18
Nitrate of potash	.0145	Potasa, nitrato ó sal de nitro	.02
Nitric acid or aquafortis	.058	Acido nítrico ó agua fuerte	.08
Nutmeg	.1305	Nuez moscada	.18
Nuts, with the shell or shelled	.029	Nueces, con cáscara ó mondadas.	.04
Oakum. (See hemp or oakum, etc.)	.0145	Estopa. (Véase cáñamo ó estopa, etc.)	.02
Oars, when not imported with the boats or launches	.0145	Remos para embarcaciones, cuando no vengan con los botes ó lanchas	.02

ARTICLE OF MERCHANDISE.	Duty per pound in U. S. currency.	ARTÍCULO DE MERCANCÍA.	Derechos por libra en moneda hondureña.
	Dollars.		*Pesos.*
Octants	.174	Octantes	.24
Oil, almond	.0145	Aceite de almendras	.02
Oilcloth, in any shape	.058	Encerados ó hules, en cualquiera forma	.08
Oil, cocoa	.0145	Aceite de coco	.02
Oil, drying, for painters	.0145	Aceite secante para pintores	.02
Oil, kerosene	.0145	Aceite de kerosene	.02
Oil, linseed	.0145	Aceite de linaza	.02
Oil, palm or drying, for painters.	.0145	Aceite de palma ó aceite secante para pintores	.02
Oil, spurge	.0145	Aceite de tártago	.02
Oil, train or codliver	.0145	Aceite de pescado ó de hígado de bacalao	.02
Oils and soaps, perfumed	.087	Aceites y jabones perfumados	.12
Oils, illuminating	.0145	Aceites para alumbrar	.02
Oils not included in other classes.	.087	Aceites no comprendidos en las clases anteriores	.12
Oil, sweet (olive)	.0145	Aceite de comer	.02
Oleic acid	.029	Acido oléico	.04
Olives	.029	Aceitunas	.04
Orange-flower water	.0145	Aguas de azahares	.02
Organs. (See pianos and organs, etc.)	.029	Organos. (Véase pianos y organos, etc.)	.04
Ornaments. (See figures, ornaments, etc.)	.058	Adornos. (Véase figuras, adornos, etc.)	.08
Ornaments, cotton. (See ribbons, braid, etc.)	.174	Adornos de algodon. (Véase hiladillos ó cintas, etc.)	.24
Ornaments, ecclesiastical. (See chasubles, etc.)	.58	Ornamentos para uso de las iglesias. (Véase casullas, etc.)	.80
Ornaments, head, of all kinds	1.088	Adornos de cabeza y redecillas de todas clases	1.50
Ornaments, iron, for house or garden. (See iron, manufactured, etc.)	.0145	Adornos para casas y jardines. (Véase hierro manufacturado, etc.)	.02
Osier, unmanufactured	.029	Mimbre sin manufacturar	.04
Paints, common, prepared with oil	.0145	Pinturas ordinarias preparadas en aceite	.02
Paints not included in other classes	.029	Colores ó pinturas no incluidos en otras clases	.04
Paletots. (See shirts, linen, etc.).	.2175	Paltós. (Véase camisas hechas, etc.)	.30
Palm, unmanufactured	.029	Palma sin manufacturar	.04
Panoramas. (See stereoscopes, etc.)	.1305	Panoramas. (Vease estereoscopios, etc.)	.18
Paper lanterns: paper collars, bosoms, and cuffs, including those lined with cloth	.058	Farolillos de papel, cuellos, pecheras y puños de papel, inclusos los forrados en género	.08

ARTICLE OF MERCHANDISE.	Duty per pound in U. S. currency.	ARTÍCULO DE MERCANCÍA.	Derechos por libra en moneda hondureña.
	Dollars.		Pesos.
Paper manufactures not included in other classes. (See paper lanterns, etc.)	.058	Papel manufacturado no especificado en otras clases. (Véase farolillos de papel,etc.).	.08
Paper of every sort, not included in other classes	.029	Papel de cualquier clase, no especificado	.04
Paper, gilded or silver-plated, stamped with figures in relief, and tinted or colored for flowers.	.174	Papel dorado ó plateado, el estampado á manera de relieve, y el pintado para flores	.24
Paper-cutter	.0145	Cuchillas para papel	.02
Paper, wall	.087	Papel pintado para tapicería....	.12
Paraffin, crude	.029	Parafina en pasta	.04
Parasol frames. (See wire manufactured into frames, etc.)....	.087	Armaduras para quitasoles. (Véase alambre manufacturado, etc.)	.12
Parasols, cotton or linen. (See umbrellas, large or small, etc.).	.174	Sombrillas, de lino ó algodón. (Véase paraguas, paragüitos, etc.)	.24
Parasols, silk. (See umbrellas, parasols, etc.)	.087	Sombrillas. (Véase paraguas, sombrillas, etc.)	.12
Parasols of wool	.1305	Sombrillas de lana	.18
Parchment and its imitations, in any form, not included in other classes	.058	Pergaminos y sus imitaciones en cualquier forma, no comprendidos en otras clases.....	.08
Pasteboard, in sheets	.0145	Cartón en pasta	.02
Paste for sharpening razors	.087	Pasta para afilar navajas	.12
Pastes, such as vermicelli, macaroni, etc	.029	Pastas semejantes á las de fideos, macarrones y tallarines	.04
Peanuts, with the shell or shelled.	.029	Manís, con cáscara ó mondados.	.04
Pearls and imitation precious stones, unmounted or mounted in any metal other than gold or silver	.174	Perlas y piedras falsas, sin montar ó montadas en cualquier metal que no sea oro ó plata..	.24
Pencil-cases	.0145	Lapiceros	.02
Pencils of all kinds	.0145	Lápices de todas clases	.02
Pencils, slate	.0145	Lapices de pizarra	.02
Penknives	.1305	Cortaplumas	.18
Pens	.0145	Plumas	.02
Pepper. (See aniseed, etc.)	.058	Pimienta. (Véase anís en grano, etc.)	.08
Percales	.174	Percales	.24
Perfumery of all sorts	.087	Perfumería de todas clases	.12
Perfumes for the toilette	.058	Aguas de olor para el tocador...	.08
Petroleum, crude	.0145	Petróleo bruto	.02
Pewter. (See steel, copper, etc.).	.029	Peltre. (Véase acero, cobre, etc.).	.04
Phosphorus	.174	Fósforo en pasta	.24
Photographs	.1305	Fotografías	.18
Pianos and organs, or any of their parts, when they come separately, including the piano stools..	.029	Pianos y organos ó cualquiera de sus partes, cuando vengan por separado, quedando incluidos aquí tambien los taburetes	.04

ARTICLE OF MERCHANDISE.	Duty per pound in U. S. currency.	ARTÍCULO DE MERCANCÍA.	Derechos por libra en moneda hondureña.
	Dollars.		*Pesos.*
Pickles, in vinegar or in brine...	.029	Encurtidos, en vinagre ó en salmuera..................	.04
Picks. (See instruments or tools, etc.).......................	.0145	Picos. (Véase herramientas é instrumentos, etc.)...........	.02
Pictures and portraits upon cloth, wood, paper, stone, or other material	.058	Pinturas y retratos sobre lienzo, madera, papel, piedra ú otra materia	.08
Pillowcases. (See skirts, fustians, wrappers, etc.).........	.174	Fundas de almohadas. (Véase enaguas, fustanes, etc.)......	.24
Pillows, not including those made of silk................	.029	Almohadas, excepto las de seda.	.04
Pincers. (See tools, etc.)	.029	Alicates. (Véase instrumentos para artes, etc.)	.04
Pins, needles, eyelets, brooches, hooks, thimbles, hairpins, and buckles for shoes, for hats, and for vests and trousers, excepting those made of silver or gold.	.087	Alfileres, agujas, ojetes, broches, anzuelas, dedales, horquillas y hebillas para el calzado, para los sombreros y para los chalecos y pantalones, excepto las de oro ó plata	.12
Pipes, mouthpieces, and cigar holders, of amber, porcelain, or any other material, excepting those made of gold or silver and those mentioned in the 4th class......................	.174	Cachimbas, boquillas y pipas para fumar, de ambar, de porcelana ó de cualquiera otra materia, excepto las de oro ó plata y las denominadas en la 4ª clase	.24
Pipes and mouthpieces, of clay or ordinary earthenware, without any other material.........	.058	Cachimbas, boquillas y pipas de barro ó de loza ordinaria sin ninguna otra materia.....	.08
Piqué. (See huckaback, etc.)....	.087	Piqué. (Véase alemanisco, damasco, etc.)..................	.12
Pistols. (See swords, sabers, daggers, etc.).................	.3625	Pistolas. (Véase espadas, sables, etc.)...................	.50
Piston glands..................	.1305	Collares	.18
Pistons	.1305	Embolos......................	.18
Pitch, black...................	.0145	Brea negra	.02
Pitch, white or light	.0145	Pez blanca	.02
Planes, jack. (See tools for art, etc.)	.029	Garlopas. (Véase instrumentos para artes, etc.)..............	.04
Plaster of Paris................	.0145	Yeso mate	.02
Plaster of Paris, manufactured into any articles except toys for children............	.029	Yeso manufacturado en cualquier forma, excepto en juguetes para niños	.04
Plumes for funeral coaches or hearses, when imported separately	1.088	Plumeros para coches fúnebres, cuando vengan separadamente	1.50
Plush, cotton. (See corduroy, cotton plush, etc.)	.174	Felpa de algodon. (Véase pana, panilla, etc.)	.24
Plushes. (See understockings, stockings, etc.)..............	.2175	Felpas. (Véase calcetas, medias, etc,)	.30
Pocket-books. (See portfolios, etc.)........................	.2175	Portamonedas. (Véase carteras, etc.)...................	.30
Poisons. (See chemicals for preserving skins.)................	.0145	Venenos. (Véase venenos para preservar las pieles)	.02

ARTICLE OF MERCHANDISE.	Duty per pound in U. S. currency.	ARTÍCULO DE MERCANCÍA.	Derechos por libra en moneda hondureña.
	Dollars.		*Pesos.*
Polishes of all sorts, excepting shoeblacking................	.0145	Betunes de todas clases, excepto el de calzado..........	.02
Polishing stone.................	.0145	Piedra de pulir..............	.02
Portfolios, etc.................	.0145	Bultos y portafolios..........	.02
Portfolios, snuff boxes, pocket-books, cigarette-cases, eyeglass-cases, match-boxes, card-cases, albums, and other similar articles, excepting those made of or containing gold or silver....	.2175	Carteras, tabaqueras, portamonedas, cigarreras, cajitas para anteojos, fosforeras, tarjeteros, albums y cualquiera otro articulo semejante, excepto los que sean ó tengan algo de oro ó plata...................	.30
Portraits. (See pictures, portraits, etc.)...............	.058	Retratos. (Véase pinturas, etc.).	.08
Posts, iron, for railings. (See iron, manufactured, etc.)......	.0145	Postes de hierro para empalizadas. (Véase hierro manufacturado, etc.)........	.02
Potash, common or calcined. (See nitrate of potash.)........	.0145	Potasa comun ó calcinada. (Vease potaso, nitrado ó sal de nitro.)................	.02
Pots. (See iron, manufactured, etc.).......................	.0145	Ollas. (Véase hierro manufacturado, etc.)................	.02
Powder-flasks.................	.1305	Polvoreras...................	.18
Presses, letter. (See iron, manufactured, etc.)................	.0145	Prensas para copiar. (Véase hierro manufacturado, etc.)...	.02
Presses, stamping, for paper. (See iron, manufactured, etc.)..	.0145	Prensas para timbrar papel. (Véase hierro manufacturado, etc.)................	.02
Prunes, dates, and figs, dried, raisins, and other similar fruits.....................	.058	Ciruelas pasas, dátiles é higos pasados, pasas y demas frutas semejantes..........	.08
Pruning hooks. (See instruments or tools).............	.0145	Calabozos. (Véase herramientas é instrumentos, etc.)......	.02
Purses. (See laces, stripes, etc.).	.58	Bolsas para dinero. (Véase encajes, tiras, etc.)..........	.80
Racks for clothes or hats. (See wire manufactured into frames, etc.)......................	.087	Armadores ó perchas para vestidos ó sombreros. (Véase alambre manufacturado, etc.) .	.12
Raisins. (See prunes, etc.)......	.058	Pasas. (Véase ciruelas, etc.)...	.08
Rattan, unmanufactured........	.029	Bejucos sin manufacturar......	.04
Ratteen. (See baize and ratteen, etc.)......................	.2175	Ratina. (Véase bayeta, etc.)....	.30
Raven's duck. (See canvas, etc.).	.058	Loneta. (Vease lona y loneta, etc.)......................	.08
Razor-strops	.087	Asentadores de navajas........	.12
Razors	.1305	Navajas......................	.18
Red lead.....................	.058	Azarcon ó minio..............	.08
Reed-mace, unmanufactured.....	.029	Enea sin manufacturar	.04
Reins	.3625	Riendas......................	.50
Resin, pine...................	.0145	Resina de pino	.02
Resins not included in other classes....................	.087	Toda clase de resina no comprendida en otras clases......	.12

ARTICLE OF MERCHANDISE.	Duty per pound in U. S. currency.	ARTÍCULO DE MERCANCÍA.	Derechos por libra en moneda hondureña.
	Dollars.		*Pesos.*
Retorts	.1305	Retortas	.18
Revolvers. (See swords, etc.)...	.3625	Revolvers. (Vease espadas, etc.).	.50
Ribbons. (See laces, stripes, etc.)	.58	Cintas. (Véase encajes, tiras, etc.)	.80
Ribbons. (See understockings, stockings, etc.)..............	.2175	Cintas. (Véase calcetas, medias, etc.)..............	.30
Ribbons, braid, laces, fringe, belts, insertings of cotton, or any other such article or ornament not included in other classes....................	.174	Hiladillos ó cintas, trencillas, encajes, flecos, fajas, tiras bordadas y caladas, de algodon, y cualquiera otro artículo ó adorno semejante, no comprendido en otras clases......	.24
Ribbons "de reata"	.087	Cintas de reata...............	.12
Rice, ground..................	.0145	Arroz molido..................	.02
Rigging......................	.0145	Jarcíar......................	.02
Rivets. (See iron, manufactured, etc.)	.0145	Remaches. (Vease hierro manufacturado, etc.)	
Rosin.......................	.0145	Brea rubia	.02
Rubber. (See bone, ivory, etc.)..	.174	Caucho. (Véase hueso, marfil, etc.)	.24
Rubber, for erasing............	.0145	Goma para borrar..............	.02
Ruching. (See cambric, batiste, etc.)	1.088	Ruches. (Véase holán batista, clarín, etc.)	1.50
Sabers. (See swords, etc.)	.3625	Sables. (Véase espadas, etc.).'.	.50
Sacks. (See shirts, linen, etc.)..	.2175	Sacos. (Véase camisas hechas, etc.)	.30
Sacks, traveling, of all sorts.....	.029	Bolsas para viaje, de todas clases....................	.04
Sadd.e-frames.................	.029	Fustes ó armazones para monturas	.04
Saddles, riding........	.3625	Sillas de montar...............	.50
Saffron	.2175	Azafrán	.30
Sago	.0145	Sagú.......................	.02
Sails, of canvas, raven's duck, or "cotonia"	.029	Velas de lona, loneta ó cotonia para embarcaciones..........	.04
Saltpeter.....................	.029	Salitre......................	.04
Salts, Epsom..................	.0145	Sal d'Epson..................	.02
Salts, Glauber	.0145	Sal de Glauber	.02
Sand for drying writings........	.0145	Arenilla	.02
Sardines, pressed, in oil, or in any other form..............	.029	Sardinas prensadas, en aceite ó en cualquiera otra forma....	.04
Sashes, linen. (See laces, stripes, etc.)	.58	Bandas (de lino). (Véase encajes, tiras, etc.)............	.80
Sashes, woolen. (See understockings, stockings, etc.).....	.2175	Bandas (de lana). (Véase calcetas, medias, etc.)	.30
Satin. (See cloth, pañete, etc.) ..	.3625	Raso. (Véase paño, pañete, etc.)......................	.50
Satin. (See drills, jeans, etc.)...	.087	Raso. (Véase driles, coquí, etc.)......................	.12
Satinet. (See drills, jeans, etc.).	.087	Rasete. (Véase driles, coquí, etc.)	.12
Sauces of all sorts.............	.029	Salsas de todas clases..........	.04

ARTICLE OF MERCHANDISE.	Duty per pound in U. S. currency.	ARTÍCULO DE MERCANCÍA.	Derechos por libra en moneda hondureña.
	Dollars.		*Pesos.*
Sausages and all sorts of food conserves in tins, not included in the foregoing classes.......	.058	Salchichones, chorizos y toda clase de conservar alimenticiar en latas, no incluidas en las clases anteriores............	.03
Saws. (See tools for arts, etc.)...	.029	Sierras y serruchos. (Véase instrumentos para artes, etc.)..	.04
Scales. (See balances, steel-yards, etc.).................	.0145	Balanzas. (Véase balanzas, romanas, etc.)................	.02
Scarfs. (See handkerchiefs, shawls, etc.)	.58	Chalos. (Véase panuelos, etc.).	.80
Scarfs. (See jerkins or doublets, etc.)..................	.1305	Bandas. (Véase almillas, etc.).	.13
Scientific instruments. (See instruments of surgery, etc.).....	.087	Instrumentos de ciencias. (Véase instrumentos de cirugía, etc.)	.12
Scissors and "chambetas".......	.1305	Tigeras y chambetas..........	.18
Screens of metal, of paper, of cloth, etc...................	.1305	Fantallas de metal, de papel, de tela, etc...................	.18
Screws, large, for blacksmiths. (See instruments or tools.).....	.0145	Tornillos grandes para herreros. (Véase herramientas é instrumentos, etc.)	.02
Sealing wax....................	.0145	Lacre	.02
Sealing wax, ordinary, in cakes..	.029	Lacre en panes ó zulaque......	.04
Seals and stamps for letters......	.0145	Sellos y timbres para cartas....	.02
Serge. (See cloth, pañete, etc.)..	.3625	Sarga. (Véase paño, pañete, etc.)......................	.50
Sextants	.174	Sextantes	.24
Shaving cases.................	.174	Cajas ó neceseres para afeitar..	.24
Shawls. (See handkerchiefs, shawls, etc.)................	.58	Pañolones. (Véase pañuelos, etc.)......................	.80
Sheepskin garments. (See sleeves, etc.).........................	.174	Chamarros. (Véase mangas, etc.)......................	.24
Sheepskin robes or rugs.........	.3625	Pellones ó zalear.............	.50
Sheetings. (See drills, jeans, etc.).....	.087	Brin crudo. (Véase driles, coquí, etc.)	.12
Shells, loose or put together into articles or ornaments.........	.174	Caracoles y conchitas sueltas ó formando piezas ó adornos..	.04
Shirt-bosoms. (See collars, etc.)..	.2175	Pecheras. (Véase cuellos, etc.).	.30
Shirtings, cotton, unlaundered, plain, and of any kind and width...................	.087	Mantas crudas, lisas y de toda clase y ancho..............	.12
Shirts. (See handkerchiefs, shawls, etc.)................	.58	Camisas. (Vease pañuelos, etc.).	.80
Shirts, linen, or of cotton with some linen, and trousers, waistcoats, jackets, drawers, coats, paletots, sacks, frock coats, and any other article of ready-made clothing for men, made of linen, wool, or cotton,		Camisas hechas de lino, ó las de algodon que tengan algo de lino, y los pantalones, chalecos, chaquetas, calzoncillos, casacas, paltos, sacos, levitas y cualquiera otra pieza de ropa hecha, para hombres,	

ARTICLE OF MERCHANDISE.	Duty per pound in U. S. currency.	ARTÍCULO DE MERCANCÍA.	Derechos por libra en moneda hondureña.
	Dollars.		*Pesos.*
excepting cotton shirts, which belong to the 7th class........	.2175	de lino, lana ó algodon, excepto las camisas de algodon, que corresponden á la 7ª clase......................	.30
Shirts made of cotton..........	.174	Camisas hechas de algodon.....	.24
Shoeblacking	.058	Betún para el calzado	.08
Shoe laces....................	.087	Cintas de botín	.12
Shoes and boots, etc., made up or in pieces	.2175	Calzado hecho ó en corte	.30
Shot belts....................	.1305	Municioneras.................	18
Shot, small. (See ammunition, etc.)........................	.029	Perdigones. (Véase municiones, etc.)	.04
Shoulder straps. (See laces, stripes, etc.)	.58	Charreteras. (Véase encajes, tiras, etc.)	.80
Shoulders (bacon)	.029	Paletas	.04
Shovels. (See instruments or tools, etc.)	.0145	Palas. (Véase herramientas é instrumentos, etc.)...........	.02
Side arms. (See swords, etc.) ...	.3625	Armas blancas. (Véase espadas, etc.)	.50
Sieves of copper wire, of horsehair, or of silk...............	.087	Cedazos de alambre de cobre, de cerda ó de seda.....	.12
Sieves of iron wire.............	.0145	Cedazos de alambre de hierro...	.02
Silk, pure or mixed with other material, manufactured into articles of any sort, and fabrics of other materials mixed with silk, excepting those articles which are specially included in other classes, such as umbrellas, parasols, church ornaments, and others....................	1.088	Seda pura ó mezclada con otra materia, manufacturada en cualquiera forma, y las telas ó tejidos de otras materias que esten mezcladas con seda, con excepción de aquellos artículos que especialmente están determinados en otras clases, como paraguas, sombrillas, ornamentos de iglesias y otros más	1.50
Silver, articles of	1.088	Los artículos de plata, etc.......	1.50
Silver, imitation. (See wire spangles, etc.)	.3625	Plata falsa. (Véase alambrillos, etc.)	.50
Silver lace, imitation. (See wire spangles, etc.)	.3625	Galones ó pasamanería de plata falsa. (Véase alambrillo, etc.).	.50
Silver leaf. (See wire spangles, etc., gold or silver leaf, etc.)..	.3625	Hojilla de plata. (Véase alambrillo, etc., libritos con hojillas, etc.)	.50
Silver thread, imitation..........	.3625	Hilo de plata, falso......	.50
Skeins, white or colored.........	.174	Madejón blanco ó de color.....	.24
Skins, tanned, not manufactured, such as patent-leather, calfskin, etc., excepting white and red sole leather, which belongs to the second class	.087	Pieles curtidas manufacturadas, como charoles, becerros, etc., excepto la suela blanca ó colorada, que corresponda á la 2ª clase	.12
Skirts. (See cambric, etc.).......	1.088	Faldellines. (Véase holán batista, clarin, etc.)	1.50

ARTICLE OF MERCHANDISE.	Duty per pound in U. S. currency.	ARTÍCULO DE MERCANCÍA.	Derechos por libra en moneda hondureña.
	Dollars.		*Pesos.*
Skirts, fustians, wrappers, and gowns, made up or in pieces, and any other article of clothing, made of cotton, for ladies, and all kinds of cotton handkerchiefs...................	. 174	Enaguas, fustanes, batas y túnicos, hechos ó en cortes, y cualquiera otra pieza de ropa hecha de algodon para señoras, y toda clase de pañuelos de algodon	. 24
Skirts, fustians, wrappers, pillowcases, and gowns, of linen or mixed with cotton, except those of cambric of linen or mixed with cotton, which belong to the eleventh class............	. 3625	Enaguas, fustanes, fustansones, batas, fundas de almohadas y túnicos de lino ó mezclado con algodón, excepto los de holán batista ó clarín de lino ó mezclado con algodon, que corresponden á la 11ª clase.....	. 50
Slate books, chalks, and pencils .	. 0145	Libros de pizarra, lapices y tizas.	. 02
Slates, with or without frames....	. 0145	Pizarras con marcos ó sin ellos.	. 02
Sleeves. (See cambric, batiste, etc.)......................	1. 088	Manquillos. (Véase holán batista, clarín, etc.)............	1. 50
Sleeves, sheep-skin garments, frieze blouses, dress patterns of cotton prints, and cloaks ("ponchos") of wool.........	. 174	Mangas, chamarras, gerga, cortes de cotón y ponchos de lana	. 24
Slippers. (See cloth or knit-goods, etc.)	. 2175	Chinelas. (Véase géneros y tejidos para chinelas, etc.)......	. 30
Soap, common..................	. 0145	Jabon comun..................	. 02
Soaps, perfumed..............	. 087	Jabones perfumados..........	. 12
Soapstone or tailors' chalk	. 0145	Jabon de piedra llamado de sastres.......................	. 02
Socks. (See laces, stripes, etc.) .	. 58	Escarpines. (Véase encajes, tiras, etc.)..........	. 80
Socks. (See understockings, stockings, etc.)	. 2175	Escarpines. (Véase calcetas, medias, etc.)	. 30
Soda	. 058	Soda ó sosa comun ó calcinada.	. 08
Soda, carbonic, crystallized......	. 058	Soda ó sosa carbónica cristalizada	. 08
Solder........................	. 058	Preparación para soldaduras....	. 08
Sole leather, white or red, not manufactured..............	. 0145	Suela colorada ó blanca, no manufacturada............	. 02
Spades. (See instruments or tools, etc.)	. 0145	Azadas. (Véase herramientas é instrumentos, etc.)..........	. 02
Spangles. (See wire, spangles, etc.)......................	. 3625	Lantejuelas. (Véase alambrillos, etc.)......................	. 50
Spatulas	. 1305	Espátulas	. 18
Spectacles. (See eyeglasses, etc.).	. 3625	Espejuelos. (Véase anteójos, etc.)......................	. 50
Spermaceti	. 029	Esperma de ballena...........	. 04
Sponges......................	. 3625	Esponjas.....................	. 50
Springs, watch. (See hands, etc.).	. 2175	Resortes (de reloj). (Véase minuteros, etc.)..........	. 30
Spurge oil.....................	. 0145	Aceite de tártago	. 02
Spurs. (See articles of German silver, etc.)................	. 3625	Espuelas. (Véase efectos de plata alemana, etc.)	. 50
Spyglasses. (See eyeglasses, etc.)	. 3625	Catalejos. (Véase anteojos, etc.).	. 50

ARTICLE OF MERCHANDISE.	Duty per pound in U. S. currency.	ARTÍCULO DE MERCANCÍA.	Derechos por libra en moneda hondureña.
	Dollars.		Pesos.
Staples or buckles covered with leather....................	.087	Argollas y hebillas forradas en cuero ó suela...., ...	.22
Starch.........................	.0145	Almidon.....................	.02
Statues, iron. (See iron, manufactured, etc.)	.0145	Estatuas de hierro. (Véase hierro manufacturado, etc.)......	.02
Stays of all kinds..............	.3625	Cotillas de todas clases	.50
Stearic acid	.029	Acido estearico...............	.04
Stearine, or tallow prepared for stearine candles	.0145	Sebo preparado para bujías, esteáricas ó estearina..........	.02
Steel, bronze, copper, brass, tin, pure or alloyed ; lead and zinc unwrought ; in bars ; in ingots ; in filings; in plates, even though these be punctured or bored....	.0145	Acero, bronce, cobre, latón, estaño puro ó ligado, plomo y zinc en pasta ó en bruto, en barras, en cabillas, en rasura ó en láminas, aunque estas últimas esten taladradas ó agujereadas	.02
Steel, copper, iron, brass, tin, tinplates, bell-metal, bronze, lead, pewter, and zinc, manufactured into forms not included in other classes, polished, japanned, tinned, bronzed, or not........	.029	Acero, cobre, hierro, latón ó azofar, estaño, hoja de lata, metal cámpanial, bronce, plomo, petre y zinc manufacturados en cualquiera forma,no comprendidos en otras clases, esten ó no estén pulidos, charolados, estañados ó bronceados	.04
Steelyards. (See balances, steelyards, etc.).................	.0145	Romanas. (Vease balanzas, romanas, etc.)	.02
Steelyards of copper or of which copper is the chief material....	.029	Romanas de cobre ó que tengan la mayor parte de este metal..	.04
Stereoscopes, cosmoramas, dioramas, panoramas, magic lanterns,and other such apparatus.	.1305	Estereoscopios, c o s m oramas, dioramas, panoramas, linternas mágicas y demas aparatos semejantes	.18
Sticks for making matches......	.0145	Palitos para hacer fósforos	.02
Stirrups. (See articles of German silver, etc.)	.3625	Estribos. (Véase efectos de plata alemana, etc.)	.50
Stockinet fabrics. (See jerkins or doublets, etc.).............	.1305	Tejidos de punto de media. (Véase almillas, etc.).........	.18
Stockings, cotton	.1305	Medias de algodon...........	.18
Stockings, woolen.............	.2175	Medias de lana...............	.30
Stockings, linen or of l i n e n mixed with cotton............	.2175	Medias de lino ó mezcladas con lana ó algodón	.30
Stockings, silk	I.088	Medias de seda...............	I.50
Stoles. (See chasubles, etc.)....	.58	Estolas. (Véase casullus, etc.).	.80
Stones, precious	I.088	Piedras finas	I.50
Stones, such as flints, touchstones, lithographic stones, and polishing stones, not included in other classes..............	.0145	Piedras semejantes á las de chispa, de toque, de litografiar y de pulir, no incluidas en otras clases................	.02
Stoves for cooking, portable, of iron or other material	.0145	Cocinas portátiles de hierro ú otra materia................	.02
Stoves. (See iron, manufactured, etc.) ....,...	.0145	Anafes. (Véase hierro manufacturado, etc.)	.02

ARTICLE OF MERCHANDISE.	Duty per pound in U. S. currency.	ARTÍCULO DE MERCANCÍA.	Derechos por libra en moneda hondureña.
	Dollars.		*Pesos.*
Straw, unmanufactured..........	.029	Paja sin manufacturar	.04
Strips. (See laces, stripes, etc.)..	.58	Tiras. (Véase encages, tiras, etc.)......................	.80
Stumps for drawing. (See canvases, prepared, etc.)..........	.058	Esfuminos para dibujos. (Véase telas preparadas, etc.)........	.08
Sugar, white or brown..........	.0145	Azúcar blanco ó prieto	.02
Sulphate of copper.............	.058	Sulfato de cobre ó piedra lípis..	.08
Sulphate of iron or copperas.....	.058	Sulfato de hierro ó caparrosa....	.08
Sulphur, in flowers or cakes......	.058	Azufre en flor ó en pasta	.08
Sulphuric acid..................	.0145	Acido sulfúrico	.02
Sunshades. (See umbrellas, large or small, etc.)...............	.174	Quitasoles. (Véase paraguas, paragüitos, etc.)	.24
Sunshades. (See umbrellas, parasols, etc.)...................	.087	Quitasoles. (Véase paraguas sombrillas, etc.)	.12
Sunshades, wool	.1305	Quitasoles de lana............	.18
Surgical instruments. (See instruments of surgery, etc.)........	.087	Instrumentos de cirugía........	.12
Suspenders of all sorts..........	.3625	Elásticas ó tirantes de todas clases	.50
Suspensories..................	.1305	Suspensorios.................	.18
Sweetmeats of all kinds........	.029	Dulces de todas clases........	.04
Swords, sabers, daggers, and fine hunting knives, blunderbusses, pistols, revolvers, muskets, capsules, fulminating caps, vents, locks, cartridges, loaded or empty, and everything connected with sidearms or firearms, excepting those adopted for the army of the republic, whose importation by private individuals is prohibited....................	.3625	Espadas, sables, puñales y cuchillos finos de monte, trabucos, pistolas, revolvers, escopetas, cápsulas, fulminantes ó pistones, chimeneas, llaves, cartuchos cargados ó vacíos, y todo lo concerniente á las armas blancas y de fuego, con excepción de las adoptadas para el ejército de la república, cuya importación es prohibida á los particulares......	.50
Syphons and machines for aërated waters..............	.087	Sifones y máquinas para aguas gaseosas	.12
Syringes	.1305	Geringes	.18
Syrups of all sorts, except those of a medicinal character.......	.029	Jarabes de todas clases, excepto los medicinales.............	.04
Table cloths. (See drills, linens, etc.)......................	.1305	Manteles. (Véase driles, creas puras, etc.)...............	.18
Table cloths. (See huckaback, etc.)......................	.087	Manteles. (Véase alemanisco, etc.)......................	.12
Table covers. (See handkerchiefs, shawls, etc.)........	.58	Carpetas. (Véase pañuelos, pañolones, etc.)............	.80
Tacks. (See iron, manufactured, etc.)	.0145	Tachuelas. (Véase hierro manufacturado, etc.)........	.02
Talc. (See bone, ivory, etc.)....	.174	Talco. (Véase hueso, marfil, etc.)	.24
Tallarin......................	.029	Tallarines..................	.04
Tallow, crude, in cakes, or pressed	.0145	Sebo en rama, en pasta ó prensado......................	.02
Tape, plain or worked, of any color	.087	Hiladillos lisos ó labrados de cualquier color	.12

ARTICLE OF MERCHANDISE.	Duty per pound in U. S. currency.	ARTÍCULO DE MERCANCÍA.	Derechos por libra en moneda hondureña.
	Dollars.		*Pesos.*
Tapioca......................	.0145	Tapioca......................	.02
Tar, mineral or vegetable........	.0145	Alquitrán mineral ó vegetal....	.02
Tarlatan. (See cambric, etc.)....	1.088	Tarlatán. (Véase holán batista, clarín, etc.).................	1.50
Tarpaulin nails. (See iron, manufactured, etc.)..............	.0145	Estoperoles. (Véase hierro manufacturado, etc.).........	.02
Tassels. (See laces, stripes, etc.)	.58	Borlas. (Véase encajes, tiras, etc.)......................	.80
Tassels. (See understockings, stockings, etc.)...............	.2175	Borlas. (Véase calcetas, medias, etc.).....................	.30
Tea............................	.087	Té	.12
Teeth, artificial	1.088	Dientes artificiales............	1.50
Telescopes. (See eyeglasses, etc.).......................	.3625	Telescopios. (Véase anteojos, etc.)......................	.50
Textiles or fabrics, ordinary, hemp, linen, or cotton, for furniture, manufactured, in broad strips or in any other shape...	.087	Telas ó tegidos ordinarios de cáñamos, lino ó algodon, para muebles, manufacturados, en cinchones ó en otra forma.....	.12
Thermometers..................	.174	Termómetros..................	.24
Thimbles. (See pins, needles, etc.)	.087	Dedales. (Véase alfileres, etc.).	.12
Thread, coarse, of hemp, of pita, of linen, or of cotton..........	.087	Hilo grueso de cañamo, de pita, de lino ó de algodon	.12
Thread, linen or cotton, for sewing, embroidering, or knitting..	.087	Hilo de lino ó de algodon, para coser, para bordar, y para téjer.	.12
Thread, shoemakers'............	.029	Hilaza ó hilo de zapateros......	.04
Tin, in the rough. (See steel, bronze, etc.)..................	.0145	Estaño en bruto, etc. (Véase acero, bronce, etc.)..........	.02
Tin, manufactured. (See steel, copper, etc.)..................	.029	Estaño, manufacturado. (Véase acero, cobre, etc.)............	.04
Tin-plates. (See steel, copper, etc.)	.029	Hoja de lata. (Véase acero, cobre, etc.).................	.04
Tinder-boxes, and the tinder or wick therefor when imported with them....................	.058	Yesqueros ó eslabones y yesca ó mecha para los yesqueros cuando venga con ellos	.08
Tinsel. (See wire, spangles, etc.)	.3625	Oropel. (Véase alambrillo, etc.)	.50
Tissue and fabrics of any material interwoven with real or imitation gold or silver, excepting the ornaments for churches and priests, which belong to the 10th class............	1.088	Tisú y las telas de cualquier materia que esten mezclados ó bordados con plata ú oro, fino ó falso, excepto los ornamentos para las iglesias y sacerdotes, que corresponden á la 10ª clase	1.50
Tobacco, in the leaf or cut.......	.3625	Tabaco en rama ó picado.......	.50
Tongs. (See tools for arts, etc.)..	.029	Tenazas y tenacillas. (Véase instrumentos para artes, etc.)....	.04
Tongues, smoked or salted, when not canned..................	.0145	Lenguas ahumadas ó saladas, cuando no vienen en latas....	.02
Tools for arts or trades, with or without handles, such as pinchers, burins, augers, compasses. masons' trowels, chisels		Instrumentos para artes ú oficios, con cabos ó sin ellos, como alicates, buriles, barrenos, compases, cucharas para	

ARTICLE OF MERCHANDISE.	Duty per pound in U. S. currency.	ARTÍCULO DE MERCANCÍA.	Derechos por libra en moneda hondureña.
	Dollars.		*Pesos.*
gouges, levels, "gúrbias", jack planes, "gullames," awls, files, hammers, saws, tongs, bench - screws, "rep l a n e s," brushes, carpenters' braces, and other similar tools, and wooden b o x e s containing any of these	.029	albañiles, escoplos,formones, niveles, gúrbias, garlopas, gullames, lesnas, limas, martillos, sierras, serruchos, tenazas y tenacillas, tornos y tornillos de banco, replanes, cepillos, berbiquies ú otros semejantes, y las cajas de madera con algunos de estos instrumentos	.04
Toothpick-holders	.0145	Palilleros	.02
Tortoise - shell, manufac tu r e d. (See bone, ivory, etc.)	.174	Carey manufacturado. (Véase hueso, marfil, etc.)	.24
Tortoise-shell, unmanufactured..	.174	Carey sin manufacturar	.24
Touchstones...	.0145	Piedras de toque	.02
Towels. (See drills, linens, etc.)	.1305	Toallas de mano. (Véase driles, creas puras, etc.)	.18
Towels. (See huckaback, etc.)..	.087	Paños de mano. (Véase alemanisco, etc.)	.12
Toys of all sorts for children....	.087	Juguetes de todas clases para niños	.12
Train oil or cod-liver oil	.0145	Aceite de pescado ó de higado de bacalao	.02
Trays. (See articles of German silver, etc.)	.3625	Azafates. (Véase efectos de plata alemana, etc.)	.50
Trimmings. (See laces, stripes, etc.)	.58	Pasamanería. (Véase encajes, tiras, etc.)	.80
Trimmings. (S e e understockings, stockings, etc.)	.2175	Pasamanería. (Véase calcetas, medias, etc.)	.30
Trousers. (See jerkins or doublets, etc.)	.1305	Pantalones. (Véase almillas, etc.)	.18
Trousers. (See shirts, linen, etc.)	.2175	Pantalones. (Véase camisas hechas, etc.)	.30
Trowels, masons'. (See tools for arts, etc.)	.029	Cucharas para albañiles. (Véase instrumentos para artes, etc.)	
Trunks contai ni ng articles, will pay the duties assessed on the contents		Baules conteniendo e f e c t o s. pagarán el aforo de los derechos que contengan	
Trunks, traveling, of all sorts....	.029	Baules para viaje, de todas clases	.04
Trusses	.1305	Bragueros	.18
Tulle. (See lace or tulle, etc.)...	.2175	Tul. (Véase punto ó tul, etc.)..	.30
Turpentine	.0145	Aguarras ó espiritu de trementina	.02
Turpentine, common or Venetian.	.0145	Trementina comun ó de Venecia	.02
Umbrella fr a m e s. (See wire manufactured into frames, etc.).	.087	Armaduras para paraguas. (Véase alambre manufacturado, etc.)	.12
Umbrellas, large or small, sunshades and parasols, of silk or mixed with wool or cotton	.174	Paraguas, paragüitos, quitasoles y sombrillas de seda ó mezclada con lana ó algodon	.24

ARTICLE OF MERCHANDISE.	Duty per pound in U. S. currency.	ARTÍCULO DE MERCANCÍA.	Derechos por libra en moneda hondureña.
	Dollars.		*Pesos.*
Umbrellas, parasols, and sunshades of linen or cotton	.087	Paraguas, sombrillas y quitasoles de lino ó de algodon....	.12
Umbrellas, woolen	.1305	Paraguas de lana	.18
Understockings. (See jerkins or doublets, etc.)	.1305	Calcetas. (Véase almillas, etc.).	.18
Understockings, stockings, fringe, tassels, lace, ribbons, sashes, cords, trimmings, plushes, caps, cloaks, belts, bows, epaulets, socks, and gloves of wool or mixed with cotton	.2175	Calcetas, medias, fluecos, borlas, encajes, cintas, bandas, cordones, pasamanería, felpas, gorras, abrigos, fajas, lazos, charreteras, escarpines y guantes de lana ó mezclados con algodon	.30
Underwaistcoats, wool. (See handkerchiefs, shawls, etc)...	.58	Guarda-camisas de lana. (Véase pañuelos, pañolones, etc.)....	.80
Underwaistcoats, cotton. (See jerkins, etc.)	.1305	Guarda-camisas de algodón. (Vease almillas, etc.)	.18
Urns, iron. (See irons, manufactured, etc.)	.0145	Jarrones de hierro. (Véase hierro manufacturado, etc.) ..	.02
Valises, traveling, of all kinds...	.029	Maletas de viaje, de todas clases.	.04
Vanilla	.087	Vainilla	.12
Varnishes not included in other classes	.029	Barnices no incluidos en otras clases	.04
Velocipedes of all sorts	.087	Velocípedos de todas clases....	.12
Velveteen. (See corduroy, cotton plush, etc.)	.174	Imitación de terciopelo. (Véase paña, pañilla, etc.)	.24
Vermicelli	.029	Fideos	.04
Vermicelli paste, broken	.0145	Sémola quebrantada para hacer fideos	.02
Vests. (See shirts, linen, etc.)...	.2175	Chalecos. (Véase camisas hechas, etc.)	.30
Vinegar	.0145	Vinagre	.02
Wafers	.0145	Obleas	.02
Waiters. (See articles of German silver, etc.)	.3625	Bandejos. (Véase efectos de plata alemana, etc.)	.50
Wall-paper	.087	Papel pintado para tapicería....	
Watches, of whatever material...	1.088	Los relojes de faltriquera de cualquiera materia que sean .	1.50
Water, aërated	1.088	Aguas gaseosas	.02
Water-filters	.0145	Aparatos ó filtradores de agua ..	.02
Water of orange flowers	.0145	Aguas de azahares	.02
Waters, mineral	.0145	Aguas minerales	.02
Wax, manufactured into articles of any sort, excepting toys for children	.1305	Cera manufacturada en cualquiera forma, excepto en juguetes para niños	.18
Wax, shoemakers'	.0145	Cerote para zapateros	.02
Wax, white, pure or mixed, unworked	.058	Cera blanca, pura ó mezclada, sin labrar	.08
Weed-hooks. (See instruments or tools, etc.)	.0145	Escardillas. (Véase herramientas é instrumentos, etc.)....	.02
Weights. (See balances, steelyards, etc.)	.0145	Pesos. (Véase balanzas, romanas, etc.)	.02
Weights, iron. (See iron, manufactured, etc.)	.0145	Pesos de hierro. (Véase hierro manufacturado, etc.)....	.02

ARTICLE OF MERCHANDISE.	Duty per pound in U. S. currency.	ARTÍCULO DE MERCANCÍA.	Derechos por libra en moneda hondureña.
	Dollars.		*Pesos.*
Weights of copper or of which copper is the chief material....	.029	Pesos de cobre ó que tengan la mayor parte de este metal	.04
Whips.........................	.1305	Látigos y foetes...	.16
Whiting, in pieces or powdered......................	.0145	Tiza ó greda blanca en pedazos ó en polvo.................	.02
Wicks for lamps...............	.087	Mechas y torcidos para lámparas	.12
Wicks, or cotton twisted for wicks.......................	.087	Pábilo ó algodon hilado para pábilo	.12
Wicks, pocket, for smokers	.174	Mechas para fumadores........	.24
Wig frames. (See wire, manufactured, etc.)..................	.087	Armaduras para pelucas. (Véase alambre manufacturado, etc.) .	.12
Window-blinds.................	.029	Celosías para ventanas........	.04
Window-glasses................	.029	Transparentes para ventanas....	.04
Wines of all sorts.............	.0145	Vinos de todas clases y en cualquier envase.................	.02
Wire, excepting for fences. (See iron manufactured, etc.)	.0145	Alambre. (Véase hierro manufacturado: en alambres, excepto los de cercos, etc.)......	.02
Wire-cloth. (See netting of iron wire, etc.)...................	.058	Telas ó tejidos de alambre de hierro......................	.08
Wire manufactured into frames for wigs, cages for birds, racks for clothes or hats, or other similar appliances, and also the frames of umbrellas and parasols....................	.087	Alambre manufacturado en armaduras para pelucas, en jaulas para pájaros, en armadores ó perchas para vestidos ó sombreros ú otros aparatos semejantes, y tambien las armaduras para paraguas y quitasoles................	.12
Wire spangles, "relumbrón," tinsel, gold or silver leaf, galloons, gold or silver lace, and any other article of gold or silver, imitation, for sewing or embroidering.............. .	.3625	Alambrillo, lantejuelas, relumbrón, oropel, hojilla, galones, pasamanería, y cualquier otro articulo de oro ó plata, falso, para coser ó bordar.........	.50
Wood, fine, for making musical instruments, cabinet work, etc. .	.0145	Madera fina para construir instrumentos de música, ebanistería, etc.........................	.02
Wood in leaves or panels for veneering...................	.0145	Madera en hojas ó sean chapas para encapar.............	.02
Wood, manufactured, in any form not included in other classes...	.0145	Madera manufacturada en cualquiera forma, no comprendida en otras clases..............	.02
Wool. (See handkerchiefs, shawls, etc.)	.58	Lana. (Véase pañuelos, pañolones, etc.)	.80
Wool. (See neckties of cotton, etc.)	.58	Lana. (Véase corbatas de algodon, etc.)...............	.80
Wool. (See skirts, linen, etc.) ...	.2175	Lana. (Véase camisas hechas, etc.)	.30
Wool, raw,....................	.029	Lana en bruto	.04
Wool, spun or twisted, for embroidering and other uses......	.2175	Lana hilada ó torcida, para bordar y otros usos.............	.30

ARTICLE OF MERCHANDISE.	Duty per pound in U. S. currency.	ARTÍCULO DE MERCANCÍA.	Derechos por libra en moneda hondureña.
	Dollars.		*Pesos.*
Woolens. (See cloth, pañete, etc.)	.3675	Telas de lana. (Véase paño, pañete, etc.)	.50
Work-baskets or boxes	.174	Costureros	.24
Worsted	.174	Estambre en rama	.24
Wrappers. (See shirts, fustians, wrappers, etc.)	.174	Batas. (Véase enaguas, fustanes, etc.)	.24
Yokes. (See muslins, fine, etc.).	.2175	Golas. (Véase muselinas finas, etc.)	.30
Zephyr. (See cambric, etc.)	1.088	Céfiro. (Véase holán batista, clarín, etc.)	1.50
Zinc, unmanufactured. (See steel, bronze, etc., unwrought)	.0145	Zinc. (Véase acero, bronce, etc., en pasta)	.02
Zinc, manufactured. (See steel, copper, etc., manufactured.)	.029	Zinc. (Véase acero, cobre, etc., manufacturados)	.04
Zinc, white, and white bole	.0145	Blanco de zinc y bolo blanco	.02

MERCHANDISE FREE OF DUTY.

Agricultural machines.
Alabaster, cut or polished, in any shape, not elsewhere specified.
Alabaster, in the rough.
Anchors, for boats and launches, when imported therewith.
Animals, live.
Apparatus for electric lighting.
Apparatus, machines, and utensils for printing offices.
Articles imported for account of the government of the Republic, for the use of municipalities, and for any public work.
Asphalt.
Axles for coaches, cars, and carts.
Baggage (personal), including only clothing and foot-wear, jewels and table service, printed books, and food, all for the use of the owner, in quantity proportioned to the latter's rank and circumstances, but not including furniture, even when already used, nor whole pieces of any sort of cloth.
Balconies, iron, in pieces.
Barrels, in pieces or put together. ·
Beans.
Beans, kidney.
Boats, in pieces or put together.
Books, printed.
Bottles, common, of black glass or ordinary white glass, for bottling liquors.

MERCANCÍAS LIBRES DE DERECHOS.

Máquinas para la agricultura.
Alabastro, labrado ó pulido, en cualquiera forma, no mencionado en otra clase.
Alabastro en bruto.
Anclas, para botes y lanchas, cuando vengan con ellos.
Animales vivos.
Máquinas ó aparatos para alumbrado eléctrico.
Máquinas, aparatos y útiles para imprentas.
Artículos que se importen por cuenta del gobierno de la república, para uso de las municipalidades y para cualquiera obra de interés público.
Asfalto.
Ejes para coches, carros y carretas.
Equipaje, entendiéndose por tal sólo la ropa y calzado, las alhajas y bajillas, libros impresos y comestibles, todo para el uso del dueño, en una cantidad proporcionada á la clase y circunstancias de este; pero no los muebles, aunque sean usados, ni las piezas enteras de cualquier tejido.
Balcones de hierro, desarmados ó en piezas.
Barriles armados ó sin armar.
Frijoles.
Habichuelas.
Botes armados ó en piezas.
Libros impresos.
Botellas comunes de vidrio negro ó de vidrio claro ordinario para embazar licores.

MERCHANDISE FREE OF DUTY—
Continued.

Bran.
Bricks.
Bridges, with their chains, flooring, and other belongings.
Cardboard, impermeable, for roofing buildings.
Carriages intended exclusively for railways.
Carriages of all sorts.
Carts of all sorts.
Cement, Roman.
Chaises.
Charcoal.
Charts, hydrographic.
Charts, navigation.
Clocks for towers, including the dials and bells.
Coaches.
Coal, mineral.
Collections of dried plants.
Copies, writing and drawing.
Corn.
Crucibles of all sorts.
Demijohns, empty.
Doors, iron, in pieces.
Effects of foreign ministers and diplomatic agents accredited to the government of the Republic and of diplomatic agents of the Republic returning to Honduras, when brought with them for their own use, and such as may be introduced for the use and consumption of the President of the Republic and of the Ministers of the Administration.
Eggs, birds'.
Electric-lighting machinery or apparatus.

Filtering stones.
Firewood.
Flags or tiles of baked clay, of marble, of jasper, or of any other material, for floors.
Flour, potato.
Flour, wheat.
Flours, not specified.
Foods, unprepared.
Fountains of iron, marble, or any other material.
Fruits, fresh, not specified.
Garden stuff.
Gas machines and apparatus.

Gigs.
Globes or spheres, celestial or terrestrial.
Gold, unmanufactured and also in lawful money.

MERCANCÍAS LIBRES DE DERE-
CHOS—Continúa.

Afrecho.
Ladrillos.
Puentes, con sus cadenas, pisos y demás adherentes.
Cartón impermeable para techar edificios.
Carruajes destinados exclusivamente para caminos de hierro.
Carruajes de todas clases.
Carretas de todas clases.
Cimento romano.
Calesas.
Carbon vegetal.
Cartas hidrográficas.
Cartas de navegación.
Relojes para torres, incluyendo las muestras y campanas.
Coches.
Carbon mineral.
Colecciones de plantas secas.
Muestras de escritura y dibujo.
Maiz.
Crisoles de todas clases.
Damesanas ó garrafones vacíos.
Puertas de hierro, desarmados ó en piezas.
Efectos que traigan consigo para su uso los Ministros Públicos y Aagentes Diplomáticos extranjeros acreditados cerca del Gobierno de la República, y los Agentes Diplomáticos de la República á su regreso á Honduras, y los que se introduzcan para uso y consumo del Presidente de la República y de los Ministros del Despacho.
Huevos de aves.
Máquinas ó aparatos para alumbrado eléctrico.
Piedras de destilar.
Leña.
Losas ó baldosas de barro cocido, de mármol, de jaspe ó de qualquiera otra materia, para pisos.
Harina de papas.
Harina de trigo.
Harinas no especificadas.
Comestibles sin preparar.
Fuentes ó pilas de hierro, mármol ó de cualquiera otra materia.
Frutas frescas no especificadas.
Legumbres.
Máquinas y aparatos para alumbrado por gas y para producirlo.
Quitrines.
Globos ó esferas celestes ó terrestres.
Oro sin manufacturar y tambien en moneda legítima.

MERCHANDISE FREE OF DUTY—Continued.

Granite, cut or polished, in any form, not elsewhere specified.
Guano.
Harness, carriage.
Hogsheads, in pieces or put together.
Hoops, of iron or wood, for casks, hogsheads, barrels, or sieves.
Houses, iron, in pieces.

Houses, wooden.
Ice.
Ink, printing.
Jasper, cut or polished, in any form, not elsewhere specified.
Launches, in pieces or put together.
Lime, common.
Lime, hydraulic.
Lumber, ordinary, for building.
Machinery or apparatus for electric lighting.
Machines and apparatus for lighting by gas and for manufacturing gas.
Machines, apparatus, and utensils for printing offices.
Machines for agriculture and mining.
Maps of all kinds.
Marble, cut or polished, in any form, not elsewhere mentioned.
Marble, in the rough.
Materials, building, not included in other classes.
Materials intended exclusively for railways.
Mining machinery.
Motors, steam, of any kind, with all their accessories.
Oars for boats and launches, when imported with them.
Oats.
Pamphlets.
Paper, white, printing, without sizing or glazing.
Periodicals.
Pine or other ordinary woods for building.
Pipes (casks), in pieces or put together.
Pipes or conduits of iron or lead.
Plants, dried, collections of.
Plants, living, of all kinds.
Potatoes.
Printing ink.
Printing-office machines, apparatus, and utensils.
Printing paper, white, without sizing or glazing.
Pumice stone.

MERCANCÍAS LIBRES DE DERE-CHOS—Continúa.

Granito, labrado ó pulido, en cualquier forma, no mencionado en otra clase.
Huano.
Arneses para los carruajes.
Bocoyes armados ó sin armar.
Arcos ó fleges de hierro ó de madera para pipas, bocoyes, barriles ó cedazos.
Edificios de hierro desarmados ó en piezas.
Edificios de madera.
Hielo.
Tinta de imprenta.
Jaspe, labrado ó pulido, en cualquier forma, no mencionado en otra clase.
Lanchas armadas ó en piezas.
Cal comun.
Cal hidráulica.
Maderas ordinarias para edificios.
Máquinas ó aparatos para alumbrado eléctrico.
Máquinas y aparatos para alumbrado por gas y para producirlo.
Máquinas, aparatos y útiles para las imprentas.
Máquinas para la agricultura y minería.
Mapas de todas clases.
Mármol, labrado ó pulido, en cualquier forma, no mencionado en otra clase.
Mármol en bruto.
Materiales de construcción no incluido en otra clase.
Materiales destinados exclusivamente para caminos de hierro.
Máquinas para la minería.
Motores de vapor de cualquiera clase, con todos accesorios.
Remos, para botes y lanchas cuando vengan con ellos.
Avena.
Cuadernos y folletos.
Papel blanco de imprenta, sin cola ó goma.

Periódicos.
Pino ú otras maderas ordinarias para edificios.
Pipas armadas ó sin armar.
Cañerías ó conductos de hierro ó plomo.
Colecciones de plantas secas.
Plantas vivas de todas clases.
Papas.
Tinta de imprenta.
Máquinas, aparatos y útiles para las imprentas.
Papel blanco de imprenta sin cola ó goma.

Piedra pómez.

MERCHANDISE FREE OF DUTY—
Continued.

Pumps, hydraulic, with their pipes and other parts.
Refractory stones for foundry furnaces.

Rice.
Roots, edible.
Sacks for coffee.
Sails, for boats and launches, when imported therewith.
Salt, common.
Samples of merchandise, in small pieces, not exceeding 25 pounds in weight.

Sawing machines.
Seeds for planting.
Shingles.
Silver, unmanufactured, and also lawful money.
Springs for coaches, cars, and carts.
Stages.
Staves for barrels, pipes, and hogsheads, imported separately.
Steam motors of every sort, with all their accessories.
Stone, of all kinds, in the rough.
Stone, such as marble, alabaster, jasper, and granite, cut or polished in any form, not elsewhere specified.

Stones for filtering.
Stones of all kinds and in any shape, for grinding or sharpening.
Stones, refractory, for foundry furnaces.

Tiles, for roofs, of clay or slate.
Tires, for coaches, cars, and carts.
Type, printers'.
Utensils intended exclusively for railways.

Vegetables.
Wheels, for coaches, cars, and carts.
Wire, iron, of any shape, for fences.

Wood, for burning.
Wood, ordinary, for building.
Wood intended for building vessels.

TARIFF CLASSIFICATION.

Merchandise from f o r e i g n countries which is introduced into t h e customhouses of the Republic is divided into eleven classes, as follows:
1. Free of duty.
2. Paying two cents a pound.

MERCANCÍAS LIBRES DE DERE-
CHOS—Continúa.

Bombas hidráulicas con sus tubos y demás piezas.
Piedras refractarias para hornos de fundición.
Arroz.
Raices alimenticias.
Sacos para café.
Velas para botes y lanchas, cuando vengan con ellos.
Sal comun.
Muestras de mercancías en pequeños pedazos, cuyo peso no exceda de veinticince libras.
Máquinas para aserrar.
Semillas para sembrar.
Tejamanil.
Plata sin manufacturar y tambien moneda legítima.
Resortes para coches, carros y carretas.
Ómnibus.
Duelas de barriles, pipas y bocoyes, cuando vengan por separado.
Motores de vapor, de cualquiera clase, con todos sus accesorios.
Piedras de todas clases, en bruto.
Piedras semejantes al mármol, alabastro, jaspe y granito, labradas ó pulidas en cualquiera forma, no mencionadas en otra clase.
Piedras de destilar.
Piedras de todas clases y en cualquiera forma, para moler y para amolar.
Piedras refractarias para hornos de fundición.
Tejas de barro ó de pizarra.
Llantas para coches, caros y carretas.
Tipos de imprenta.
Utensilios destinados exclusivamente para caminos de hierro.
Hortaliza.
Ruedas para coches, carros y carretas.
Alambre de hierro en cualquiera forma para cercos.
Leña.
Maderas ordinarias para edificios.
Madera á proposito para la construcción naval.

CLASIFICACIÓN ARANCELARIA.

Las mercaderias procendentes del extranjero que se introduzcan por las Aduanas de la República se dividen en once clases:
1. Que no pagará derecho alguno.
2. Que pagará dos centavos por libra.

TARIFF CLASSIFICATION—Continued.

3. Paying four cents a pound.
4. Paying eight cents a pound.
5. Paying twelve cents a pound,
6. Paying eighteen cents a pound.

7. Paying twenty-four cents a pound.

8. Paying thirty cents a pound.
9. Paying fifty cents a pound.

10. Paying eighty cents a pound.

11. Paying one dollar and a half a pound.

CLASIFICACIÓN ARANCELARIA—Continúa.

3. Que pagará cuatro centavos por libra.
4. Que pagará ocho centavos por libra.
5. Que pagará doce centavos por libra.
6. Que pagará diez y ocho centavos por libra.

7. Que pagará veinte y cuatro centavos por libra.

8. Que pagará treinta centavos por libra.
9. Que pagará cincuenta centavos por libra.

10. Que pagará ochenta centavos por libra.

11. Que pagará ciento cincuenta centavos por libra.

Appendix E.

RECIPROCAL COMMERCIAL ARRANGEMENT BETWEEN THE UNITED STATES OF AMERICA AND HONDURAS.

Concluded April 29, 1892; proclaimed April 30, 1892.

BY THE PRESIDENT OF THE UNITED STATES OF AMERICA.

A PROCLAMATION.

Whereas, pursuant to section 3 of the act of Congress approved October 1, 1890, entitled "An act to reduce the revenue and equalize duties on imports, and for other purposes," the Secretary of State of the United States of America communicated to the Government of Honduras the action of the Congress of the United States of America, with a view to secure reciprocal trade, in declaring the articles enumerated in said section 3 to be exempt from duty upon their importation into the United States of America;

And whereas the consul-general of Honduras at New York has communicated to the Secretary of State the fact that, in reciprocity for the admission into the United States of America free of all duty of the articles enumerated in section 3 of said act, the Government of Honduras will, by due legal enactment as a provisional measure, and until a more complete arrangement may be negotiated and put in operation, admit free of all duty from and after May 25, 1892, into all the established ports of entry of Honduras, the articles or merchandise named in the following schedule, provided that the same be the product or manufacture of the United States:

SCHEDULE.

of products and manufactures from the United States which the Republic of Honduras will admit free of all customs, municipal, and any other kind of duty.

1. Animals for breeding purposes.
2. Corn, rice, barley, and rye.
3. Beans.
4. Hay and straw for forage.
5. Fruits, fresh.

6. Preparations of flour in biscuits, crackers not sweetened, macaroni, vermicelli, and tallarin.

7. Coal, mineral.

8. Roman cement.

9. Hydraulic lime.

10. Bricks, fire bricks, and crucibles for melting.

11. Marble, dressed, for furniture, statues, fountains, gravestones, and building purposes.

12. Tar, vegetable and mineral.

13. Guano and other fertilizers, natural or artificial.

14. Plows and all other agricultural tools and implements.

15. Machinery of all kinds, including sewing machines, and separate or extra parts for the same.

16. Materials of all kinds for the construction and equipment of railroads.

17. Materials of all kinds for the construction and operation of telegraphic and telephonic lines.

18. Materials of all kinds for lighting by electricity and gas.

19. Materials of all kinds for the construction of wharves.

20. Apparatus for distilling liquors.

21. Wood of all kinds for building, in trunks or pieces, beams, rafters, planks, boards, shingles, or flooring.

22. Wooden staves, heads, and hoops, and barrels and boxes for packing, mounted or in pieces.

23. Houses of wood or iron, complete or in parts.

24. Wagons, carts, and carriages of all kinds.

25. Barrels, casks, and tanks of iron for water.

26. Tubes of iron and all other accessories necessary for water supply.

27. Wire, barbed, and staples for fences.

28. Plates of iron for building purposes.

29. Mineral ores.

30. Kettles of iron for making salt.

31. Sugar boilers.

32. Molds for sugar.

33. Guys for mining purposes.

34. Furnaces and instruments for assaying metals.

35. Scientific instruments.

36. Models of machinery and buildings.

37. Boats, lighters, tackle, anchors, chains, girtlines, sails, and all other articles for vessels, to be used in the ports, lakes, and rivers of the Republic.

38. Printing materials, including presses, type, ink, and all other accessories.

39. Printed books, pamphlets, and newspapers, bound or unbound, maps, photographs, printed music, and paper for music.

40. Paper for printing newspapers.

41. Quicksilver.

42. Lodestones.

43. Hops.

44. Sulphate of quinine.

45. Gold and silver in bars, dust, or coin.

46. Samples of merchandise the duties on which do not exceed $1.

It is understood that the packages or coverings in which the articles named in the foregoing schedule are imported shall be free of duty if they are usual and proper for the purpose.

And that the Government of Honduras has further stipulated that the laws and regulations adopted to protect its revenue and prevent fraud in the declarations and proof that the articles named in the foregoing schedule are the product or manufacture of the United States of America, shall impose no additional charges on the importer nor undue restrictions on the articles imported.

And whereas the Secretary of State has, by my direction, given assurance to the consul-general of Honduras at New York that this action of the Government of Honduras in granting freedom of duties to the products and manufactures of the United States of America on their importations into Honduras, and in stipulating for a more complete reciprocity arrangement, is accepted as a due reciprocity for the action of Congress as set forth in section 3 of said act:

Now, therefore, be it known that I, Benjamin Harrison, President of the United States of America, have caused the above-stated modifications of the tariff laws of Honduras to be made public for the information of the citizens of the United States of America.

In testimony whereof, I have hereunto set my hand and caused the seal of the United States to be affixed.

Done at the city of Washington, this 30th day of April, one thousand eight hundred and ninety-two, and of the independence of the United States of America the one hundred and sixteenth.

[SEAL.]   BENJ. HARRISON.

By the President:

    JAMES G. BLAINE,

       Secretary of State.

[Honduras.]

NOTE.

Appendix F, Commercial Directory, page 175 to page 180, inclusive, omitted in reprint.

NEWSPAPER DIRECTORY.

CHOLUTECA.

La Verdad.

COMAYAGUA.

El Diario.
El Orden.

JUTACALPA, OLANCHO.

El Eco.

SANTA BARBARA.

El Progreso.

SANTA ROSA, COPAN.

El Copaneco.

TEGUCIGALPA.

El Monitor.
El Orden.
Gaceta Oficial.
Honduras Mining Journal.
La Nación.
La Paz.
La República.
La Academia.

TRUJILLO.

La Voz de Trujillo.

YORO.

La Nueva Era.

INDEX.

A.

B.

C.

D.

183

Bull. 57——12

O

www.ingramcontent.com/pod-product-compliance
Lightning Source LLC
Chambersburg PA
CBHW030830270326
41928CB00007B/977